How to Form Your Own

NEW YORK

CORPORATION

by Attorney Anthony Mancuso

Nolo Press • 950 Parker St., Berkeley, CA 94710

important

Nolo Press is committed to keeping its books up-to-date. Each new printing, whether or not it is called a new edition, has been revised to reflect the latest law changes. This book was printed and updated on the last date indicated below. Before you use this book, you may wish to call Nolo Press (415) 549-1976 to check whether a later printing or edition has been issued.

printing history

New "Printing" means there have been some minor changes, but usually not enough so that people will need to trade in or discard an earlier printing of the same edition. Obviously, this is a judgment call and any change, no matter how minor, might affect you.

New "Edition" means one or more major, or a number of minor, law changes since the previous edition.

FIRST EDITION	June 1984
Second Printing	February 1986
Third Printing	November 1986
SECOND EDITION	August 1988
Second Edition	August 1988
Illustrations	Mari Stein
BOOK DESIGN	Jackie Clark
COVER DESIGN	Toni Ihara
PRINTING	Delta Lithograph

Library of Congress Catalog Card Number: 84-60605
ISBN 0-917316-74-6
Copyright © 1984, 1986 and 1988 by Anthony Mancuso
All Rights Reserved

acknowledgments

Thanks to Lewis R. Rosenbluth, New York attorney, for his help in co-authoring the first edition of this book. Also, to Glenn Relyea, Esq., former Director, Division of Corporations, Bob Blumberg, Esq., and Sharon Babala, for their invaluable assistance and feedback related to the particular requirements of New York corporate law and procedure. Also, to Ron Lomax, Research Librarian, Alameda County Law Library, for sharing his gift for locating helpful research materials and to Mike Rodriquez for providing research assistance.

A special thanks to the publisher and editor, Ralph Warner, for his commitment to this book and to David Cole, Nolo marketing director, for undertaking the arduous task of distributing this book to New York readers.

Also to Jackie Clark and Toni Ihara for the production and design of this new edition, Janet Bergen for final proofreading, and Mari Stein for her imaginative illustrations. A heartfelt thanks to the hard-working people at Nolo Press for their help in making it all happen.

UPDATE SERVICE
INTRODUCTORY OFFER

Our books are as current as we can make them, but sometimes the laws do change between editions. You can read about law changes which may affect this book in the NOLO NEWS, a 24-page newspaper which we publish quarterly. In addition to the Update Service, each issue contains comprehensive articles about the growing self-help law movement as well as areas of law that are sure to affect you (regular subscription rate is $7.00).

To receive the next 4 issues of the NOLO NEWS, please send us $2.00:

Name _____

Address_____

Send to: NOLO PRESS, 950 Parker St., Berkeley CA 94710

RECYCLE YOUR OUT-OF-DATE BOOKS &
GET 25% OFF YOUR NEXT PURCHASE!

Using an old edition can be dangerous if information in it is wrong. Unfortunately, laws and legal procedures change often. To help you keep up to date we extend this offer. If you cut out and deliver to us the title portion of the cover of any old Nolo book we'll give you a 25% discount off the retail price of any new Nolo book. For example, if you have a copy of TENANT'S RIGHTS, 4th edition and want to trade it for the latest CALIFORNIA MARRIAGE AND DIVORCE LAW, send us the TENANT'S RIGHTS cover and a check for the current price of MARRIAGE & DIVORCE, less a 25% discount. Information on current prices and editions is listed in the NOLO NEWS (see above box). Generally speaking, any book more than two years old is of questionable value. Books more than four or five years old are a menace.

OUT OF DATE = DANGEROUS

This offer is to individuals only.

NYC 8/88

TABLE OF CONTENTS

INTRODUCTION

1

**ADVANTAGES AND DISADVANTAGES OF FORMING
A NEW YORK CORPORATION**

2

A CLOSER LOOK AT NEW YORK CORPORATIONS

3

THE SMALL NEW YORK CORPORATION

4

CORPORATE TAXATION

5

STEPS TO FORM YOUR CORPORATION

6

AFTER YOUR CORPORATION IS ORGANIZED

7

LAWYERS AND ACCOUNTANTS

APPENDIX

INTRODUCTION

The business activity of the United States was at one time comprised primarily of individual and family enterprises providing a limited line of products or services to a local market. Today, however, after decades of technological change and the growing concentration of the methods and means of production into the hands of a decreasing number of corporations, it might be more appropriate to refer to our nation as the Corporate States of America or, more succinctly, United States, Inc.

Despite the trend toward economic concentration, there are still many small businesses striving to compete successfully with large corporations which seek an inexpensive means of taking advantage of the formality and economic flexibility of the corporate form. This book is written for these New York businesses and the people who are trying to make them work.

In this book we give you the instructions and forms necessary to organize a business corporation which has less than 10 New York shareholders and which plans to engage in any lawful activity permitted by the Business Corporation Law of New York. This book can also be used if your corporation will be offering its initial shares to a limited number of New York residents (who have close personal, business or family ties) for a relatively small amount of money. We have provided chapters which give you general information on the advantages and disadvantages, tax

consequences, etc., of incorporating. *You cannot use this book to form a nonprofit or professional corporation* (see these sections in Chapter 1), although you might find much of the background information contained in this book helpful.

Lawyers can charge up to $2,000 for an incorporation. This book is intended to minimize your reliance on attorneys' services with respect to filling in standardized boiler-plate forms, and to help you ask specific, informed questions related to the specific needs of your corporation when it becomes necessary to seek a lawyer's advice. Although not required by law, we recommend that you consult an attorney to check over your incorporation papers. Despite the trend of higher and higher attorneys' fees, the process outlined in this book, including a consultation with a lawyer, should make the cost of incorporating extremely reasonable.

This book is a tool to be used to comply with the legal formalities necessary to form a valid corporation. It does not and cannot substitute for a careful examination of the economic realities facing each business. Only you can make informed decisions regarding the consequences of organizing your business as a corporation. Since accountants can often assist you with decisions regarding the tax consequences and other financial aspects of incorporating your business, we have included a section on choosing an accountable accountant.

How to Use This Book

Completing the Certificate of Incorporation, Bylaws, Minutes, and other forms necessary to form a small New York corporation isn't difficult. You will find the how- to-do-it material clearly set out in Chapter 5. But before you start filling in blanks, we have a favor to ask, two favors actually. First, please read the material in the first four chapters carefully. This material is designed to give you background information about how corporations work and to warn you about potential danger areas. You may find some of this information more technical than you need, especially if you are incorporating a small, relatively noncomplex business. Fine, you haven't lost much by reading it, and we are confident you will learn some things you need to know.

And now for the second favor. If you are confused by anything you read here, check it with an expert. Remember, if you do form your own corporation, the ultimate responsibility for making the right decisions is yours.

ADVANTAGES AND DISADVANTAGES OF FORMING A NEW YORK CORPORATION

Chapter 1

ADVANTAGES AND DISADVANTAGES OF FORMING A NEW YORK CORPORATION

THIS CHAPTER PROVIDES YOU with general information on the advantages and disadvantages of incorporating. By way of a brief comparison, we will also look at the fundamental legal characteristics of other forms of doing business.

A. Different Ways of Doing Business

AS BUSINESS OWNERS, we know that there are many ways to run or operate a business. But the law, in its concern for the recognition and classification of form, places most businesses into one of three broad categories: sole proprietorship, partnership, or corporation. Because this is a how-to-incorporate book, we won't spend a lot of time looking at the noncorporate forms of ownership.

1. Sole Proprietorship

A sole proprietor is the sole owner of a business. Employees may be hired and may even receive a percentage of the profits as wages. The owner, however, is personally liable for all the debts, taxes and liabilities of the business, including claims made against employees acting within the course and scope of their employment. The owner must report and pay taxes on the profits of the business on his individual income tax returns.

At death, a sole proprietorship simply ends. The assets of the business normally pass under the terms of the deceased owner's will, or by intestate succession (under the state's inheritance statutes) if there is no will. Unfortunately, in either case the probate process can take up to a year and can make it difficult for the inheritors to either operate or sell the business or its assets. Often, the best way to avoid this is to place the business assets into a living trust, a legal device which avoids probate and allows the business assets to be transferred to the inheritors promptly.[1] A good source of information on how to start and operate a small sole proprietorship is *Small Time Operator* by Kamaroff, Bell Springs Press (available through Nolo Press).

2. Partnership

A partnership is a business owned by two or more people. The owners normally have a written partnership agreement specifying their respective rights and liabilities. However, while not advisable, a simple oral agreement is enough to create a partnership. The purpose of a partnership agreement is to provide detailed operating rules, such as the manner of dividing profits and losses. The drafting of a partnership agreement often proves to be more complex than the preparation of standard incorporation papers. One reason for this is that many partnerships sensibly wish to custom-tailor their agreement to deal with such issues as what happens when a partner dies, or otherwise leaves the business. If no specific agreement is made to deal with these and many other central partnership issues, the statutory rules (contained

---

[1]For detailed information on living trusts and estate planning, see *Plan Your Estate* by Clifford (Nolo Press).

in the New York Partnership Law[2]) will apply to the operation and termination of the partnership. An excellent source of "how-to" information on this subject is *The Partnership Book* by Clifford & Warner (Nolo Press).

General partnership law principles include the following. Each partner is an agent for the partnership and can individually hire employees, borrow money, and perform any act necessary to the operation of the business. Unless otherwise agreed, partners share equally in the profits. The partners themselves include their share of profits on their individual tax returns and pay taxes on them in the year in which they are earned at their individual income tax rates. Each partner is personally liable for the debts and taxes of the partnership. In other words, if the partnership assets are insufficient to satisfy a creditor's claim, the partners' personal assets are subject to attachment and liquidation to pay the business debts. Technically, when a partner ceases to be associated in the carrying on of the business of the partnership (e.g., upon the death, disability, or withdrawal of any one of the partners), the partnership is dissolved. However, commonly the partnership agreement provides in advance for these eventualities with the share of the departed partner being purchased by those who remain.

One final point about partnerships—the law also allows for the formation of a special kind of partnership, called a limited partnership. A limited partner, in conjunction with one or more general partners (the type discussed above), is allowed to invest in a partnership without the risk of incurring personal liability for the debts of the business. If the business fails, all that the limited partner can lose is her capital investment (the amount of money or the property she paid for an interest in the business). However, generally, the limited partner is not allowed to participate in the management or control of the partnership. If she does, she loses her limited liability status and can be held personally liable for partnership debts, claims, obligations, etc.

A limited partnership cannot be established by verbal agreement alone. Under the New York Partnership Law[3], a limited partnership is formed by filing a certificate of limited partnership in the office of the county clerk of the county in which the principal office of the partnership is located. A copy of the certificate must be published and proof of publication must be filed with the clerk.

Tax Note: Generally, under the federal tax law, expenses and losses from a limited partnership are considered "passive" (non-active) items and cannot be used as deductions or offsets to regular active business income such as wages, salaries, profits from an active business, etc. These limited partnership items can, as a general rule, only be deducted against other passive income (e.g., only against the individual's share of any partnership income on his individual return). Exceptions to this passive loss rule have been carved out however. For example, Treasury Regulations[4] allow limited partners to treat partnership losses as active losses (which can offset active income) if the limited partner "materially participates" in the partnership business under one of several tests.

---

[2] See New York Partnership Law, Sections 1-82. New York's partnership statutes are based upon the Uniform Partnership Act (a standard set of partnership rules adopted, in whole or part, in the various states).

[3] New York Partnership Law, Sections 90-126 (New York has adopted the Uniform Limited Partnership Act).

[4] See Temp. Reg. § 1.469-5T(e) or simply ask your tax advisor about the Treasury regulations which have been issued under Section 469 of the Internal Revenue Code.

We summarize several of these material participation tests later in this book (see "What Constitutes Material Participation?" in Chapter 4C—only a few of the tests listed apply to limited partners). Note, however, that a limited partner may be caught in the following bind: if he materially participates in the business of the limited partnership to obtain favorable tax treatment, he may loose his limited liability status under New York partnership law (remember, if a limited partner takes part in the control of the business, he becomes personally liable for partnership debts). This entire area is complex and tricky. Check with your tax advisor for further information on these special partnership passive loss rules and material participation tax regulations.

3. Summing Up

With the exception of the limited partnership, these noncorporate ways of doing business have the advantage of requiring little official red tape. However, doing business this way can be risky. This is because the owners (except in the case of a limited partner) are personally liable for the debts of the business. One unsuccessful business venture can wipe out most, or all, of their personal assets. In addition, noncorporate ways of doing business often result in reduced flexibility in tax planning. Any profits realized from the business are automatically passed along to the owners and fully taxed to them at the end of each year. By contrast, as discussed in Section B below, the corporate form of ownership allows for considerably more flexibility when it comes to tax planning.

The death of the owner or owners of a small business also raises problems for the sole proprietorship or partnership. It often means the end of a business that has been built up after years of hard work. While the death of a central figure also is likely to cause problems for the small corporation, the formal structure of the corporation often makes the continuance or sale of the business easier.

It is true, particularly with the partnership form, that some of the problems associated with noncorporate businesses can be solved by careful planning and by the use of custom-tailored, written partnership agreements. Further, in some instances, the owners of newly-formed small business are not ready emotionally or from a tax perspective to incorporate their business. In these cases, starting off as a sole proprietorship or a partnership (backed up by a carefully considered partnership agreement) makes good sense.

B. The Corporation

NOW, LET'S LOOK at the basic attributes, advantages and disadvantages of the corporation. A corporation is a statutory creature, created and regulated by state laws. In short, if you want the "privilege" (that's what the courts call it) of turning your business enterprise into a New York corporation, you must follow the requirements of the New York Business Corporation Law.

What sets the corporation apart from all other types of businesses, and makes it special for legal, practical and tax purposes, is that it is a legal entity separate from any of the people who own, control, manage, or operate it. It is a legal "person" capable of entering into contracts, incurring debts, and paying taxes. It is this distinction between the business and the people who own the business (the shareholders), from which many of the advantages of the corporate entity flow.

Unlike sole proprietorships or partnerships, the corporation is a separate taxable entity. Business income can be sheltered in the corporation and reported and taxed at the business (corporate) level only. The decision as to how much money should be kept in the business and how much should be paid out to the owners is, of course, completely in the hands of the people who own the business. In addition, since the corporation is a separate taxable "person," the instant you incorporate your business, you become an employee of your own business, eligible for tax deductible employee fringe benefits—in effect, once you incorporate, you are truly working for yourself.

And, best of all, while you enjoy this dual tax entity status with the ability to place a respectable distance between your business income and the amount of individual income you must report on your individual tax return, you also enjoy the corporate advantage of limited liability. By forming a corporation you substantially insulate your personal assets from lawsuits and claims made against your business. In other words, people with claims against the business can, as a general rule, only reach as far as the corporate assets and can't take the personal assets of the people who own and operate the corporation. We discuss the concept of limited liability in more detail below.

Example: There are numerous ways to make the most of the split personality of the corporate form. Let's jump ahead of ourselves here to mention one typical tax technique used when incorporating a prior business:

You incorporate your prior business which has been valued at $250,000. You transfer (sell) all assets of your unincorporated business to your corporation. However, instead of taking back the entire selling price in shares of stock, you decide to take $50,000 in stock and the remainder, $200,000, back as a note from your corporation. In other words, you loan your corporation $200,000 to buy your business. The principal and interest on the note are paid back to you by your corporation over five years. Since the payments of principal on the note are

considered by the IRS as nontaxable "returns of capital, " you pay taxes only on the interest on the note. Between these substantial principal repayments and the tax-free fringes available to you as a corporate employee, you may be able to live virtually tax-free over the next five years (the term of the note). We cover these technical areas of capitalizing your corporation and corporate fringe benefits in Chapters 2 and 4, respectively.

Let's now look a little closer at some of the advantages of incorporating.

1. Limited Liability

An important reason for incorporating is to limit the personal liability of the business owners for the debts and liabilities of the business. A corporate director, officer, or shareholder is normally not personally liable for the debts of the corporation. This means that a person who invests in the corporation normally only stands to lose the amount of money or the value of the property which he has contributed for stock. As a result, if the corporation does not succeed and cannot pay its debts or other financial obligations, creditors cannot usually seize or sell the corporate investor's home, car or other personal assets.

Example: Rackafrax Dry Cleaners, Inc., a New York corporation, has several bad years in a row. When it files for bankruptcy it owes $50,000 to a number of suppliers and $8,000 as a result of a lawsuit for uninsured losses stemming from a fire. Stock in Rackafrax is owned by Harry Rack, Edith Frax, and John Quincy Taft. Are the personal assets of any of these people liable to pay the money Rackafrax owes? Absent unusual circumstances, the answer is No.

Exceptions to the Rule of Limited Liability

In certain circumstances, you, as an officer, director or shareholder of a corporation, may be responsible for paying some or all of your corporation's liabilities (that is, the money it owes to other people). Here are a few of the most common exceptions to the rule:

Bank Loans. Often when a bank or other lender loans money to a small corporation, particularly a newly-formed corporation, it requires that the people who own the corporation independently pledge some of their personal assets as security for the debt. Be aware that if you do this you have waived the shield of limited liability with respect to these pledged personal assets.

Federal and State Taxes. Another common situation where limited liability may not protect corporate officers or directors is when the corporation has failed to pay income, payroll or other taxes. The IRS and the state Department of Taxation and Finance do not recognize the concept of limited liability in this instance and

attempt to recover unpaid taxes from "responsible" employees if they can't collect these taxes from the corporation. In other words, make sure to withhold, deposit, report and pay corporate income and employment taxes on time. Detailed information on corporate taxes is provided in Chapter 6.

Employee Wages. Under the provisions of Section 630 of the Business Corporation Law, the 10 largest shareholders (determined by the value of their shares) of privately-held (non-public) corporations are personally liable for the payment of wages and other payments due to the corporation's employees (but not for debts owed to contractors). Generally, the employees may sue one or more of these 10 shareholders for unpaid wages, etc., if they cannot collect on a judgment first obtained against the corporation for these amounts.

Unlawful or Unauthorized Transactions. If you use the corporation as a devise to defraud third parties, or if you do something on behalf of the corporation which you are unauthorized to do, or if the corporation itself does anything it is not permitted to do, you can be held individually liable for any damages caused to others (damages means, in this case, monetary losses).

There are other types of situations which can cause you to be personally liable for corporate obligations. Fortunately, almost all of them can be avoided by following a few simple rules. First, don't do anything which is dishonest. Second, make sure that before you sign or approve anything for the corporation you have the authority to do so (the limits of your authority as an officer are spelled out in the bylaws which are discussed in Chapter 5, Step 4). Finally, make sure that you remain aware of what is going on, and, particularly, that no one else associated with the corporation is doing anything illegal or dishonest. Ignorance may not be a sufficient excuse to avoid personal liability.

2. Tax Planning, Financial Flexibility and a Brief Summary of Corporate Tax Rules

In this section, we take a preliminary look at some of the tax aspects of incorporating which can provide a significant amount of financial flexibility to the owners of an incorporated business.

Taxation is a significant area where a corporation can give the owners of a small or medium-sized business flexibility in decision making and financial planning. As we've said, by forming a corporation, the owners immediately become eligible to split business income between themselves personally, and the separate taxable entity, the corporation. For example, corporate income can be paid out to the owner-employees in the form of salaries, bonuses, fringe benefits, etc. These payouts are deductible by the corporation and, therefore, are not taxed at the corporate level. Such salaries and bonuses will only show up and be taxed on the individual's income tax return.

In conjunction with the payment of deductible salaries and other amounts to the owner-employees, a portion of corporate income can be left in the corporation to meet the future needs of the business or paid out as salaries or other deductible amounts to the owner-employees in later years (this way, the owners can control the amount of individual income they realize from their business in each year).

For small corporations with modest-to-medium profits this can often result in substantial tax savings since initial corporate tax rates on profits left in the corporation are low (i.e., 15% and 25%—we discuss corporate tax rates in Chapter 4B1 and provide examples of corporate tax savings in Chapter 4B2). The ability to split up and shelter such business income is a unique attribute of the corporation—the Internal Revenue Code specifically allows most corporations to accumulate up to $250,000 of retained earnings in the corporation, no questions asked (amounts above this limit can be accumulated for the reasonable needs of the business).

Note: Certain personal service corporations (those whose principal function is the performance of services in the fields of health, law, engineering, architecture, accounting, actuarial science, performance arts, or consulting and whose stock is owned by the professional employees of the corporation) are subject to a flat federal corporate tax rate of 34%. In other words, any taxable income left in the corporation at the end of the corporate tax year is taxed at the maximum federal corporate income tax rate (again, see Chapter 4B1).[5]

---

[5]Also note: Corporations engaged in the practice of these specific professions or activities are limited to an automatic accumulated earnings credit of $150,000

Partnerships and sole proprietorships, on the other hand, must report all business income on their individual tax returns in the year in which it is earned. In a very good (high income and high tax) year, this can sometimes result in unincorporated individuals wishing, in part, they had not done quite so well.

Also, owner-employees of a corporation are eligible for certain deductible fringe benefits not available to (deductible by) noncorporate business owners, such as sick pay, group term-life insurance, accident and health insurance, reimbursement of medical expenses, disability insurance and other employee benefits. The reason for this favorable tax treatment is simple: as we've said, when you incorporate your business, you become an employee of your own corporation, eligible for employee benefits. These benefits are deductible by the corporation and, for the most part, are tax-free to the owner-employees (they do not have to show these benefits as income on their individual tax returns).[6] See Chapter, 4G for further information on corporate fringe benefits.

What about the old bugaboo of double taxation? Isn't it true that corporate income is taxed twice–once at the corporate level and again a second time when it is paid out to shareholders? In theory this is possible. However, in practice it seldom occurs in the

---

(instead of the standard $250,000 credit—see Chapter 4H).

[6]These special corporate fringe benefits are not available to shareholders who own 2% or more of the stock in S corporations (Chapter 4C). Also note that unincorporated business owners are allowed to deduct a portion (25%) of the premiums paid for themselves and their spouses for health insurance. This deduction does not, however, reduce the individual's liability for self-employment (social security) taxes and is not available if the individual is eligible to participate in an employer sponsored plan.

context of the small corporation. The reason is simple. Employee-owners don't pay themselves dividends (which are taxed twice), but pay themselves salaries and bonuses (taxed to the individual, not the corporation). If this is not practical because the business owner has absolutely no role in corporate operations or planning, owners also have the option of electing S corporation tax status which, we will see in the next paragraph, also avoids double taxation.

An added tax flexibility allowed to many corporations is the ability to elect to have profits and losses pass through the corporation directly to the shareholders and reported on their individual tax returns (in effect, allowing the corporation to be taxed as if it were a partnership) by electing S corporation tax status. In some circumstances it is wise to do this. For example, an S corporation is a handy way of passing initial start-up losses through to the shareholders to be deducted on their individual tax returns while retaining the legal status and benefits of a corporation.

The S corporation election also makes sense if the owners of the business find that corporate taxable income (net corporate income after subtracting all deductions including business expenses, salaries, bonuses, depreciation, etc.) will be subject to more taxes at the corporate level than if taxed to the individuals personally. However, your corporation must be substantially profitable before electing S corporation status for this reason. This is because, as a rough rule of thumb, corporate taxes on the first $185,000 of taxable income are lower than individual taxes on the same income.

Exception: If you form one of the special personal service corporations listed above, you will be taxed at the maximum corporate tax rate of 34% and may, therefore, wish to elect S corporation status to have any taxable income left in the corporation at the end of the tax year pass through to the individual shareholders to be taxed at their lower individual tax rates (see Chapter 4B1).

In Chapter 4B2 we discuss individual versus corporate taxation and what is really involved for the typical small corporation in more detail.

There are several other unique tax advantages of the corporate form, such as the ability, in many cases, to have the corporation keep its books and pay taxes based upon a tax year which is unrelated to the tax year of the owners of the business (i.e., to elect a non-calendar tax year for the corporation).[7] As a result, many corporations can choose to prepare tax returns and year-end financial statements at a time which is most convenient for them and which best reflects their own unique business cycle.

Although corporate pension and profit sharing plans are, for the most part, similar in terms of their advantages to noncorporate Keogh plans, corporate plans still provide the added advantage of allowing plan participants to borrow as much as $50,000 of the funds contributed to the plan without penalty. Also, corporate defined benefit plans allow a significantly larger level of contributions to be made to the plan by participants than those permitted to Keogh participants (see Chapter 4G2).

---

[7]As a general rule, S corporations and personal service corporations (defined here as those whose principal activity is the performance of personal services substantially performed by the employee-shareholders of the corporation) are required to choose a calendar tax year for the corporation. However, exceptions to this calendar year rule for these corporations do exist. For example, S and personal service corporations are allowed to elect a non-calendar tax year if they can show a valid business purpose or if the non-calendar year results in a deferral of income of three months or less—see Chapter 4D for more information.

Other specific tax provisions favor the corporate form, one example being the ability of a corporation to make tax deductible charitable contributions—other businesses cannot deduct such contributions as a business expense.

There is, however, one tax rule that may make it disadvantageous to incorporate under some circumstances. At the risk of totally confusing you with legal gobbledygook, this is called the repeal of the General Utilities doctrine and it affects who pays taxes on gains from business liquidation. Simply put, both the corporation and its shareholders may have to pay taxes when the corporation is sold or dissolved.

While this sounds bad (why incorporate if you're going to get taxed twice if you wind up a profitable business?), there are a number of reasons why this does not normally produce this unhappy result for smaller corporations. Here are two: First, this corporate tax rule only applies towards appreciated assets held by the corporation. Many corporations (particularly those that provide services) do not hold significant assets which have appreciated during the life of the corporation (often the fair market value of assets will decrease rather than increase) and will not be subject to this corporate level tax even if they do liquidate. Second, if a corporation anticipates that its assets (such as real estate) will appreciate, it may elect federal S corporation tax treatment prior to any substantial appreciation and avoid this corporate tax since appreciation occurring while the corporation maintains its S corporation tax status is generally not taxable under this rule.

Of course, these are just some of the tax provisions which apply to corporations. The relative importance of these special provisions will vary from one business to another.

In determining whether or not to incorporate your particular business for tax reasons, the only sound advice we can give you is to actually sit down (usually with your accountant or financial planner) and determine if the corporate form will really save you money, based upon a careful examination of your own unique situation, taking into account such factors as:

• The specific sources and amount of income and expenses associated with your particular business;

• The amount of money you will wish to continue to receive individually (as a corporate salary);

• The nature and extent of deductible fringe benefits you wish to provide for yourself;

• The amount of money you wish to keep in the corporation to meet the future needs of your business (or simply to shelter from individual taxation).

Moreover, as we've said, tax considerations are just one factor in arriving at your decision to incorporate. For example, depending on the type of business you are engaged in, the corporate advantage of limited liability (particularly in these days of overpriced or unsatisfactory liability insurance coverage) may be far more important to you. Also, the availability of special corporate fringe benefits to the owner-employees of the corporation and the certainty and formality of the corporate form as a means of acquiring and disposing of ownership interests in the incorporated business through stock ownership are often of equal, or greater, importance in arriving at the decision to incorporate.

3. Formality

A more subtle, but very real, reason many people choose to incorporate is the sense of business respectability that goes with being a corporation. While this benefit is obviously intangible, many proprietorships and partnerships feel (often justifiably) that their operations are seen by the business or financial community as too informal. Incorporating is one way for business people to put others on notice that theirs is an established business whose operations are carefully planned and routinely reviewed. In other words, although placing an "Inc." after your name will not directly increase sales, it forces you to pay serious attention to the structure and organization of your business, something that is likely to improve all aspects of your business including sales in the corporation. Besides, in a world where everyone else proclaims the professionalism of their business, you too are entitled to a little self-validation.

4. Commercial Loans and Capital Investment

The corporate form often "lends" itself to a number of arrangements for the borrowing of funds for business operations. Lending institutions are familiar with the various types of debt instruments which have been developed through the years to provide corporations with funds and the risk-conscious corporate lender with special preferences. Examples include corporate bonds (secured promissory notes) and debentures (unsecured notes) which can confer voting or management rights on the lender or can be convertible by the lender into shares which carry special dividend, liquidation or other rights. Furthermore, although this book is not designed to show you how to make a public offering of stock, this is one valuable future option that can provide a successful corporation with needed capital.

5. Perpetual Existence

A corporation is, in some senses, immortal. Unlike a sole proprietorship or partnership which terminates upon the death or withdrawal of the owner or owners, a corporation has an independent legal existence which continues despite changeovers in management or ownership. Of course, like any business, a corporation can be terminated by the mutual consent of the owners for personal or economic reasons and, in some cases, involuntarily, as in certain bankruptcy proceedings. Nonetheless, the fact that a corporation does not depend for its existence on the life or continual ownership interests of particular individuals does influence creditors, employees and others to participate in the operations of the business. This is particularly true as the business grows.

C. Summing Up—Advantages and Disadvantages of Incorporation

WE HAVE DISCUSSED the general characteristics of the corporate entity. They are included only by way of comparison with other forms of doing business. We will look more closely at particular legal and tax provisions in later chapters— provisions that give the corporate form additional special characteristics. For now, however, let us summarize the relative advantages of incorporating the small business.

Advantages

- The business owners are not personally liable for the debts of the business except for loans secured by their own personal assets, unpaid taxes, for the wages of corporate employees, and for the results of unauthorized or illegal acts.

- The corporation has increased financial and tax flexibility in terms of tax reporting, income-splitting, obtaining capital and operating revenues, providing employee incentives (fringe benefits), lower income tax rates in many situations, as well as the opportunity of electing the benefits of corporate legal status and partnership tax status under the S corporation provisions of federal and state corporate tax laws.

- The formality associated with the corporate form provides insiders with an opportunity to review and reflect upon business decisions, and it gives outsiders increased confidence in the stability of the business.

- The corporation has an independent legal existence which is unaffected by death or changes in ownership or management.

Disadvantages

- One disadvantage of the corporate form involves complying with the formalities of the New York Business Corporation Law, and other state laws, rules and regulations concerning corporations. For small corporations, such as those formed with this book, these are not generally onerous, but as we will explain, they do exist. In addition, there are initial filing fees of at least $110 and annual franchise tax payments of a minimum of $250.

- The other main disadvantage of incorporating has traditionally been the $1,000 or more that you could expect to pay an attorney. This book, together with a little effort on your part, should significantly reduce, if not eliminate, this cost.

- Another perceived disadvantage of incorporating in New York, in the view of some incorporators, is that New York incorporation fees and on-going formalities are more cumbersome than those found in other states. This last issue is addressed in the next section.

D. Incorporating Out-Of-State (or the Myth of the "Trouble-Free, Tax-Free" Delaware Corporation)

NO DOUBT YOU HAVE HEARD about the possibility of incorporating in another state, most notably Delaware, where initial and ongoing fees are lower and regulations may be less restrictive than in New York.

Even though New York's corporation laws are competitive with other corporate-friendly jurisdictions (for example, New York has enacted liberal director immunity and indemnification statutes and modern anti-takeover provisions—see Chapter 2D2 for a discussion of some of these provisions), some larger, publicly-held corporations may prefer to incorporate in another state. For most New York-based businesses, however, out-of-state incorporation is not desirable.

It is true that you may incorporate in any state you please. No matter where your business is incorporated, however, if your out-of-state corporation is considered to be transacting business intrastate (i.e., within New York), you must file certain papers with the Department of State of New York which permit your corporation to do business in New York.

Although the rules regarding what constitutes doing business are quite technical, generally, if a corporation has permanent or regular dealings within the state, it is considered to be doing business here.[8] If an out-of-state (legally referred to as a "foreign") corporation is doing business in New York without having qualified to do so, the Attorney General of the state can obtain an injunction forbidding the

---

[8]See Section 1301(b) of the Business Corporation Law for a statutory examples of activities that do not constitute doing business in New York.

corporation from continuing its business in New York. There are, in addition, other penalties for unauthorized business operations within the state. Among them is the inability to initiate a court action within the state (although your corporation can be sued here).

To qualify to do business in New York, a foreign corporation must file an application for authority with the Department of State. This procedure is similar to that for setting up and qualifying a New York corporation (as discussed in Chapter 5). Once qualified, a foreign corporation is given the powers allowed it under the laws of its home state (as long as these powers are not greater than those allowed under New York law).[9] Also note that the directors and officers of foreign corporations doing business in New York are specifically made subject to the same liability for their actions or misconduct as are the directors and officers of New York corporations.[10]

The fee for filing an application to do business in New York for a foreign corporation is $200, plus a license fee based on the value or amount of its capital stock employed in New York. A foreign corporation is also subject to New York franchise taxes and must pay an annual maintenance fee of $200 (this fee is credited towards any franchise taxes paid by the foreign corporation).

The conclusion to this is simple. It is expensive as well as time-consuming to incorporate in another state and become qualified in New York. If you are going to do most of your business in New York, then incorporate here.

[9]See § 1306 of the BCL.

[10]See § 1317 of the BCL.

A CLOSER LOOK AT
NEW YORK CORPORATIONS

Chapter 2

A CLOSER LOOK AT
NEW YORK CORPORATIONS

THIS CHAPTER GIVES YOU some background on the particular legal and tax provisions of concern to New York corporations. Much of the information discussed here will be important to you in considering whether or not to incorporate. Some information relates to the day-to-day operations of the corporation. The rest is simply nice to know.

A. Kinds of New York Corporations

NEW YORK CLASSIFIES CORPORATIONS in several, sometimes overlapping ways. The first classification is "domestic" vs. "foreign." A domestic corporation is one which is formed under the laws of New York by filing a Certificate of Incorporation with the Department of State in New York and fulfilling other requirements of the law which will be discussed later. A corporation which is formed in another state, even if it is physically present (that is, has an office here) and is doing business in New York, is a foreign corporation.

Corporations can also be classified as business corporations, not-for-profit corporations, professional corporations, etc. For the purposes of this book, we will usually refer to a regular business corporation (the type you will form) as a "for-profit" or "profit" corporation. The following sections provide a brief discussion of these kinds of corporations.

1. Nonprofit Corporations

A nonprofit corporation is a nonstock corporation, formed by one or more persons under the New York Not-For-Profit Corporation Law. Not-for-Profit corporations are generally defined as nonprofit groups organized for mutual benefit purposes, or organized and operated for religious, charitable, scientific, literary or educational purposes, or civic clubs and fraternal organizations. In other words, your corporation must be designed for some public or quasi-public purpose in order to incorporate under the Not-For-Profit Law.

The Not-For-Profit Corporation Law prohibits the distribution of the corporation's profits to its members or nonmembers except under specific circumstances. Most nonprofit corporations dedicate all corporate assets to another nonprofit corporation upon dissolution to comply with the stricter provisions of state and federal tax laws and to obtain exemptions from payment of corporate income tax (the main reason for organizing as a nonprofit corporation).

Nonprofit corporations, like regular business corporations, have directors who manage the business of the corporation. Instead of shares of stock, membership certificates can be issued whose purchasing price, if any, is levied against the members and paid as enrollment fees or dues. Like regular corporations, a nonprofit corporation may sue or be sued, incur debts and obligations, acquire and hold property, and engage, generally, in any lawful activity not inconsistent with its purposes and its nonprofit status. It also provides its directors and members with limited liability for the debts or liabilities of the business and continues perpetually unless steps are taken to terminate it.

It is unlikely that the corporation you have in mind will fall into this category. You probably wish to incorporate a business with the hope that it will make a profit which will then be distributed to you and your fellow shareholders. If this is the case, you must follow the provisions of the New York Business Corporation Law discussed in the remainder of this book. If you do wish to form a nonprofit corporation, this book will not help you.

2. Profit Corporations

There are several types of profit corporations. You are probably familiar with the large ones with listings on stock exchanges and many thousands or millions of shares of stock. These corporations are regulated by governmental agencies and require considerable red tape before they are permitted to set up and operate. Just qualifying shares of stock for sale with the New York Attorney General's Office and the federal Securities and Exchange Commission can be a major undertaking. If you are interested in setting up a corporation with shares sold by public subscription, see a lawyer—you will quickly get into areas of law which are beyond the scope of this book. If you are going to start on a smaller scale, read on.

a. The Professional Service Corporation (Doctors, Lawyers, Etc.)

Under the terms of the Professional Service Corporation Act[1], certain professionals may incorporate their practices by complying with the standard state incorporation formalities. The Act provides that professional services may be rendered by a professional service corporation only through individuals who are licensed to practice the particular profession in which the corporation is engaged. It also limits ownership of corporate shares to such licensed individuals and makes the corporation subject to the rules, regulations and disciplinary powers of the regulating body. The written consent of the State Education Department, Division of Professional Licensing must be obtained prior to incorporating a professional service corporation and a certificate of approval from the Division must be filed with the corporation's Certificate of Incorporation.The following is a list of

professions which may, if they desire, incorporate. If they do so, the corporation must be organized as a professional service corporation. *A professional service corporation cannot be formed by using this book.*

Accounting (Certified Public Accounting and Public Accounting)
Acupuncture
Animal Health Technology
Architecture
Attorney[2]
Audiology
Chiropractic
Dental Hygiene
Dentistry
Engineering
Land Surveyor
Landscape Architecture
Massage
Medicine
Nursing (Licensed Practical Nursing and Registered Professional Nurse)
Occupational Therapist Assistant
Occupational Therapy
Opthalmic Dispensing
Optometry
Pharmacy
Physical Therapist Assistant
Physical Therapy
Physician's Assistant
Podiatry
Psychology
Shorthand Reporting
Social Work
Specialist's Assistant

---

[1]Section 1501-1516 of the Business Corporation Law.

[2]Although attorneys must also incorporate as a professional corporation, they must obtain the approval of the appellate division of the supreme court where they are enrolled, not the Department of Education.

Speech Language Pathology
Veterinary Medicine

Important Note: Professions are occasionaly added to this list. If you plan to incorporate any type of professional practice, call the State Education Department, Division of Professional Licensing, in Albany (518-474-8225) to see if you must form a professional corporation (with the help of a lawyer).

Tax Note for Certain Professionals: As mentioned earlier and explained in Chapter 4B1, professionals engaged in the fields of health, law, engineering, architecture, accounting, actuarial science or consulting will be subject to the maximum 34% federal corporate tax rate if substantially all the stock of the corporation is owned by the employees who perform professional services for the corporation—this rate will be applied to any taxable income left in the corporation (not paid out as salary, fringe benefits, etc.) at the end of the corporation's tax year whether or not the individuals involved are organized as a New York professional or New York for-profit corporation.

b. The Small New York Corporation

This is the type of New York corporation for which this book is written. More specifically, we show you how to form a small for-profit corporation by filing your Certificate of Incorporation with the New York Department of State. For our purposes, a small corporation is one which has less than ten shareholders and which is making an intrastate offering of shares. An intrastate offering means an offer and sale of shares within New York to New York residents. You will also see that most of the information in this book also applies generally to corporations which are offering their initial shares to a limited number of people who have close personal, business or family ties, for a relatively small amount of money. Forming a small corporation is not difficult, but it is important that you meet all the qualifications.

B. Corporate Powers

THE BUSINESS CORPORATION LAW gives profit corporations carte blanche to engage in any lawful business activity. Generally this means that a for-profit corporation can do anything that a natural person can do. The law, by way of illustration and not limitation, lists the following corporate powers:

- To adopt, use, and alter a corporate seal;

- To adopt, amend, and repeal bylaws;

- To qualify to do business in any other state, territory, dependency or foreign country;

- Subject to certain restrictions, to issue, purchase, redeem, receive, take or otherwise acquire, own, hold, sell, lend, exchange, transfer, or otherwise dispose of, pledge, use, and otherwise deal in and with its own shares, bonds, debentures and other securities;

- To make donations, regardless of specific corporate benefit, for the public welfare or for community fund, hospital, charitable, educational, scientific, or civic or similar purposes;

- To pay pensions, and establish and carry out pension, profit-sharing, share-bonus, share-pension, share-option, savings, thrift, and other retirement, incentive and benefit plans, trusts and provisions for any or all of the directors, officers and employees of the corporation or any of its subsidiary or affiliated corporations and to indemnify and purchase and maintain insurance on behalf of any fiduciary of such plans, trusts, or provisions;

- Except with respect to certain restrictions as to loans to directors, officers and employees which we discuss later, to assume obligations, enter into contracts, including contracts of guaranty or suretyship, incur liabilities, borrow and lend money and otherwise use its credit, and secure any of its obligations, contracts or liabilities by mortgage, pledge or other encumbrance of all or any part of its property, franchises and income;

- To participate with others in any partnership, joint venture or other association, transaction or arrangement of any kind, whether or not such participation involves sharing or delegation of control with or to others.

C. Corporate Purposes

CORPORATIONS MAY BE FORMED for any "lawful" purpose. In legalese, "lawful" doesn't just mean noncriminal, it means not otherwise prohibited by law. As we've said, prior to the enactment of the law permitting lawyers and other professionals to incorporate, it was "unlawful" to incorporate certain professions. Now, it is lawful to incorporate almost any business. Of course, different professions or businesses may be subject to their own special regulations and added controls, but the "privilege" of incorporating is open to virtually everyone. Moreover, unless you're incorporating a professional corporation, bank, trust company, insurance company, certain types of transportation companies, or other types of businesses that require special permission from certain state authorities, you do not even need to mention in your Certificate of Incorporation the specific type of business you will be engaged in. Those of you who use the forms included in this book to incorporate your business will be forming a corporation for the purpose of engaging in any business except those types discussed above.

D. Corporate People

WHILE A CORPORATION is a "legal person" capable of making contracts, paying taxes, etc., it needs real people to carry out its business. These corporate people are classified in the following ways:

- Promoter

- Incorporator

- Director

- Officer

- Shareholder

   Note: Distinctions between these different roles often become blurred in a small corporation setting since one person may simultaneously serve in more than one, or all, of these capacities.

   The courts and the Business Corporation Law have given these corporate people varying powers and responsibilities. Here we discuss these provisions and a few court-developed rules. Don't let this information intimidate you.

If you read it through several times you will see that many of the do's and don'ts are based on common sense concepts of honesty and fair dealing.

1. Promoters and Incorporators

A "promoter" is a person who starts in motion the process of forming a corporation. You don't need any permission or authority or license to be a promoter. All you have to do is want to form a corporation and start doing something about it. However, as a "promoter," you are subject to some aspects of the law, so you must be a bit cautious in how you go about things. As long as you attempt to induce people to invest in a corporation, you will legally be considered a promoter. In the case of most people who read this book, you will stop being promoters once the corporation is formed and the stock is all issued. Of course, if more stock is sold later you could become a promoter again.

If you are the promoter of a corporation not yet formed, be careful about signing contracts on behalf of the corporation (this includes leases). You may wind up being personally liable if the corporation does not accept them. One way to attempt to avoid this is to make clear to the other party that you are acting on behalf of a corporation which is not yet in existence, and the contract you are signing is subject to ratification by the corporation once it comes into existence.

Also, as a promoter, you must be open about your dealings in matters concerning the corporation—you can't make secret profits and can be held liable for misrepresentations or fraudulent statements. However, someone has to take the first steps. If you are honest, and are careful about what agreements you sign–in short, if you use common sense–you should have no problems. This is especially true if you are incorporating a small business in which all shares are to be owned by a few family members or close business associates.

An incorporator can be anyone who is at least eighteen years of age and who is involved in the formation of a corporation. Generally this involvement consists of signing and filing the Certificate of Incorporation discussed in Chapter 5. There is very little difference between an incorporator and a promoter other than a commonly held perception that a promoter is more active in raising money and getting the corporation off the ground. The same rules which apply to promoters also apply to incorporators.

2. Directors

Except for certain specific management decisions which the law reserves to the shareholders and other specific circumstances discussed more fully in Chapter 3B, the directors are given the authority and responsibility of managing the affairs of the corporation. The directors meet and make decisions collectively as a board of directors. However, the Business Corporation Law does permit the board to delegate, by resolution, most of the management of the corporation to an executive committee or other committees consisting of three or more directors.

(Obviously, if your corporation has fewer than three directors, you can't do this.) This arrangement is often used when one or more of the directors is unwilling or unable to assume an active voice in corporate affairs and the remaining directors wish to assume full control. The passive directors should still keep an eye on what the other directors are up to, as the courts have held them liable for the mismanagement of the active directors.

Directors must act in its best interests of the corporation and exercise care in the making of management decisions. What does this mean? The Business Corporation Law says that directors must perform their duties "...in good faith and with that degree of care which an ordinarily prudent person in a like position would use under similar circumstances."[3] (this duty is sometimes referred to as the directors' "duty of care."). Courts, in turn, decide whether directors have met this broad statutory standard on a case-by-case basis. Traditionally, in the absence of evidence of fraud, self-dealing or bad faith, there is a presumption that the acts of a director are proper, fair and honest. Broadly speaking, the courts say that honest errors in business judgment are OK (this court-developed rule is known as the "business judgement rule"), while fraudulent or negligent behavior isn't.

The BCL specifically permits a director to rely on information, opinions, reports or statements prepared or presented by:

- officers of the corporation whom the director believes to be reliable and competent in the matters presented;

- lawyers and accountants and other persons as to matters which the director believes to be within such person's professional or expert competence, or

---

[3]BCL § 717(a).

- committees of the board upon which the director does not serve if the director believes the committee merits confidence and if the matters are within the committee's designated authority.

In all cases, the director must rely on these sources in good faith and with the degree of care specified above. A director will not be considered to have relied in good faith if the director has knowledge concerning the matter in question that would cause such reliance to be unwarranted. If a director performs his duties according to these rules, the BCL states that the director "...shall have no liability by reason of being or having been a director of the corporation."

The director owes the corporation loyalty and usually must give the corporation a "right of first refusal" as to business opportunities she becomes aware of in the capacity of corporate director. If the corporation fails to take advantage of the opportunity after full disclosure (purchase of inexpensive land, for example) or clearly would not be interested in it, the director can go ahead for herself. It is best to have this type of transaction approved at a board meeting and inserted in the corporate records.

Directors normally serve without compensation since their work, as directors serving on the board, is usually done because they are intimately involved with the business of the corporation and will gain financially if the corporation does well by being able to pay themselves a better salary and/or eventually selling the business. Reasonable compensation is allowed, however, if given for the performance of real services to the corporation and if it is provided for in advance. A director may be authorized to receive advancement or reimbursement for reasonable out-of-pocket expenses (e.g., travel expenses) incurred in the performance of any of his corporate duties.

The board of directors may properly vote on a matter in which one or more of the directors has a substantial financial interest, provided the following conditions are met:

- The material facts of the director's interest are disclosed in good faith or known to the board and the board vote to approve the transaction is sufficient without counting the vote of the interested director (even if these votes are insufficient, the transaction may be approved by the unanimous vote of the disinterested directors);

- The material facts of the director's interest are disclosed in good faith or known to the shareholders and the shareholders approve the transaction; or

- The contract or transaction is proven to be fair and reasonable as to the corporation at the time it was approved by the board or shareholders.

The BCL provides other means of approving transactions or contracts in which a director has a substantial financial interest.[4] Unless otherwise provided in the Certificate of Incorporation or Bylaws, the board is specifically allowed under the BCL to fix the compensation of directors for services in any capacity.

The corporation cannot make a loan to a director unless it is authorized by vote of the shareholders (the shares of a director who would be the borrower are not entitled to vote on approval of the loan).[5]

If you wish to put additional restrictions on business transactions between the directors and your corporation, they can be inserted in the Certificate of Incorporation (discussed in Chapter 5). This may include a provision prohibiting all such transactions if desired. You should note that the rules concerning transactions or contracts between a director and the corporation also apply to transactions between two corporations with one or more common directors.

Generally, if a director violates one of the above rules (e.g., he does not meet the requisite duty of care when approving corporate transactions, takes advantage of corporate opportunities, participates in unlawful transactions), he can be personally liable for any loss that the corporation, shareholders or creditors suffer.

In the event a director enters into an undisclosed transaction with the corporation, he can be made to pay to the corporation all of the profits made on the transaction. Generally, if a transaction entered into between a director and the corporation is honest to begin with, and all aspects of it are fully disclosed to the board of directors or the shareholders *before* the transaction is completed, any profits made by the director can be retained and need not be paid to the corporation.

Director Protection Note: New York, like other jurisdictions friendly to corporate formation such as Delaware and California, has enacted special provisions which help protect directors from personal liability and expenses incurred in the event of lawsuits by shareholders. See the shaded box below for a discussion of New York's special director immunity and indemnification rules.

---

[4]See BCL § 713.

[5]BCL § 714.

New York Director Immunity and Indemnification Rules

Specifically, Section 402(b) of the Business Corporation Law allows a corporation to limit or eliminate the personal liability of directors to the corporation or the shareholders for breach of the director's duty as a director (in other words, for breach, by a director, of the statutory duty of care discussed above). However, a corporation cannot limit or eliminate a director's personal liability if a judgment or other final adjudication establishes that the director's acts or omissions consisted of, or involved, any of the following:

- Bad faith;
- Intentional misconduct;
- A knowing violation of law;
- The personal gain of financial profit or other advantage to which the director was not entitled;
- A violation of Section 719 of the BCL (liability of directors in certain cases such as the unlawful declaration of dividends, purchase of shares, distribution of assets and making of loans).

To take advantage of these director immunity provisions, special language must be included in the corporation's Certificate of Incorporation (any personal liability of director's occuring prior to the adoption of this special language cannot be eliminated). In Chapter 5 we show you how to prepare and file a Certificate of Incorporation which contains language elimi-nating the personal liability of your directors under these provisions [under Section 402(b) of the BCL].

The BCL also helps directors (and officers) by allowing (and sometimes requiring) a corporation, under certain circumstances, to indemnify (pay back) a director or officer for reasonable expenses (including legal fees) incurred in defending a lawsuit or other proceeding, as well as fines, judgments, settlements and other amounts which may be charged against a director or officer in connection with these proceedings. Indemnification can apply to lawsuits brought against the directors by the shareholders, as well as lawsuits brought by outside parties.

The statutory rules for indemnification are complex. Generally, to be entitled to indemnification under the statute,[6] a director (or officer) must have acted in

---

[6]New York's statutory indemnification rules are contained in BCL §§ 721-726.

good faith, for a purpose which the director reasonably believed to be in the best interests of the corporation (in criminal proceedings, the director must also have had no reason to believe that the conduct was unlawful). In actions where a director is sued by or in the right of the corporation (e.g., in a shareholder's derivative suit where a shareholder sues a director in the name of the corporation—see subsection 4 below for a further discussion), special indemnification rules must be met if the case is pending or settled out-of-court or where the director is judged to be liable in the proceeding.

Further, a corporation is specifically permitted to go beyond the statutory indemnification provisions of the BCL and to provide indemnification for directors and officers in situations not covered by the indemnification statutes. This non-statutory indemnification can be provided for in the Certificate of Incorporation, the Bylaws, or, if authorized by the Certificate of Incorporation or Bylaws, by a resolution of the directors or shareholders or according to the terms of separate agreements. Although this non-statutory indemnification can be customizeded to fit the partuicular needs of each corporation, there are still a few situations where this extra indemnification cannot be provided (situations involving bad faith, deliberate dishonesty, or unjustifiable personal gain on the part of the director or officer[7]).

The main point of this discussion is that directors and officers are entitled to, or may be granted, indemnification rights which allow them to be paid by the corporation for various amounts they may incur in connection with lawsuits and other proceedings brought against them. As we've said, these rights can arise by operation of law (under the explicit terms of New York's indemnification statutes) or by agreement (non-statutory indemnification provided for, or authorized by, the corporation's Certificate of Incorporation or Bylaws). Most incorporators of smaller corporations will probably feel that New York's statutory indemnification rights are sufficient and will not feel it necessary to provide non-statutory indemnification for their directors and officers. The Bylaws, prepared as part of Chapter 5, contain language which authorizes the corporation to provide for non-statutory indemnification should you wish to do so (you will need to see a lawyer to prepare special resolutions or agreements actually providing for such non-statutory indemnification).

[7]See BCL § 721.

Reality Note: Of course, if you are forming your own closely-held corporation with, let's say, just you and your spouse acting as the corporation's only directors, officers and shareholders much of the discussion in this and the subsequent sections regarding director immunity from, or indemnification against, shareholder suits, as well as other formal corporate director, officer and shareholder procedures and rules will not be as important to you. In such cases, since there will be an identity of interest between you and your closely-held corporation, it's not so important that you deal with your corporation at arm's length or worry about disgruntled shareholders (after all, you're not likely to want to sue yourself). However, if even a few others invest in your corporation, all the rules and legal principles regarding fair dealing discussed here do apply and you will want to make sure, as a matter of law and basic fairness, to protect your shareholders' interests when making corporate decisions.

3. Officers

Officers (president, vice-president, secretary, treasurer) are elected or appointed by the board of directors and, customarily, are charged with supervising (or, in the context of the small corporation, carrying out) the day-to-day business of the corporation. The powers, duties, and responsibilities of officers are set by the Certificate of Incorporation, the Bylaws, or by resolution of the board of directors. Like directors, officers must perform their duties in good faith and with due care.

Another Reality Note: In smaller corporations, the board of directors and the officers will often be the same people. However, the directors, as such, should still meet as a board to authorize the officers to enter in major corporate transactions (such as the issuance of stock, sale or pledge of significant corporate assets, etc.) to ensure that courts and the IRS will treat your business as a viable corporate entity (see Section I below for a further discussion of this issue).

Officers are considered by the courts to be agents of the corporation and can subject the corporation to liability for their negligent or intentional acts which cause damage to people or property if such acts were performed within the course and scope of their employment. The corporation, moreover, is bound by the contracts and obligations entered into or incurred by the corporate officers if they had legal authority to transact the business. This authority can be actual authority (a bylaw provision or resolution by the board of directors), implied authority (a necessary but unspecified part of duties set out in the bylaws or a board resolution), or apparent authority (where a third party reasonably believes the officer has certain authority). Generally, the courts allow a third party to rely on the signature of the president, vice-president, secretary or assistant secretary, treasurer, or assistant treasurer on any written instrument, whether or not the officer had any actual or implied authority to sign the instrument on behalf of the corporation, as long as the third party did not know, or did not have reason to know, that the corporate officer didn't have authority to sign it.

Note: Of course, any act performed by an officer without the legal authority discussed above binds the corporation if it accepts the benefits of the transaction or if the board of directors ratifies the transaction after the fact.

Corporate officers are normally compensated for their services to the corporation, either as officers or simply as employees of the corporation. The compensation should be reasonable and given for services actually performed for the corporation.

Example: Jason Horner and Elmore Johnson form their own publishing company. Jason is the President and Elmore is the Treasurer of the corporation. Jason is paid a salary for acting as the Publisher (not for serving as President). Elmore is paid a regular annual salary as Treasurer (for the bookkeeping, bill paying and other ongoing work related to the financial operations of the corporation). The point here is that the title of the person being paid is not critical (officer title versus an employee title). What does matter is the nature and extent of the work for which the person is being compensated.

Officers, like directors, can be indemnified against judgments, fines and other amounts under the rules discussed in the previous subsection.

4. Shareholders

Again, when reading this material, remember our earlier reality note: If you are forming a closely-held corporation and will not bring in any outside shareholders (by outside shareholders we mean outsiders who do not also manage and operate the corporation as directors and officers), you will not need to protect yourself or your own corporation against your own actions and much of the following discussion will not apply to you. Also realize that the directors of closely-held corporations without passive investors are not likely to wish to pay themselves dividends, preferring instead to compensate themselves directly as employees by way of deductible salaries and bonuses (see Chapter 1B2).

Shareholders, generally, have no specific statutory responsibility to the corporation beyond paying the corporation the full value of the shares they purchase. This value is determined by the board of directors and may change from time to time.

Exception: As noted earlier, the 10 largest shareholders of privately-held corporations can be held personally liable for wages and other amounts owed to corporate employees.

Shareholders vote for the board of directors and do, therefore, have an indirect voice in the management of the corporation. In addition, the shareholders can amend, repeal or adopt new bylaws and therefore influence the rules under which the corporation is managed, and expand or limit their authority accordingly.

The Business Corporation Law requires shareholder approval of certain corporate acts, including the following:

- The amendment of the Certificate of Incorporation;

- The sale, lease, exchange or other disposition of all or substantially all of the corporate assets other than in the usual or regular course of its business;

- The approval of a plan of merger or consolidation of the corporation.

Also, shareholder approval must, or may, be sought with respect to loans to directors, transactions or contracts in which a director has a substantial financial interest or indemnifications given by the corporation in favor of an officer or director. Shareholders also have the power to act independently of the board of directors in certain limited situations, the most important, aside from electing directors, being a unilateral shareholder decision to dissolve the corporation.

In the absence of provisions to the contrary contained in the Certificate of Incorporation or Bylaws, shareholders are given one vote per share (i.e., if you own 100 shares, you cast 100 votes for or against a shareholder action), with a majority vote usually necessary to decide an issue subject to shareholder approval. Shareholders whose names appear on the records book of the corporation as of a certain date specified by the board of directors are entitled to vote on the matter in question. The record date must be no more than 50, nor less than 10, days prior to the shareholder meeting.

Aside from the limited participation in corporate affairs discussed above, shareholders' rights primarily include the right to participate in the profits of the corporation through dividends and the right to participate, after the creditors are paid, in the liquidation proceeds of a dissolved corporation.

The person or persons who own a majority of the stock of a corporation, for all practical purposes, control the corporation. Assuming that there are no shareholder or other agreements which prevent such action (shareholder agreements are discussed in Chapter 3, Section B4), majority shareholders can take over control of the corporation, either directly by electing themselves directors and officers, or indirectly by vetoing corporate actions. Despite this enormous power, the majority shareholders have no specific legal or fiduciary responsibility to the minority shareholders. However, if the majority act in a manner which is contrary to the corporation's best interests, or do anything which injures

(financially) the minority shareholders, they can be sued. In short, if you are a majority shareholder, you must act in good faith towards other shareholders and not do anything which harms the corporation's business.

A shareholder, like any other person, can sue the corporation for *personal* wrongs or damages suffered on account of corporate action. If, however, the shareholder is damaged in her capacity as a shareholder (e.g., wasting of corporate assets by the officers or directors which devalues stock), the law says that the real injury is to the corporation. An injured shareholder, in this case, must ask the board of directors to bring suit or take the appropriate action. Of course, where the damage was caused by the mismanagement, negligence, or fraud of the officers or directors, the shareholder is, in effect, asking them to take action against themselves and, as you might guess, this doesn't always bring immediate results.

If the shareholder can't get the officers or directors to bring suit, as in the situation described above, or if an attempt to get them to do this through intra-corporate channels would be futile, the shareholder can bring suit in his own name. This legal action is called a *shareholder's derivative suit* since, as the theory goes, the shareholder derives the right to sue from, and on behalf of, the corporation which is considered to be the party sustaining the injury. An attorney can tell you more about this type of suit if it ever becomes an issue (fortunately, in the context of the closely-held corporation, it rarely does).

E. Capitalization

A CORPORATION NEEDS people and money to get started. In the common sense definition of the term, the money or dollar value of assets used to set up a corporation is called capital and the process of raising the money or other assets is called capitalizing the corporation. There are no minimum capitalization requirements for corporations in New York—theoretically, you could start a corporation with next to no money, property, or other assets. There must be some consideration, e.g., money, given for shares, even if it's only a one-person corporation, but there are no statutory requirements as to how much is necessary.

In a practical sense, however, the idea of starting a corporation without assets is absurd. Profit corporations are in business to make money, and if you don't have assets to start with, it is unlikely that you're going to be much of a success. In a legal sense, too, an undercapitalized corporation is risky. Even though New York doesn't require a corporation to have a minimum amount of assets, courts in New York have been known to disregard the corporate existence and hold the shareholders of a corporation personally liable if there is the appearance of fraud, illegality or some other wrongdoing. The fact that very little money has been put into the corporation merely reinforces

any suspicions which may already exist. The court decisions very much rely upon the specific facts of a situation, so it is impossible to spell out hard and fast rules. Since you are going to be doing business through your corporation, in any event, to be on the safe side and to give yourself the best chance of making a success of your corporation, you should pay into the corporation enough money and other assets to start operations and cover, at minimum, foreseeable short-range expenses and the liabilities that might occur in the particular business in which you plan to engage.

There are several ways to get the assets necessary to capitalize a corporation. Often this is no problem at all, as the incorporators are simply formalizing the operations of an already existing business (partnership or sole proprietorship). The assets of the existing business are transferred to the new corporation in return for shares of stock.

In most other situations, a corporation is capitalized with money, property, or past services contributed to the corporation in return for shares of stock, or with money loaned to the corporation.

It should be realized that the term capitalization refers loosely to the assets that a corporation starts out with and, as we've said, there should be enough to guarantee a good start. In bookkeeping terms, however, capitalization has a specific meaning and refers to the way the organizational assets are carried on the corporate books—as stated capital, surplus, or debt.

Under the Business Corporation Law, the portion of the money or the dollar value of the property received by the corporation for its shares which represents the par value of the shares is considered to be the "stated capital" of the corporation.[8] If the stock has no par value, all the money or property received for the issued stock will be considered to be stated capital, although the board of directors, within 60 days of the time the no par value stock is issued, may elect to allocate some, but not all, of the money given for the stock to "surplus." This technical distinction between stated capital and surplus can be important since the Business Corporation Law restricts the ability of the corporation to reduce the amount in the stated capital account. Some portions of the receipts from the sale of no par shares must be allocated to the stated capital account (the remainder can be allocated to the surplus account). You will see that the corporate minutes included with this book provide for this allocation in Chapter 5, Step 8. Since the requirements for each corporation differ significantly, and since technical restrictions on making this allocation apply in special circumstances (contained in Section 506 of the BCL), we suggest you speak with an accountant prior to making this allocation.

Debt is, quite logically, money borrowed by the corporation in return for promissory notes or other debt instruments which usually specify a maturity rate and a given rate of interest.

It is often true that the nature of the capitalization assets will, in and of themselves, determine whether they will be carried on the books as equity or debt. In many cases, however, particularly in small corporations, the incorporators can choose whether their contribution to the corporation will be treated as equity or debt. For example, they can loan money to the corporation or contribute it in return for shares of stock. Because there are

significant practical, legal, and tax differences between equity and debt capital, it is often important to seek the advice of an experienced accountant or other financial advisor before opting for a particular capitalization method. We'll take a brief look at these differences to give you a general idea of some of the considerations relevant to your decision.

In practical terms, a contribution of equity capital to a corporation in return for shares of stock is a risk investment. The shareholder will receive a return on this investment if, and only if, the corporation makes a profit and is able to distribute dividends to shareholders or, upon its dissolution, has assets left after payment of the corporate creditors to distribute to the shareholders. When equity contributions are made to a new business which hasn't operated previously in noncorporate form, this is indeed a high risk investment. A debt transaction is a bit safer, with the contributor relying on the terms of the loan agreement as to the date of repayment and the rate of return (interest) and, as we've already mentioned, often demanding that the personal assets of the incorporators be pledged for security. A standard note, however, unlike a stock certificate, doesn't carry with it the attractive possibility of providing the contributor with a percentage of the profits or the liquidation assets of a successful enterprise.

The situation is altered somewhat for a closely-held corporation in that the shareholders of the corporation are not normally passively investing in an enterprise but are rather simply incorporating their own business which will pay them a salary in return for their efforts and provide them with favorable corporate tax advantages. Nonetheless, if the incorporators lend money to the corporation, they too will be able to look to the specific terms of a promissory note in seeking a guaranteed rate of return on their investment, rather than relying solely on

---

[8]We discuss the concept of par value in Section G2 of this chapter. The great majority of small New York corporations issue stock with no par value, so, generally speaking, it's not something you will have to worry a lot about.

the profits of the corporation to pay them money by way of salary.

For tax purposes, an equity contribution may result in the recognition of income by the shareholders: dividends paid to shareholders are taxed to them at their own individual income tax rates. In addition, payment of dividends to shareholders is a distribution of profits, and the corporation is not allowed a business expense deduction for these payments. Debt capital, on the other hand, provides certain tax advantages to the corporation and to the noteholder. Interest payments, like dividends, are taxed to the recipient as income, but the repayment of principal is simply a return of capital giving rise to no individual tax liability. The corporation, moreover, is allowed to deduct interest payments as a business expense on its tax return.

Here's an example of how these rules might work in the context of the incorporation of a one-person business:

Let's assume that Phil Spectrum owns and operates a small unincorporated 24 track recording studio, Spectrum Sound. The studio has been doing well; so well in fact, that Phil's accountant, Malcolm, tells him that he can't afford not to incorporate—the net profits are resulting in excessive individual tax liability for Phil. Phil only needs a portion of these net profits to meet his personal needs, the rest of these profits are always put right back the business. Malcolm values the business at $150,000 (book value) and advises Phil to transfer 1/3 of the business assets to the new corporation in return for $50,000 worth of stock in Spectrum Sound Inc., and to transfer the other $100,000 in return for a promissory note from his corporation which will be repaid to him in monthly installments consisting mostly of principal repayments together with a smaller amount representing a reasonable rate of interest.

The net result is that Phil is still "taking home" the same amount of money, this time in the form of a salary from his corporation and in monthly principal and interest payments on the note. However, he only pays individual taxes on the salary amount and the interest payments on the note—the principal payments on the note are a non-taxable return of capital. As a result, he has substantially lowered the amount of money he must report on his individual tax returns. Phil's corporation, on the other hand, pays corporate taxes (at the lower graduated corporate tax rates) on the net profits of the business, deducting, as we've said, salary and interest payments to Phil.

Warning: Debt to Equity Ratios Should Be Reasonable. Absent any other capital contribution, it's a mistake to transfer all assets of an unincorporated business to a corporation in return for a note. As we've said, your corporation should begin with a reasonable amount of equity in its capital account. One reason for this is that the courts and the IRS have often been suspicious of corporations with a high ratio of debt to equity, feeling that creditors were inadequately protected and that the corporation was a sham designed to insulate incorporators from personal liability and to grant them undeserved tax benefits (see Chapter 2I for more on this). For instance, if a disproportionate amount of money is "loaned" to the corporation by the incorporators of a closely-held corporation rather than paid in for stock, and the repayment terms are unduly permissive or generous, it might be held that the contribution was, in essence, an equity transaction contrived as debt to obtain favorable tax treatment. In this situation, the interest payments are subject to being treated as dividends, with the corporation unable to deduct these payments as a business expense and the lender-shareholder having to report repayment of the principal of the loan as income rather than a return of capital.

Another practical reason for watching your debt to equity ratio is that banks are unlikely to loan money to your corporation if this ratio is particularly lopsided (too much debt/not enough equity).

A rule-of-thumb (which is subject to loads of exceptions depending on specific circumstances) is that a 3 to 1 debt to equity ratio (e.g., $30,000 of debt, $10,000 of equity) is considered to be relatively safe, while higher debt to equity ratios are considered to be progressively more risky, particularly those which exceed 10 to 1. (In the "Phil Spectrum" example above, Spectrum Sound Inc. will be incorporated with $50,000 worth of debt and $25,000 in assets, resulting in a debt-to-equity ratio of 2 to 1—an accountant will normally consider this to be an acceptable ratio). Obviously, rules of thumb really provide very little guidance, so ask your accountant or other tax advisor for her opinion before deciding on a particular level of debt when capitalizing your corporation with loans.

The courts have listed a number of criteria which they will consider when attempting to determine if a purported debt arrangement should be treated as a real debt obligation or whether it should be reclassified to the less

favorable status of an equity contribution. Briefly stated, the courts have indicated that the debt instrument should be drawn up as a regular promissory note with a fixed maturity date and a specified rate of interest, and the corporation should have the right to enforce the terms of the note. The corporation should not arbitrarily grant the person making the loan any special preferences over other lenders or allow this person to postpone payments on the note. If the corporation is "thinly" capitalized (has a high ratio of debt to equity), can obtain loan funds from outside lenders, or uses the loan proceeds to acquire capital assets, these factors will make disallowance of the loan more likely.[9]

F. Initial Sale of Stock

CORPORATE STOCK may be sold for:

- money
- tangible or intangible property, or
- labor or services actually received by, or performed for, the corporation or for its benefit or in its formation or reorganization.

If shares are sold for other than money, the board of directors should state, by resolution at their meeting, the fair market value of the services, property, or other form of payment given for the shares. Shares cannot be issued in return for promissory notes of the purchaser or in return for the performance of future services. The details of issuing stock are discussed in Chapter 5, Step 9.

---

[9]For a case listing and explaining eleven different debt/equity characterization criteria, see *Hardman, Inc. v. United States*, 87 Daily Journal D.A.R. 6566 (9th Cir. 1987).

Example: Thomas and Richard, after a bit of brainstorming, decide to form a Manhattan hang gliding tour service, called "Two Sheets in the Wind, Inc." Unfortunately, they know only one person who would be willing to actually strap himself in as their tour guide, a fellow flying enthusiast, Harold. Harold sees the unique possibilities associated of this enterprise and insists on owning shares in the corporation rather than being a mere employee. Since all parties concede that not just any Tom, Dick or Harry would be willing to assume this position, it is decided that Harold will receive one-third of the corporation's shares in return for entering into an employment contract with the corporation. Although this arrangement may seem extremely fair under the circumstances, the New York Business Corporation Law, as we've said, does not allow shares to be issued in return for future services and Harold will have to contribute something else of value for his shares. Harold suggests that the corporation issue its shares to him in return for a long-term note (he'll pay for them after he's survived a few tours). Again, since shares cannot be issued in return for promissory notes, this idea is discarded, and Harold decides to pay (or borrow) enough cash to purchase his shares outright.

G. Stock Certificates and Shares of Stock

YOUR OWNERSHIP of a portion or all of the corporation is represented by the stock certificate you receive. A single stock certificate can represent more than one share. For example, if you own 75 shares of a corporation, you may only actually have one stock certificate. Later in this book we will explain how a stock certificate is actually issued. We also provide tear-out certificates which you can use for your corporation.

The stock certificate is a very important document for several reasons. First, the owner of the certificate is the only person who is entitled to vote on corporate decisions, to receive dividends, and to take part in other corporate activities. Secondly, the stock certificate indicates, in short form, any limitations which may be placed on the shares you own. The types of limitations which can be placed on ownership rights are varied and legally complex. We will discuss some of the more common ones in Chapter 5. Generally, these limitations will be in the Certificate of Incorporation before you purchase your stock. You should be aware of any such limitations before you purchase your shares.

1. Types of Shares

The shares of stock of a corporation can legally be divided into different classes and/or series, each with different rights and privileges. The classes you are probably most familiar with are common and preferred stock. As the name suggests, owners of preferred shares are given preference in certain corporate matters such as the right to receive dividends before common shareholders. In this book, we will discuss how to set up a corporation with only one class of stock, i.e., common voting stock with no par value. Issuance of more than one class of stock often presents complex legal, tax and business management questions which require the help of an expert. However, for most small business incorporations, one class of stock will be adequate, at least to begin with.

2. Par Value

The stock you issue can have either a par value or no par value. The concept of par value is, for the most part, only of historical importance, having to do with accounting and financial practices no longer commonly used or relied upon. Basically it means that each share of stock is represented by a sum of money in the corporation's stated capital account equal to the par value of the shares. There is no necessary correlation between the par value of the shares and the actual price at which they are sold—in fact, if par value shares are issued, they are usually sold at a price well above their (usually minimal) par value. For example, if 100 shares of stock are issued for $50.00 per share with a par value of $1.00, the corporation must have at least $100.00 in its stated capital account.

Under today's accounting and financial systems, there is generally little reason to issue shares with par value. This book is only designed to show you how to issue stock with no par value.

3. Other Limitations

There are other limitations which can be placed upon the rights of shares of stock. These limitations may be contained in the Certificate of Incorporation, the Bylaws, or in agreements between the shareholders. Any such limitations must be clearly spelled out on the stock certificates. Typically, these limitations are: (1) restrictions on rights to transfer stock, and (2)

voting agreements between shareholders. We discuss some common limitations in more detail in Chapter 3B.

4. How Much Stock Should You Authorize And Issue?

You will see, in Chapter 5, Step 2, that you will first need to authorize the corporation to issue a certain number of shares in your Certificate of Incorporation. There is no statutory requirement restricting the number of shares you can authorize the corporation to issue. It's important to realize that the mere fact of authorizing a certain number of shares in your Certificate doesn't allow you to treat these shares as paper money or legal tender, nor will you necessarily initially issue all of the shares authorized by your Certificate of Incorporation. Each time you issue shares, as you'll see with your initial issuance, you will need to strictly follow the requirements of state and federal securities laws as well as the other provisions of New York law. As you will see in Chapter 5, Steps 2 and 3, many incorporators authorize 200 no-par shares in the Certificate of Incorporation since this is the largest amount of shares which may be authorized for the smallest filing fee (provided, of course, that this number is sufficient to cover your initial stock issuance).

The actual number of shares which you will initially issue is based upon the actual payments made by your shareholders and is essentially a matter of mathematics and working with whole numbers. You will see in Chapter 5, Step 9, that even though your shares have no par value, they will be sold to all of the initial shareholders at a set price per share (if you discounted the price for one of the shareholders, this might be fraudulent and would dilute the value of shares sold to others). Let's assume that you plan to issue shares to three persons: Mr. C will invest $1,000 cash, Mr. L will transfer land worth

$12,000 for his shares, and Ms. M will sign over $5,000 worth of machinery to the corporation. Setting a price of $100 per share will result in Mr. C receiving 10 shares, Mr. L receiving 120 shares, and Ms. M receiving 50 shares—nice round, manageable numbers. If, on the other hand, you set the share price at $120, Mr. L would receive an even 100 shares, but Mr. C and Ms. M would receive fractional portions of a share—an undesired result.

As you can see, the amount of money or other consideration to be paid for the shares, together with the price per share figure you arrive at, will determine the number of shares you should issue. Generally the results of these computations allow for flexibility. If an accountant or lawyer advises you that a fixed number of shares or a fixed price per share figure should be used due to specific tax or legal circumstances associated with your incorporation, you should, of course, follow his or her advice.

H. Dividends

DIVIDENDS REPRESENT that part of the corporation's earnings which the board of directors may set aside periodically to be divided among the shareholders of the corporation. While usually this payment is in the form of money, the law does not require this. Dividends can be paid, for example, in property, bonds or shares of the corporation. A dividend payment can take any form unless that form is expressly prohibited in the Certificate of Incorporation or the corporation's Bylaws.

Reality Note: As discussed in Chapter 4, smaller corporations rarely declare and pay dividends since they result in double taxation of corporate profits.

The right of the board of directors to declare and pay a dividend is closely controlled by the Business Corporation Law. The purpose of the legal guidelines is basically to prevent a fraud from being perpetrated upon the creditors of the corporation. Therefore, A DIVIDEND CANNOT BE PAID UNLESS:

1. the net assets of the corporation which remain after payment of the dividend equal or exceed the stated capital of the corporation, and

2. the dividend is paid out of surplus only (surplus is the amount by which the net assets of the corporation exceed its stated capital), and

3. the corporation is solvent at the time the dividend is declared or paid, and payment of the dividend will not make the corporation insolvent.[10]

Note: In addition to these rules, the Certificate of Incorporation or the Bylaws may list other circumstances under which the directors will be prohibited from declaring or paying a dividend.

The question of whether a dividend can be legally declared or paid really depends upon the value of the corporation's assets and the amount of its liabilities at the time the dividend is declared or paid. What this means is that you should consider the actual value of the assets, not what you think they should be worth before declaring a dividend (a good rule of thumb is to consider what a third person would pay for them or what you would pay to buy them). Anticipated profits or anticipated payments of debts owed to the corporation should not generally be listed as assets in determining whether dividends can be paid. Goodwill, that is, the value of the corporation's reputation, can be considered as an asset for dividend purposes, but the value to assign to it is a tricky matter and

---

[10]Insolvency means either (1) the inability to pay debts when they come due and (2) when liabilities exceed assets.

you should talk to an accountant if you have to rely on goodwill for paying a dividend.

Finally, all these rules for valuing assets and liabilities must be considered on the date the directors "declare" a dividend. This is the date on which the resolution declaring payment of a dividend is passed at a board of directors meeting. It can be and usually is prior to the date the dividend is actually paid. This means that if circumstances occurring after the declaration date alter the amount of surplus or change the value of the assets, the dividend is not illegal (provided that after paying it the corporation is not insolvent). Once a dividend has been declared, the shareholders become creditors of the corporation up to the amount of the dividends owed them. You should take care to follow the rules set out above since directors and even shareholders who participate in the payment of, or receive, an illegally declared dividend can be sued by creditors of the corporation.

Generally, the matter of declaring dividends is totally within the discretion of the board of directors. They can determine the time, amount, and manner of payment. In a corporation where all the shareholders are also directors, they can distribute the corporation's surplus without going through the formality of declaring a dividend. However, it may be wiser to have the board of directors meet and formally declare a dividend just so a clear record is kept. In all other corporate situations, dividends can only be declared at a formal meeting of the board of directors.

The entire area of declaration and payment of dividends is complex and requires a degree of understanding of technical accounting and legal rules and standards. You should consult with your lawyer and accountant before declaring or paying out a dividend.

I. Piercing the Corporate Veil
(or, If You Want to be Treated Like a Corporation, It's Best to Act Like One)

AFTER YOU'VE SET UP A CORPORATION, you must act like one if you want to be sure to qualify for the legal protections and tax advantages the corporate form offers. Filing your Certificate of Incorporation with the Department of State brings the corporation into existence and transforms it into a legal entity. You should be aware, however, that this is not enough to ensure that a court or the IRS will treat you as a corporation.

Courts occasionally do scrutinize the organization and operations of corporations, particularly closely-held corporations where the shareholders also manage, supervise, and work for the corporation as directors, officers, and employees. If a corporation is inadequately capitalized, doesn't issue stock, diverts funds for the personal use of the shareholders, doesn't keep adequate corporate records (e.g., minutes of annual or special meetings), or, generally, doesn't pay much attention to the theory and practice of corporate life, a court may disregard the corporate entity and hold the shareholders liable for the debts of the corporation. Using the same criteria, the IRS has been known to treat corporate profits as the individual income of the shareholders. In legalese this is called "piercing the corporate veil."

Please Note: Piercing the corporate veil is the exception, not the rule. If you follow the basic precautions mentioned below, you should never face this problem.

To avoid problems, your corporation should be adequately capitalized; issue its stock; keep accurate records of who owns its shares; keep corporate funds separate from the personal funds of the shareholders, officers and directors; and keep accurate records of all votes and decisions which occur at formal meetings of the board of directors and the shareholders. These formal meetings should be held at least annually and whenever you wish to document a change in the legal or tax affairs of your corporation (such as an amendment of your bylaws, board approval of an important tax election, etc.) or an important business transaction (purchase of corporate real estate, authorization of a bank loan, etc.).

Reality Note: Of course, many corporations, regardless of their size, hold frequent meetings of directors, shareholders, staff, department heads, committees, etc. Here, we are talking about more formal legal or tax related meetings documented by formal minutes. For one-person or other small corporations, these formal meetings will often be held on paper, not in person, to document corporate actions or formalities which have already been agreed to ahead of time by all the parties.

J. Dissolution of a Corporation

WHEN A CORPORATION IS DISSOLVED, it means it goes out of business and, in essence, ceases to exist. It should first be noted that a corporation can't just close its doors and dissolve. There are specific rules which state how this must be done. These rules will be discussed below. Also, keep in mind that once a corporation is dissolved, it is gone forever—it cannot be revived. There are two major types of dissolution: involuntary dissolution, in which less than all of the shareholders, under specific conditions, may desire to dissolve the corporation, or where state authorities step in to dissolve the corporation; and voluntary dissolution, where the shareholders agree to dissolve the corporation, or where the Certificate of Incorporation contains terms which automatically dissolve the corporation. These are more specifically discussed below.

1. Involuntary dissolution

An involuntary dissolution occurs pursuant to a court proceeding where the appropriate or legally required parties present a petition to the court asking the court to dissolve the corporation. The rules concerning involuntary dissolution are contained in Article 11 of the Business Corporation Law. There are three ways in which this can be done:

a. Director's Petition

A majority of the board of directors can present a petition if they adopt a resolution stating that:

1. the assets of the corporation are insufficient to pay its liabilities, or

2. dissolution will be in the best interests of the shareholders.

b. Shareholders' Petition

1. a majority of the shareholders (or a greater number if the Certificate of Incorporation requires it), at a shareholders meeting, can adopt a resolution calling for a petition to be filed upon the grounds that:

- the corporation's assets are insufficient to pay its liabilities, or

- dissolution is in the best interests of the corporation.

A meeting for this purpose can be called by 10% of the shareholders, unless the Certificate of Incorporation allows less, but this type of resolution can't be presented more than once every 12 months.

2. holders of 50% of the outstanding shares entitled to vote for directors (or only 1/3 of the shareholders under some circumstances) may present such a petition without a meeting on any of the following grounds:

- that the directors are so deadlocked that the board can't manage the corporation, or

- the shareholders are so deadlocked that they can't elect directors.

3. The holders of 20% or more of the shares entitled to vote for directors of a corporation whose shares are not publicly traded, may present a petition on any of the following grounds:

- the directors have been guilty of illegal, fraudulent, or oppressive action towards the complaining shareholders, or

- the property or assets of the corporation are being looted, wasted or diverted for noncorporate purposes.

4. One or more shareholders can present a petition if the shareholders of the corporation are so deadlocked that for a period of at least two consecutive annual meeting dates, the shareholders have failed to elect successors to directors whose terms have expired.

c. Attorney General

The Attorney General of New York can bring an action to dissolve a corporation upon any of the following grounds:

a. the corporation procured its formation through fraudulent misrepresentation or the concealment of a material fact, or

b. the corporation has conducted its business in a persistently fraudulent or illegal manner, or

c. the corporation has exceeded its legal authority, or

d. the corporation has violated a law and has automatically forfeited its charter, or

e. the corporation has violated the public policy of the state, or

f. the corporation has failed to file tax reports or pay taxes for two or more consecutive years.

2. Voluntary Dissolution

There are three circumstances by which a corporation can be voluntarily dissolved. A corporation is voluntarily dissolved by filing a Certificate of Dissolution with the Department of State. At any time after the Certificate of Dissolution is filed, the corporation, its officers, directors, shareholders, creditors, or the Attorney General, can petition to have the courts both determine the validity or fairness of the dissolution and to supervise the dissolution. The three circumstances by which a corporation may be voluntarily dissolved are:

- The Certificate of Incorporation contains terms which provide for automatic termination under certain circumstances.

- If the Certificate of Incorporation states that the life of the corporation is less than perpetual, then the corporation automatically ceases to exist after that time elapses.

- Two-thirds of the shareholders of all the outstanding shares of stock, entitled to vote, vote to dissolve.[11]

In the case of voluntary dissolution, all creditors of the corporation must be notified of the dissolution by publishing that fact at least once per week for two successive weeks in a newspaper of general circulation[12] in each place where the corporation had an office or place of business. Also, you must mail notice of the fact to each creditor at their last known address. Creditors must file claims against the corporation within six months of receiving notice or the claims will not be recognized. In the case of involuntary dissolution, all creditors of the corporation, and all of its officers, directors, and shareholders must be notified as directed by the court.

Before a dissolution becomes final, a corporation must obtain the consent of the Tax Commission. To get this permission, the corporation must file a report with the Tax Commission showing all net income not previously reported, up to the date of dissolution, and pay the amount of taxes due on that income.

K. Summing Up—More Questions

THE PRECEDING SECTIONS of this chapter on general corporate law and practices may have raised more questions than they have answered. We could not (and at this stage you probably wouldn't want us to) squeeze a complete corporate law course into this book. The unanswered questions should give you an appreciation of some of the complexities of corporate law as well as an awareness that corporations are closely regulated by statute, subject to scrutiny by courts, and that there are certain problem areas which often require the advice of a financial or legal expert.

This doesn't mean you can't organize and operate a corporation on your own (we obviously believe you can) or that you should suffer mental anguish wondering whether your debt-equity ratio is the right size, whether you're forming a "thin" or a "fat" corporation, etc. The great majority of small, sensibly run corporations will not face any of these problems. It does mean that you should use your own business judgment as to when and why to pay a financial or legal advisor to answer specific questions related to your individual problems. The fact that you can competently do many things yourself (prepare standard organizational forms) does not mean that you will never need to see an accountant or a lawyer.

---

[11]If the Certificate of Incorporation has any of these sort of provisions, the stock certificates of the corporation must disclose them.

[12]This is generally the local newspaper if it is published at least once a week.

THE SMALL NEW YORK CORPORATION

Chapter 3

THE SMALL NEW YORK CORPORATION

SO FAR WE'VE GIVEN YOU general information applicable to most for-profit corporations. This chapter will discuss more specifically the special rules and considerations relevant to the type of corporation you wish to form: the small New York corporation. The topics covered here include: (1) the number and kind of corporate people needed to organize a small corporation, (2) special rules and regulations which may be used by small corporations to customize operating procedures, (3) shareholder and subscription agreements, (4) New York State and federal securities laws as they apply to the small corporation.

Note: This is a good time to again remind you to relax and read this information carefully. Not all of it will apply to you, especially if you are incorporating a small, noncomplex business. However, it's valuable background information for all business people and we believe it will be of value to you.

Finally, some of the information in this chapter (primarily the sections which relate to your initial stock issuance) may seem complicated. It will make better sense when you integrate it with the actual steps necessary to prepare your papers, which you will find set out in Chapter 5. So for now, relax, read this information carefully and, if it still seems muddy, read it again when you go through Chapter 5.

A. How Many People May Organize the Corporation?

THE BUSINESS CORPORATION LAW states that a corporation may be formed by one or more natural persons of the age of eighteen years or over . The corporation is formed by the filing a Certificate of Incorporation with the New York Department of State (technically, the people who execute and file your Certificate are the incorporators of your corporation).

The BCL also requires that directors be at least 18 years of age. Aside from these particular age requirements, New York does not impose residency or other special qualifications on the people who organize or operate your corporation (e.g., your directors and officers are not required to be New York residents).

The Bylaws or the Certificate of Incorporation must provide for at least three directors, except that a corporation with less than three shareholders must have a number of directors at least equal to the number of shareholders (e.g., if you have two shareholders, you must have at least two directors). A corporation with one shareholder may have only one director.

Although the Business Corporation Law does not specify which officer positions must be filled, we assume you will elect at least a President, Secretary and a Treasurer (many corporations will also wish to elect a Vice President). If your corporation has only one shareholder, one person may fill all officer positions. However, if your corporation has two or more shareholders, then the office of President and Secretary must be filled by different persons.

Summing this up, a corporation should provide for and fill the have the following minimum number of titled positions:

- If one shareholder: one incorporator, one director, one president, one secretary and one treasurer.

- If two shareholders: one incorporator, two directors, one president, one secretary and one treasurer (the offices of president and secretary must be filled by different persons).

- If three or more shareholders: one incorporator, three directors, one president, one secretary and one treasurer (again, with the offices of president and secretary held by a different persons).

Notice that these are the *minimum* number of titled positions. The law allows one person to act as incorporator, director, and to fill the officer positions of the corporation. The same person, however, cannot occupy more than one director position (or both the president and secretary officer positions if the corporation has two or more shareholders,). This means that a corporation can be organized and operated by the following minimum number of people:

- If one shareholder: one person.

- If two shareholders: two people (two directors, with a separate president and secretary).

- If three or more shareholders: three people (three directors; again, with a separate president and secretary).

These are the minimum number of positions and people necessary to incorporate a business in New York. However, a corporation may have as many incorporators, directors, officers, and shareholders as are desirable or expedient to carry out its business. As a practical matter, it is quite likely that major corporate shareholders will wish to fill not only a directorship position, but will also wish to participate as officers in supervising or carrying out the day-to-day operations of the corporation. As we've said, you should elect a President, Secretary and Treasurer (many corporations will also elect a Vice President). Subject to providing for and filling the required positions, the details of these arrangements are up to you.

B. Rules for Organizing a Small Corporation

AS WE'VE SAID, corporations which have only a small number of shareholders are occasionally referred to as "close" or "closely-held" corporations. These are merely terms of convenience, and while used frequently by lawyers and accountants, have no specific legal significance or meaning under the laws of New York. In fact, clear definitions of these terms are not even given in the New York statutes.[1] Generally, however, if the shares of your corporation are not publicly traded or listed on a stock exchange and you have fewer than ten shareholders, you can consider your corporation to be a closely-held corporation.

Although small corporations of this sort may not differ legally from large corporations in most respects, in a very practical sense they differ quite a bit. Since frequently the shareholders of a small corporation are also its directors and

---

[1]The Internal Revenue Code contains a definition of this term which we will refer to when explaining special corporate tax rules. Specifically, under Internal Revenue Code Sections 469(j)(1), 465(a)(1)(B) and 542(a)(2), a closely-held corporation is one where more than 50% of the value of the corporation's stock is owned by five or fewer individuals during the last half of the corporation's tax year.

officers, the lines of ownership and management are not as clearly delineated as they are in a corporation with thousands of shareholders. Also, in most cases the shareholders have invested a large share of their personal wealth in the corporation and therefore have a great interest in controlling the destiny of the corporation. The Business Corporation Law recognizes these differences and deals with them in the manner discussed below.

Due to the sharing of corporate titles and responsibilities and the financial and personal interests at stake, small corporations tend to act informally, that is, without formal meetings and without regard to other legal "niceties." We urge that you avoid this temptation and conduct your corporate business in the manner discussed in Chapter 2I when possible. We also recognize that this is sometimes impractical, and, therefore, will discuss below various ways in which your corporate status, and your personal interests as a shareholder, can be protected even though you occasionally operate with less than strict formality.

There are four sources of rules which govern the management of the kind of small corporation discussed in this book. These are the Business Corporation Law of New York, the Certificate of Incorporation of your corporation, the Bylaws of your corporation, and an agreement between the shareholders of your corporation (called a shareholders' agreement). A shareholders' agreement is optional; the rules contained in the corporation law, your Certificate and Bylaws will always apply to your corporation. Let's look at all four.

1. The Business Corporation Law

This is a body of laws which creates the general framework of establishing, managing and dissolving a corporation. Generally, as explained below, some of the rules contained in the Business Corporation Law can be modified by the shareholders. The important point to note is that some of these requirements cannot be modified, and many of these laws must be followed to the letter. If they are modified or disregarded, corporate action may be invalid. In the Certificate of Incorporation and Bylaws provided in this book, we have generally included the minimum requirements contained in the Business Corporation Law. They are reasonable and adequate guidelines for corporate management.

In addition to these minimum requirements there are five specific sections of the Business Corporation Law which are particularly applicable to small corporations and the protection of shareholder interests. None of these has to be used, but you should be aware of their existence. They are as follows:

a. SECTION 616. This section provides that the Certificate of Incorporation can require higher quorum and voting requirements for shareholder action than otherwise provided in the BCL (for example, rather than a majority for either being required, you can require two-thirds or some other higher percentage).

b. SECTION 709. This section provides that similar super-majority rules may be specified for the quorum and voting requirements applicable to director's actions.

c. SECTION 715. This section permits the Certificate of Incorporation to contain a provision for officers to be elected directly by the shareholders rather than by the directors (the latter procedure is more common).

d. SECTION 1002. This permits the Certificate of Incorporation to provide for dissolution upon a vote of the shareholders or upon the occurrence of a specified event.

e. SECTION 620. This section permits shareholders to accomplish two objectives. First, it permits shareholders to enter into a written agreement in which they agree to vote their shares in a specified manner (for example, to elect specific persons to specific offices, etc.). Secondly, it permits the Certificate of Incorporation to include a provision effectively placing management of the corporation in the hands of the shareholders. To take advantage of the second part, you must meet three requirements:

1. All the holders of all shares in the corporation must agree to it;

2. None of the shares of stock of the corporation can be listed, quoted or traded on a national securities exchange; and

3. If this provision is adopted, thereafter shares of the corporation can only be issued or transferred to persons who have knowledge or notice of this provision or who have agreed to it in writing.

Several points should be noted here. First, all of the above items are optional. Second, if they are used, they must be inserted as provisions in the Certificate of Incorporation. Third, the Bylaws and any agreements between the shareholders should be consistent with any and all provisions contained in the Certificate of Incorporation or, in other words, if you put them in your Certificate, put them in your Bylaws, too. Fourth, if any of these provisions are used, the stock certificates must indicate this fact. More on this in Chapter 5.

2. Certificate of Incorporation

This is the basic charter of your corporation. It is your most important corporate document. Any set of rules which the corporation or its shareholders may attempt to establish which are inconsistent with the Certificate of Incorporation will be invalid. The Certificate of Incorporation

we have included in this book in Chapter 5 meets the basic requirements of the law, but purposely does not include any of the optional provisions just discussed.

We have elected to include only these basic legal rules in the Certificate of Incorporation and to put more routine operational procedures in the Bylaws because of the following disadvantages encountered in using the Certificate of Incorporation for this purpose:

- It is virtually impossible to think of every provision your corporation will need when you prepare the certificate, and in fact, you may inadvertently include things that hinder corporate operations.

- It takes at least a majority of shareholders, at a shareholders meeting, to change the certificate. The need for this formality, and the time it may take, greatly reduces the flexibility and efficiency of corporate operations.

- All changes which you make in the certificate must be filed with and approved by the Department of State. This takes time and costs money.

A more practical reason for our decision to make the tear-out Certificate of Incorporation included in this book as simple as possible is the fact that each set of incorporators will have a different relationship to each other and different interests they wish to protect—we can't, of course, provide for the special circumstances of each incorporation. Moreover, many (if not most) small corporations will wish to keep things simple. The most obvious case is the situation of a single incorporator. Simplicity may also be best for many family businesses. Generally, the Certificate of Incorporation should include only those special provisions which you feel are needed to insure that the terms of any shareholders' agreement will be followed.

3. Bylaws

The Bylaws of your corporation is the document which contains the rules by which your corporation is managed. This is a document which is prepared by the incorporators of the corporation and initially approved by them. The Bylaws can be changed either by the shareholders at a meeting, or by the board of directors if the Certificate of Incorporation gives them that power.[2] The advantage of putting most of the corporate rules in the Bylaws, in addition to the ease with which they can be changed, is that, as mentioned above, no state approval is needed for any changes that are made (although they must still comply with the Business Corporation Law).

The tear-out Bylaws which we have included in this book cover most of the situations which a small corporation may encounter. Other items can be included when needed in the course of the corporation's life.

4. Shareholders' Agreement

A shareholders' agreement is a contract between the shareholders of a corporation. Usually this type of contract is entered into when there are only a few shareholders and they wish to (1) more closely control the operations and future of the corporation, and (2) agree among themselves in advance on certain matters relating either to the management of the corporation itself or positions or the authority they will exercise within the corporation. As discussed above, Section 620 of the Business Corporation Law can legitimize this type of centralization of management in the shareholders. Generally, a shareholders' agreement is entered into before a corporation is formed so that everyone who will be an incorporator is fully aware of what he is entitled to.[3]

a. Advantages of Shareholders' Agreements

The main reasons for entering into a shareholders' agreement are:

- To arrange for the election of specified shareholders to agreed upon offices, or as directors, and to determine initial salaries.

- To arrange for the distribution of money, as well as the timing of distributions, and whether they will be paid out as salaries, dividends, bonuses, etc. If one shareholder wishes to be entitled to a distribution disproportionate to his or her holdings (e.g., a 10% shareholder being entitled to 25% of the profits), this can be spelled out.

---

[2]If the Certificate of Incorporation doesn't give the board of directors this power, the shareholders may vote to give them this power later.

---

[3]If you do not qualify under Section 620, a shareholders' agreement can still be entered into, but the areas it covers cannot directly include management matters.

- To determine how and to whom shares of stock will be sold or transferred in the future. Usually in the case of a corporation with few shareholders, they will wish to keep all the stock within that group. For example, in the case of death of a shareholder, or if a shareholder wishes to sell stock, a method by which the corporation can purchase the stock, rather than an outsider, can be covered in the agreement.[4]

- To make sure that each shareholder votes her stock in a manner that does not violate the terms of the shareholders' agreement.

Note: There are many more provisions which can be put into this type of agreement which are beyond the scope of this book.

b. Disadvantages of Shareholders' Agreements

There are potential disadvantages of shareholders' agreements. Here are a few:

- Shareholders assuming managerial control of the corporation are subject to the same responsibilities and liabilities as directors. This means they might be deemed to have a fiduciary responsibility to passive (non-managing) shareholders.

- Tax-free exchange of business assets for stock under Section 351 of the Internal Revenue Code might not be available. We discuss this provision in Chapter 4, Section F.

- In some circumstances the right to receive an amount of proceeds disproportionate to stock ownership may be deemed by the IRS to constitute the creation of a second class of stock and thus make the election of S status

---

[4]In this case, the stock must indicate that the transferability of the stock is limited. More on this in Chapter 5.

unavailable. We discuss S status in Chapter 4C.

Because of the legal, tax and practical problems which may arise, and also due to the fact that the terms of any shareholders agreement must necessarily meet individual needs, we have not included a standardized tear-out shareholders' agreement in this book. See an attorney if you feel you need this type of contract.

Please Read This

What we have attempted to do in this section is give you an idea of the rules which do or can govern corporate operations and management. When setting up a corporation with your fellow shareholders, you want to make sure that each of you knows what she is entitled to, what your responsibilities are, and how things are to be organized. Each of the documents discussed above helps you to do this. As a general rule, those aspects of corporate life which are most important to you, and which you don't think you will wish to change in the future, should be put into the Certificate of Incorporation. Most others should be in the Bylaws. Anything you put in a shareholders' agreement can be overruled by the Certificate of Incorporation or the Bylaws, so make sure that (1) the documents are consistent, and (2) they reflect and are consistent with any agreements made between the incorporators. Most incorporators of small corporations should find the basic tear-out forms in this book suitable to their needs.

C. Subscription Agreements

SUBSCRIPTION AGREEMENT is a term which you might have heard of and which we feel should be explained. Generally, subscription agreements are rarely used when only a few people are getting together to form a corporation and, in the typical case, you will not be entering into this type of agreement since it will be clearly understood who will be getting how much stock, at what price, and when.

Briefly, a subscription agreement is a contract by which a person (or persons) agree to purchase shares in a proposed corporation. In this type of contract, each individual agrees to purchase from the corporation a specified number of shares at a stated price per share. Like all contracts, this agreement can contain any number of terms, so long as they do not involve a violation of law. If you feel the need to enter into a subscription agreement, you should really see an attorney. It's too important to do yourself.

D. New York Securities Law

THIS SECTION AND THE FOLLOWING section (Federal Securities Law) discuss the laws controlling the issuance of stock. They are designed to prevent people from being cheated through assorted schemes and misrepresentations. Generally, these laws are intended to cover situations where strangers are dealing with one another. Even though most of the readers of this book will not be in this situation, you must still be aware of these rules since they also apply to many sales of stock made after the corporation is organized.

A Note of Caution and a Caveat: The entire subject of state and federal securities laws is very complex. What we have attempted to do here is give you a basic outline of these laws. Since the penalties for violating these rules can be quite harsh (including criminal penalties), since the securities laws and rules are subject to change, and since each corporate situation can differ, we advise you to consult an attorney to check your conclusions and to make sure your stock offering and issuance meets the current requirements of all applicable securities laws.

In New York, securities transactions are governed by the Martin Act. In particular, there are three areas covered by this law which are most important for the readers of this book. The first deals with fraudulent activities. The second concerns the disclosure of the stock offering itself. The third relates to the registration of dealers and issuers. The latter two areas may require the filing of certain rather complex forms issued by the Attorney General's office. The preparation of these forms and associated supporting documents requires the services of an attorney and probably an accountant. In addition, the fees for filing these forms are relatively high. Fortunately, as explained below, the law exempts certain types of transactions from most of these filing requirements. Most of the readers of this book should qualify for this special treatment and, therefore, should not have to meet complicated filing requirements.

1. The Law

The New York Martin Act (General Business Law, Article 23-A) regulates the issuance and sale of securities. This includes the stock in your corporation. Certain activities are clearly prohibited by the Martin Act under all circumstances, regardless of any exemptions or other exceptions to the law which may apply to you. Most importantly, you cannot use "fraud, deception, concealment, suppression, false pretense or fictitious or pretended purchasers or sales to promote or induce the sale of securities." You also can't make any promises about the future expectations of the corporation, such as potential profits, which are beyond reasonable expectations, and you can't misrepresent facts or say things that you don't actually know to be true. These provisions of the law apply to securities transactions made within or from New York.

The stock registration provisions of the Martin Act deal primarily with *intrastate* offerings of securities, that is, offers or sales of stock of a New York corporation, made within New York to residents of New York. The question as to what constitutes an intrastate, as opposed to an interstate, offering can be complex and unclear, even to lawyers. For example, if you use a means of *inter*-state commerce such as the telephone or the mails to offer your shares, does this automatically make your stock offering an inter-state offering? Technical debates of this sort are beyond the scope of this book. Suffice it to say that you can generally stay on the safe (intrastate) side by only offering and selling your shares to people who live in New York while they are within the state borders.[5]

More specifically, Section 359-ff of the General Business Law (part of the Martin Act) states that before you can sell, or offer to sell, any security which is part of a security issue being sold to New York residents only (an intrastate offering), you must prepare an offering prospectus, file it with the Attorney General's office, and present it to the person to whom you are making the offer. This prospectus must disclose all the material facts about the corporation which would be important in helping the person make a decision, including, among other things, the nature of the corporation's business, the purpose of the offering, and the use of the proceeds of the sale.[6]

As we've said, the Martin Act regulates persons who sell securities in addition to regulating the stock offering itself. Section 359-e of the General Business Law requires that certain persons who sell securities register with the Attorney General's office before they do so (remember, a corporation is considered a legal person). Included among these persons are dealers. Dealers are defined to include "...any person, firm, association, or corporation engaged in the business of buying or selling securities from or to the public ..." *and* "...also include(s) a person, firm, association, or corporation selling or offering for sale from or to the public within this state securities issued by it." Under these definitions, your corporation may be classified

---

[5]If you do make an interstate offer, you are no longer governed by the terms of the Martin Act as they relate to offerings. Rather, the provisions of the federal Securities Act of 1933 apply. However, the Martin Act still is applicable with regard to dealer registration requirements and fraud. If you have any questions on whether or not you are making an intrastate offering you should talk to a lawyer.

[6]This section relating to the intrastate offering prospectus does not apply to you in certain cases where the corporation has, or will, register its share offering with the federal Securities and Exchange Commission or where you are relying on a federal SEC exemption (other than the federal intrastate offering exemption) for the issuance of your shares— see Section E, below, for a discussion of the federal exemption rules. Since we assume that you will not need to register your shares with the SEC and that you will, in many cases, be relying on the federal intrastate exemption in issuing your shares, we assume that these particular exemptions do not apply to you.

as a dealer and the organizing people (or promoters) may also be considered dealers. To register as a dealer, you must complete certain forms supplied by the Attorney General's office and pay prescribed fees.

The preparation of an intrastate offering prospectus to satisfy the requirements of Section 359-ff can be somewhat expensive and time-consuming. Fortunately, there are exemptions which should be available to you. Similarly, under certain circumstances, you may be able to eliminate the need to register as a dealer under Section 359-e. The following sections discuss these exemptions.

Important Note: Throughout the remainder of this discussion we assume that you will be making an intrastate offering, that is, an offer and sale of your initial shares in New York to New York residents only (see above explanation). If this assumption isn't true for you, you may not qualify for exemptions from the prospectus and dealer registration requirements and should see a lawyer.

2. Prospectus Requirement— Automatically Exempted Transactions

We assume that most readers of this book will be in a situation where, either individually, or together with a few friends, business associates, or family members, they want to form a corporation and issue all of the shares to themselves and these other people. In this case, the law provides certain automatic exemptions from the intrastate offering prospectus regulations which we have previously

discussed.[7] The critical factors which determine whether or not you are eligible for these exemptions depend on (1) the total number of the people involved, (2) the amount of money that you are trying to raise, and (3) the relationship of the parties to each other or to the corporation. In addition, these provisions apply only to your initial issuance of stock.

a. Automatic Prospectus Exemption for Issuance to Less Than Ten Persons

If your stock offering is made to *less than ten people* (this is a critical number to keep in mind) you are automatically exempted from the intrastate offering prospectus requirements of section 359-ff of the Martin Act. This exemption is available without having to apply for it.

Note: This exemption is interpreted quite literally and applies to both offers and sales. More specifically, the term "offering" is defined as a written or oral request to participate in an investment initiated by either a potential seller or buyer of a security. Thus, if you ask ten people if they want to buy shares, strictly speaking you don't qualify for this exemption, even if only nine accept the offer and purchase the initial shares of the corporation.

b. Automatic Prospectus Exemption for Certain Small Offerings

An automatic exemption from the intrastate prospectus requirements also exists for certain small offerings, regardless of the number of people to whom shares are offered or sold. Specifically, if you are making a "small offering" to a "promoter group" or a "related group," you

---

[7]These exemptions from the intrastate prospectus requirements of the Martin Act are found in Section 80.9 (and related sections) of the New York Intrastate Financing Act.

are also automatically exempt from the prospectus requirements of the Martin Act. This exemption may come in handy if you are unable to meet the numerical requirements of the "less-than-ten" exemption discussed above. However, these terms are very specific and you must fall clearly within their definitions in order to qualify for this exemption. Let's define some terms:

A "small offering" is defined as an offering which seeks to raise no more than $40,000, not including the personal investment of promoters. In addition, the offering must be "fair, just and equitable." What this means is, as we have said throughout this book, that all of your dealings should be honest and "above-board." The term "promoter" has a distinct definition, different from the general one which we've given you in Chapter 2, Section D1. In this context, the term promoter includes all officers, directors, principals or controlling persons of a venture (in this case, of your corporation). A "promoter group" consists, therefore, of these particular types of corporate people. Finally, a "related group" is defined as a group where a family or long-time business or personal relationship exists between one or more of the promoters and each and every member of the group. As you can see, these definitions are overlapping and can result in some fairly complex calculations. Here are a few guidelines and examples:

If you plan to utilize one of these small offering exemptions, you will first want to make sure that you meet the definition of a small offering. In other words, your first hurdle is making sure that you will offer and sell shares at a total sales price of $40,000 or less. Remember, you don't have to count money paid by people defined as promoters such as directors or officers. So, if you and your neighbor, Sam, are going to form a corporation together with his brother, Alfred, and you and Sam plan to be directors while Al will be a passive investor, you

don't have to count the money which you and Sam are paying for your shares. As long as Alfred is paying $40,000 or less for his shares, you will be making a "small offering."

The next hurdle is determining if your small offering is being made to a promoter or a related group according to the above definitions. Under the facts of the above example, your small offering is not being made to a promoter group since Alfred is not a promoter. Also, the example does not clearly indicate that you are making your offering to a related group since at least one promoter (either you or Sam) must have the required family, business or personal relationship with each and every member of the group. All we know is that Sam is related to Alfred. If Sam also has a long-time business or personal relationship with you, then the "related group" prospectus exemption requirements are met.

If this sounds a bit confusing, you're right, it is. If you are like most other small corporations you should be automatically exempt from having to prepare and file an intrastate prospectus under the simpler less-than-ten rule discussed above. If you find yourself having to resort to the small offering exemption and are getting bogged down, arrange to have a consultation with a lawyer to sort out the details. This type of legal deciphering is one of the most valuable services a lawyer can perform for you. Finally, various sections of the Intrastate Financing Act contain other exemptions from having to issue a prospectus. However, these other exemptions require that you prepare and file an application for exemption with the Attorney General's office or file a short-form prospectus and are somewhat complex. You should also see a lawyer if you need to explore these alternative exemptions.

A Few Reminders: First, make sure that you are making an intrastate offering. For example, don't ask any out-of-state relatives to become shareholders in your corporation or call a friend who lives in New York to become a shareholder while she is vacationing in another state. This might seem picky, but as someone once said, its better to be safe than sued later (corporate lawsuits often hinge on technical violations of the securities law). Second, despite your exemption from the Martin Act's prospectus requirements, you are still required to comply with all other provisions of the Act, including those sections dealing with misrepresentations and fraud (and dealer registration requirements if they apply—see below). Third, these automatic exemptions only apply to the initial issuance of stock. If, after the corporation is in business, you decide to issue more stock, you may be required to issue a prospectus.

Another Reminder: As we've said throughout this book, the offer and sale of shares is, perhaps, the most crucial and complex phase of your incorporation. Since you should be completely safe when issuing shares, we advise you to consult a lawyer to make sure you are exempt from these prospectus requirements. As you'll see in the following sections of this chapter, we also suggest you have a lawyer review the complex issues which can arise under the dealer registration requirements of the Martin Act and the stock issuance exemptions of the federal securities law. One consultation with a lawyer can serve to cover all three of these areas and, in view of the potential liabilities involved with the issuance of shares, is, in our opinion, well worth the price.

3. Dealer Registration Requirements

In contrast to the preceding exemptions from filing an intrastate prospectus under Section 359-ff, spelled out in regulations promulgated by the Attorney General's office, the question of whether you are also exempt from the dealer registration requirements of Section 359-e of the Martin Act is not so easily pinned down. The regulations (Section 80.16 of the New York Intrastate Financing Act) specifically state that an exemption from Section 359-ff (the intrastate prospectus requirement) does not exempt you automatically from the dealer registration requirements. Unfortunately, the law is not clear on this point, and it has not, to our knowledge, been considered by the courts of New York.

Despite this lack of statutory authority with respect to dealer registration exemptions, the key in determining whether you, or your corporation, must register as a dealer usually hinges on the question of whether or not you are offering to sell stock to the public. Some guidelines can be offered on this point. Generally, if you meet each of the following requirements, you are probably not making a public offering and will usually not have to register as a dealer:

- A pre-existing relationship exists between all the shareholders of the new corporation (either personal or family ties or existing business associations);

- All of the new shareholders are going to actively participate in the control and management of the new corporation, either as directors or officers;

- All new shareholders will be employees of the new corporation;

- A promoter is not involved (in the sense of someone who will be paid for selling the stock and then have no further dealings with the corporation);

- You do not advertise the fact that you are offering or selling shares.

By the way, if you are forming the corporation by yourself and will be the only corporate shareholder and director, you should be able to meet all of these requirements.

You should be aware of an important distinction here. Except with regard to small offerings to promoter groups (promoters are defined as directors, officers or controlling persons of the corporation), the automatic exemptions from the prospectus requirements of the Martin Act do not require any of people who are offered or sold shares to participate in the management or actual carrying out of the corporation's business. Here, however, the general guidelines for not being subject to the dealer registration requirements are more rigorous and require that all of the people to whom shares are offered or sold participate in the corporation in an active manner as directors or officers and as employees. As you can see, the fact that you meet the requirements for exemption from issuing a prospectus does not also necessarily mean that you also meet the guidelines for not having to register as a dealer.

If you do not meet each of the above requirements, you may or may not need to register. For example, if you are making a limited offering to forty or fewer persons, you can apply to the Attorney General's office for an exemption from these dealer registration requirements. This application procedure involves interpreting technical language and is beyond the scope of our discussion.

We suggest you consult a knowledgeable lawyer at this point and follow his or her advice on the whole issue of complying with New York's dealer registration requirements. If you must register, make sure you prepare and file the appropriate papers with the Attorney General's (and Department of State's Miscellaneous Records) office such as an Issuer Statement, State Notice, and Further State Notice. Most lawyers feel that small corporations organized by a small number of people who have had past business dealings or close family or personal ties and which are making a private (unadvertised) offering of initial shares will not usually be subject to these dealer registration requirements, even if one or more people will not be employees of the corporation. However, we strongly advise you to obtain the opinion of a lawyer after explaining your particular circumstances. The issuance of your stock is too important a matter, and the dealer registration requirements relatively too slight a formality, to leave this matter to guesswork.

E. Federal Securities Act

THE FEDERAL SECURITIES ACT also applies to the offering of shares by a corporation. You must register your initial offering of stock with the Securities and Exchange Commission (SEC) unless you fall under a specific exemption from registration. There are several exemptions available and most small profit corporations eligible for an exemption from issuing an intrastate offering prospectus under the New York Martin Act (as discussed in the previous section) should not need to register with the SEC.

Here's a very brief description of the more obvious choices available to issuers in order to effect an unregistered private offering of securities under the federal Securities Act of 1933 and exemption rules promulgated under this Act.

Traditionally, most small, closely-held corporations wishing to privately issue their initial shares to a limited number of people have been able to rely on the SEC "intrastate offering" or "nonpublic offering" exemptions. One of these exemptions will still probably be your most obvious choice in seeking an exemption from registration or notification of your initial stock offering with the SEC.

The intrastate offering exemption is contained in Section 3(a)(ll) of the Act and exempts certain intrastate offers and sales of stock. Generally it applies to the issuance of shares offered and sold only to persons resident within a single state if the issuer (the corporation) is resident and doing business within the state. This is, perhaps, the most popular exemption relied on by small corporations when issuing their initial shares. SEC Rule 147 defines more precisely the technical language used in this statute and provides a set of guidelines and procedures to follow to make reliance on this exemption a bit safer. For instance, limitations should be placed on resales of shares, precautions should be taken against later interstate offers and sales, and purchasers should make written representations as to their residency within the state.

The nonpublic offering exemption is a one-line exemption contained in Section 4(2) of the Securities Act for "transactions by an issuer [corporation] not involving any public offering.". The courts have discussed the basic elements which should be present when relying on this exemption:[8]

- the offerees and purchasers are able to fend for themselves due to their previous financial/business experience, relationship to the issuer (the corporation, its directors, officers), and/or significant personal net worth;

- the transaction is truly a nonpublic offering involving no general advertising or solicitation;

- the shares are purchased by the shareholders for their own account and not for resale;

- the offerees and purchasers are limited in number;

- the offerees and purchasers must have access to or be given information relevant to the stock transactions in order to evaluate the pros and cons of the investment (the same type of information supplied on an SEC registration statement).

In order to better understand the factors which should, and should not be, present when relying on this exemption, the SEC has issued Release No. 33-4552. This release contains several statements and examples regarding the nonpublic offering exemption—see the accompanying shaded box for a summary of this release.

---

[8]A leading case on this exemption is *SEC v. Ralston Purina Co.*, 346 U.S. 119 (1953).

SEC Release 33-4552

Here is a summary and restatement of some the factors contained in this release issued to help explain the scope of the federal nonpublic offering exemption:

• Whether a transaction is one not involving any public offering is essentially a question of fact and requires a consideration of all surrounding circumstances, including such factors as the relationship between the offerees and the issuer (corporation), the nature, scope, size, type and manner of the offering.

• The number of persons to whom shares are offered is not determinative of whether this exemption is available. The real consideration is whether these people have sufficient association with and knowledge of the issuer so as to make the exemption available.

• Negotiations or conversations with, or general solicitations of, an unrestricted and unrelated group of prospective purchasers for the purpose of ascertaining who would be willing to accept an offer of securities makes the transaction a public offering and renders the exemption unavailable, even though only a few knowledgeable purchasers ultimately buy the shares.

• Limitation of the offering of shares to certain employees designated as key employees may not be sufficient to qualify for this exemption. However, an offering made to executive personnel who, because of their position, have access to the same kind of information that the Act would make available in the form of a registration statement (financial statements, etc.) may qualify for the exemption.

• The sale of stock to promoters who take the initiative in founding or organizing the business would come within this exemption.

• If the amount of the stock offering is large it may be considered a public offering not eligible for the exemption.

- An important factor is whether the securities offered have come to rest in the hands of the initial informed group or whether the purchasers are merely conduits for a wider distribution. If the purchasers do, in fact, acquire the securities with a view to public distribution, the corporation assumes the risk of possible violation of the registration requirements of the Act and the imposition of civil penalties.

- The nature of the purchaser's past investment and trading practices or the character and scope of his or her business may be inconsistent with the assumption that the purchaser is buying the shares solely for investment purposes and not for resale. In particular, purchases by individuals engaged in the business of buying and selling securities require careful scrutiny for the purpose of determining whether they may be acting as mere conduits for a wider distribution of shares.

- The issuer may help control the resale of the securities and thereby make reliance on this exemption a little safer. For example, the corporation may secure a representation from the initial purchasers that they are acquiring the securities only for investment and place a legend to this effect on the stock certificates.

- What may appear to be a separate offering to a properly limited group will not be so considered if it is one of a related series of offerings (if, for example, you offer and sell shares after your initial stock offering, this future issuance, if similar in structure, purpose and scope, may be considered part of your initial stock issuance and may jeopardize your initial exemption).

- Whether or not an exemption is available for your stock offering, you cannot engage in any fraudulent activity (and should disclose all material facts to all potential shareholders) to avoid the possible imposition of penalties under other sections of the Act.

More recently, the SEC adopted a number of "500 series" rules as part of Regulation D, a series of provisions "...designed to simplify and clarify previous exemptions, to expand their availability, and to achieve uniformity between federal and state exemptions in order to facilitate capital formation consistent with the protection of investors." For the most part, these rules, together with Section 4(6) of the Act, allow corporations to privately sell a limited amount of securities to no more than 35 investors and to an unlimited number of accredited investors (those meeting certain sophisticated investor standards related to personal net worth, annual individual income, position of responsibility within the corporation, etc.). Generally, these rules also require the disclosure of information to prospective purchasers, prohibit general solicitation or advertising, and impose limitations on resale of the securities (they cannot be resold without being registered or being eligible for an exemption from registration). Reliance on these Regulation rules or on Section 4(6) requires a Notice of Sales of Securities form to be filed with the SEC. For more information on Regulation D, you may wish to obtain a copy of SEC Release No. 33-6389.

Most lawyers will probably feel that your initial stock issuance (which, we assume, will be eligible for an exemption from issuing an intrastate offering prospectus under New York's Martin Act) will not require registration with, or notification to, the SEC. Nonetheless, this is a complex area with more than a few ambiguities and pitfalls and we advise you to check with a lawyer to ensure that you are in fact eligible for an exemption under the federal Securities Act for your initial stock offer and issuance (e.g., an attorney may wish your prospective shareholders to sign written disclosure/representation letters, place a non-registration or other legend on your stock certificates, and follow other formalities suggested by the exemption guidelines discussed above). Note that whether or not you have to register or provide notification to the SEC of your stock offering, the anti-fraud provisions of the Securities Act always apply, so DISCLOSE, DISCLOSE, DISCLOSE!

Finally, if your offering of securities involves a state outside of New York (e.g., if your offer is made outside of New York or if a purchaser is not a New York resident), you should consult an attorney to make sure you comply with the requirements of the securities laws of that state.

CORPORATE TAXATION

Chapter 4

CORPORATE TAXATION

CORPORATIONS, LIKE INDIVIDUALS, are subject to the payment of state and federal taxes. In this chapter we will discuss some of the tax consequences of starting and operating a corporation and talk about some special tax elections many small corporations will want to make. This information is meant to introduce you to the most important areas of corporate taxation and to provide the necessary background to study them in greater depth with a tax consultant.[1]

A. New York Taxes

1. New York Corporate Franchise Tax

Corporations doing business in New York must pay an annual franchise tax, determined upon the basis of the entire net income of the corporation in each tax year. Each corporation must file a report of its income on March 15 following the close of each calendar year, or if the corporation uses a fiscal year, within two and one-half months after the end of its fiscal year. This report must be certified by the president of the corporation or any other officer authorized by the bylaws of the corporation to do so. (A certification merely is a statement signed by these officers stating that the contents of the report are true.)

To determine the franchise tax that your corporation will owe, you must make several calculations. We won't describe the various calculations and special rules here.[2] The general rule is that for-profit corporations are subject to a 9% state tax rate on income earned in New York or allocated to New York sources (you must pay more this 9% amount if the other calculations, based upon the corporation's capital base or minimum taxable income bases, exceed this 9% figure). In any case, a *minimum* state franchise tax of $250 must be paid for each corporate tax year.

Small Corporation Tax Note: Small business corporations (generally this means corporations with smaller net incomes which qualify as a small business corporation under Internal Revenue Code § 1244—see Section E below) qualify for lower franchise tax rates under special provisions of New York law.[3]

Obviously, the actual amount of franchise tax you will owe each year will depend on a number of factors, including the amount of business your corporation does in New York, tax deductions and credits to which your corporation is entitled, etc. Obviously the determination of the amount of franchise tax you owe can be complex and the services of an accountant or bookkeeper is usually required.

Remember: If you fail to pay corporate franchise taxes, your corporate privileges can be taken away. A more detailed discussion of other taxes for which your corporation may be liable is found in Chapter 6.

---

[1]We've tried to include major changes which affect the tax areas discussed in this and other chapters. However, tax laws and regulations are constantly changing. Please see the most recent IRS and New York tax publications mentioned throughout this book (for example, see the box titled "For More Information" in the introduction to Chapter 6) and consult your tax advisor to make sure you have all the current information.

---

[2]The statutory formulas for calculating the New York corporate franchise tax are contained in New York Tax Law § 210.

[3]See New York Tax Law §§ 210(1)(a) and (1)(f).

2. New York Personal Income Tax

Corporate profits are reported on the personal income tax.returns of individual shareholders (and taxed to them at their personal income tax rates) when and if these profits are distributed to them as dividends or salaries. Dividends are taxed twice: at the corporate and individual levels (dividend payments cannot be deducted by the corporation). As a practical matter, however, most small corporations rarely pay dividends (and, therefore, are not subject to double taxation on corporate profits). Why? Because one of the primary reasons to incorporate is to have the flexibility to either retain earnings in your corporation at corporate tax rates or to pay out profits to the employee-shareholders in the form of salaries, fringe benefits, etc., which are deductible by the corporation. Either way, only one tax is paid (corporate or individual) and double taxation is avoided.

In addition, a New York corporation may wish to elect state and federal S corporation tax status: These tax elections allow the corporation to bypass regular corporate level taxes on corporate taxable income, with the taxable income of the corporation passed through to the shareholders to be taxed only once on their individual tax returns (see the next subsection and section C below).

3. New York S Corporation Tax Election

Sections 209(8) and 660 of the New York Tax Law do provide for and implement an optional New York S corporation tax election, available to corporations that have elected S corporation tax status with the IRS. The effect of this state tax election parallels the federal election: generally, corporate income, losses, deductions and reductions are passed through the corporation and reflected instead on the individual New York returns of the shareholders. Although New York S corporations are exempt from paying the New York corporate franchise tax discussed in subsection 1 above, they must pay a flat annual filing fee to the New York Department of Taxation and Finance ($25 for 1988; $50 in 1989; $100 each year starting in 1990).

If you plan to elect, or have elected, federal S corporation tax status (see Section C below for information on electing federal S corporation tax status), you may also wish to make this New York S corporation tax election by submitting form CT-6 to the New York State Department of Taxation and Finance. For newly-formed New York corporations wishing to make this election for their first tax year, form CT-6 must be filed on or before the 15th day of the third month following the date of incorporation.

Contact the New York State Department of Taxation and Finance in Albany for forms and information regarding the specific requirements and procedures for electing S corporation tax status with the state (request New York tax forms CT-6 and CT-3S). Also consult your tax advisor for guidance in making your state (and federal) S corporation tax election.

B. Federal Taxes

1. Federal Corporate Income Tax

The federal government taxes the first $50,000 of taxable corporate income at 15%, the next $25,000 at 25%, and the remainder of taxable income over $75,000 at 34%. To make larger corporations pay back the benefits of these lower graduated tax rates, corporate taxable incomes between $100,000 and $335,000 are subject to an additional 5% tax. We have included a comparison of corporate and individual tax rates as they apply to owners of small corporations in subsection 2 below.

Maximum Corporate Tax Rate on Certain Personal Service Corporations: Under special provisions of the Internal Revenue Code, the taxable income of certain personal service corporations is taxed at a flat corporate tax rate of 34% (the lower 15% and 25% federal corporate tax brackets do not apply to these corporations). Specifically, this flat maximum federal corporate tax rate is applied to corporations (1) where substantially all the stock of the corporation is held by the employees performing professional services for the corporation and (2) where substantially all the activities of the corporation involve the performance of one of the following professions or activities:

- health
- law
- engineering
- architecture
- accounting
- actuarial science
- performing arts
- consulting

A few comments on this special federal flat corporate tax:

First, remember that the practice of most of the professions engaged in these fields is required to be incorporated as a New York professional corporation, not as regular New York for-profit corporation [see Chapter 2A2(a) for further information]. Similarly, performing arts groups typically incorporate as New York not-for-profit corporations—see Chapter 2A1.

Second, if this flat tax provision applies to you (because you are forming a for-profit or professional corporation engaged in one of these fields and all of your corporation's stock will be owned by the professionals), this doesn't mean that you will be paying 34% of your income to the IRS each year—this tax only applies to any taxable income left in the corporation at the end of the corporate tax year. If, like many professionals, you have no need to accumulate money in your corporation and prefer to pass corporate profits to yourself each year in the form of a deductible salary, fringe benefits, a substantial contribution to your pension plan, etc., then this tax provision will have little, if any, impact on your corporation's tax liability. Further, if you do end your corporate tax year with income left in the corporation and wish to avoid the imposition of this tax, electing S corporation tax status will pass corporate profits to you automatically each year and avoid corporate level taxes on these profits (however, this election will limit your ability to pay yourself deductible fringe benefits—see Section C below).

Third, this flat tax provision contains some general terminology which may require you (or your tax advisor) to explore current and future Treasury regulations. For example: When is all the stock of one of these personal service corporations substantially owned by the professional employees? What is "consulting" for purposes of provision?[4] If you may be subject to this flat tax rate, we suggest you consult your tax advisor for further guidance.

Fourth, this special tax provision applies to the same professions and activities to which the lower federal corporate accumulated earnings credit of $150,000 applies (see Section G below for a further explanation of this credit).

2. Federal Individual Income Tax

The federal government taxes corporate profits when distributed to shareholders as dividends or salaries. The shareholders must pay individual income tax on the amounts received. As we've mentioned earlier, however, since the payment of dividends results in double taxation (the income is taxed to both the corporation and the shareholder), owners of small corporations normally use one of several methods to get money out of the corporation without being subject to double taxation. When the owner works for the corporation, the simplest is to pay out corporate profits in the form of deductible salaries, bonuses, and benefits rather than in dividends. As long as salaries aren't unreasonable and the benefits are paid in accordance with IRS guidelines (see Section F below), the IRS should have no objection. Of course, money paid in salaries and bonuses is a deductible business expense of the corporation and is thus not taxed to the corporation, only to the individual.

In effect then, incorporating a business you actively participate in allows you to split your income between two tax entities, the corporation and yourself, as an employee-shareholder, in order to obtain the most favorable (smallest) tax rate on this income. You can pay salaries to yourself and other employees which will be taxed at individual tax rates while retaining earnings in the corporation which will be taxed at the lower corporate tax rates of 15% or 25% (again, certain personal service corporations pay corporate taxes at a flat 34% rate as explained in the previous subsection).

This feature of income splitting is unique to the corporate way of life—partnerships and sole proprietorships are not tax entities separate from their owners. All income realized by these unincorporated businesses is automatically counted as part of the individual income of the business owners each year, and is taxed at their individual income tax rates. In other words, even if profits are needed to expand the business and don't end up in the unincorporated business owner's pocket, individual income taxes must be paid. In contrast, as you'll see in Section G below, the IRS allows most corporations to accumulate up to $250,000 of earnings in the corporation for this type of income splitting, no questions asked. Amounts above this amount may be accumulated to meet the reasonable business needs of the corporation.

If you anticipate, or find, that corporate taxable income (net corporate income after subtracting all deductions including business expenses, salaries, bonuses, depreciation, etc.) will be subject to more taxes at the corporate level than if taxed to you and the other shareholders personally, your corporation may be able to elect S corporation tax status—as explained in Section C below, this election passes corporate income through to your shareholders where it is reported and taxed on their individual tax returns only.

---

[4]For answers to these questions and examples of corporate activities subject to this tax rate, see the regulations issued under IRC § 441 and § 448 (starting with Temp. Regs. § 1. 441-1T and § 1.448-1T).

A Comparison of Individual and Corporate Tax Rates and Payments for Owners of Smaller Corporations

As we pointed out in our discussion of the tax benefits of incorporating in Chapter 1B2, incorporating and paying taxes as a corporate entity generally results in paying less tax on business income than you would pay as an individual (or as a partner) if your corporation has a taxable income of $185,000 or less. There are two basic reasons for this corporate advantage:

1. Corporate tax rates on taxable incomes of $75,000 or less are 15% on the first $50,000, and 25% on the next 25,000, as opposed to the 15% and 28% individual rates,[5] and

2. More importantly, while individual rates jump to 28% at very modest levels of taxable income, the lower corporate rates stay in effect for the first $75,000 of taxable income; corporate taxable incomes above this amount are taxed at a 34% rate.[6] (Remember the exception discussed

---

[5]Higher income individuals pay taxes on all taxable income at a flat rate of 28%. The advantage of the initial 15% bracket is wiped out by an additional 5% "pay-back" or "phantom" bracket of 33%.

[6]Although corporations are also subject to an additional 5% pay-back bracket of 39% on taxable incomes between $100,000 and $335,000, this increased rate does not take away the benefits of the

above for certain personal service corporations—these corporations pay taxes at a flat 34% corporate rate).

Taking all this into consideration (and ignoring personal service corporations for the moment), the result is that a fairly high level of taxable income must be reached before it makes sense for your corporation to choose to be taxed at individual rates (by electing S corporation tax status) rather than the standard corporate rates. Again, remember, since salaries, employee fringes and other expenses of doing business are deducted by the corporation first, it is rare for the majority of smaller businesses to report more than $185,000 of taxable income.

In fact, the majority of small corporations will probably show a taxable income of less than $50,000, and will, therefore, pay taxes at a flat 15% minimum corporate tax rate. After the corporation pays deductible salaries and corporate fringe benefits to the owner-employees of the corporation (and to other corporate personnel) and deducts other corporate business expenses, gross receipts, even in the millions of dollars range, are commonly reduced to a small taxable income amount and are taxed at the lower corporate tax rates.

Here is an example of how, with proper planning, a smaller incorporated business is able to split income between the corporation and its owners, retain money in the corporation for necessary expenditures and lower the corporation's tax liability to an amount that is actually less than what would have to be paid by the principals of the same business if it was not incorporated:

Example: Sally and Randolph run their own incorporated lumber supply company (S & R

---

lower 15% and 25% brackets until corporate taxable income reaches $335,000.

Wood). With the boom in home renovations, their sales increase to a $1.2 million yearly pace. After the close of the third quarter S & R's accountant reports that they are on course to make $110,000 net profit (net taxable corporate income) for the year. Sally and Randolph are pleased and call a meeting. They decide to reward themselves and other key employees with moderate raises in pay, provide a small year-end bonus to other workers, and purchase some needed equipment, including another cross-cut saw to increase their productivity. As a result, their net taxable corporate income is reduced to $45,000—an amount they feel is prudent to retain in the corporation for future expansion or in case next year's operations are less profitable. Taxes are therefore paid at the lowest 15% corporate rate.

Incidentally, if Sally and Randy wanted to get a larger personal return they could have increased their salaries (which are a tax deductible corporate expense) a little more as long as the total was reasonable. They see no reason to declare a stock dividend (as a big corporation would) since doing so would subject them to a double tax of 15% at the corporate level plus 28% personally.

If S & R Wood had not incorporated but instead operated as a partnership, the entire net profits of the business ($110,000 minus the bonuses to workers and expenditures for equipment) would pass through to Sally and Randy. The result would be that the $45,000 (which was retained in the business in the corporation example above) would be taxed at their 28% individual rate, rather than the 15% corporate rate.

But now suppose that the owners of smaller corporations anticipate corporate taxable income so substantial (roughly over $185,000 as we've said) that they would really benefit from being taxed at the slightly lower maximum individual rates. Fine. They have the opportunity to do so

by electing S corporation tax status. By doing this these owners can take advantage of the legal, financial and other advantages of the corporation (e.g., limited liability, ease of obtaining investment capital, etc.) while having corporate earnings and profits taxed at individual rates. This tax election, which is available, generally, to corporations with 35 or fewer shareholders, passes corporate income, losses, deductions, credits, etc., directly through to the owners of the corporation. In essence, the S corporation achieves the tax status of a partnership while enjoying the legal and other benefits of the corporate form. (Again, see Section C just below for further information on federal S corporations.)

C. Federal S Corporation Tax Status

A CORPORATION WHICH HAS 35 or fewer shareholders and which meets other basic requirements may elect to fall under special federal tax provisions contained in Subchapter S of the Internal Revenue Code.[7] Corporations which make this election are known as S corporations. Generally, a corporation which

---

[7]This discussion is intended to treat the general aspects of S corporation tax status—for more detailed information regarding special rules, see IRS Publication 589, *Tax Information on S Corporations.*

elects to become an S corporation has its profits and losses passed through the corporation to its shareholders. This means, with exceptions, that profits and losses are not taxed to, or deducted by, the corporation, but by the individual shareholders in proportion to their stockholdings. The corporation side-steps taxation on its profits and its shareholders (like partners) get the tax benefit of the losses, credits, deductions, etc., of the corporation. Profits of the S corporation pass through to shareholders on a per-share, per-day basis, whether or not such profits are actually distributed to them.[8] Consequently, S corporation tax status can be a very flexible planning tool, providing corporations with the ability to live in two different worlds, enjoying a corporate legal life (including limited liability status for its owners) and partnership tax status.

This pass-through of corporate income and losses to the shareholders can be advantageous to some newly-formed or existing corporations. Here's a few typical situations where electing S corporation tax status can save tax dollars:[9]

1. In start-up businesses that expect initial losses before the business begins to show a profit, S corporation tax status can pass these initial losses to the individual tax returns of the shareholders who actively participate in the business (see the "Note on Active Participation"

below). This allows them to offset income from other sources with the losses of the corporation.

Example: Will and Bruno decide to form a part-time air charter business and incorporate it. They'll continue to work during the week at their salaried jobs until their new business gets off the ground. They know that the first few years of corporate life will generate substantial losses (modest profits from weekend flying charters accompanied by large expenditures for the purchase of a plane, required charter insurance, etc.). Rather than take these losses at the corporate level and carry them forward into future profitable years of the corporation, they decide they would be better off electing S corporation tax status and deducting these losses immediately against their individual full-time salary income on their individual tax returns.

2. If corporate taxable income is substantial, S corporation tax status can be a handy way of taking advantage of the lower individual rates (if corporate taxable income is high, these profits can be passed through and taxed at the shareholders' lower individual rates—remember, individual taxes are generally lower than corporate taxes when taxable income exceeds $185,000 —see Section B2 above for more on this point).

Example: Tomas and Gerald form their own video production company. They anticipate a first year profit of $2 million and, after deducting all salaries, business expenses, depreciation, etc., a corporate taxable income of $350,000. Since corporate taxable incomes above $335,000 are taxed at a flat rate of 34%, they decide to elect S corporation tax status and have this income passed through to them individually since it will be taxed to each of them at a flat 28% individual rate.

3. As discussed in Chapter 1B2, regular corporations with appreciated assets are subject to a corporate level tax when the corporation dissolves. S corporations are generally not

---

[8]IRS rulings indicate that S corporation shareholders may have to estimate and pay individual federal income tax during the year on their pro rata share of the undistributed taxable income of the S corporation—previously S corporation shareholders included this income on their individual federal tax return at the end of the year. Please check with your tax advisor for current developments on this issue.

[9]Another potential advantage of S corporation status is that corporate profits which are passed through to the individual returns of shareholders are not subject to self-employment (Social Security) taxes.

subject to this tax.[10] For some corporations, this can be a decisive factor in electing S corporation tax status.

Example: Sam and his sister Terry decide to form a corporation to hold title to real property. During the anticipated ten-year life of their corporation, they expect the property to appreciate considerably. In order to avoid a corporate level tax on this appreciation when the corporation is dissolved and the property sold, they decide to elect S corporation status prior to the purchase of any property by their corporation.

The point of these examples is simple. In some businesses, at least some of the time, it is better for business owners to be taxed as if the business was a sole proprietorship or partnership. With some technical exceptions, electing S corporation status allows you to do this. If later, for the reasons discussed in Section B above (e.g., to split business income between your corporation and yourself, with part kept in and taxed at the corporate level) or for any other reason, you no longer wish to be an S corporation, you can revoke or terminate this tax status as discussed below.

Please Note: These are generalized and necessarily simplistic examples of what can be complicated tax strategies. In all cases you'll want to consult your tax advisor to ensure favorable tax results before electing S corporation tax status.

Here now are some potential disadvantages of S corporation tax status:

• The amount of losses which may be passed through to the business owners

---

[10]S corporations are subject to a "built-in gains" tax for any appreciation which occurred prior to the S corporation election (if these assets are disposed of within 10 years after the effective date of the S corporation tax election). Please consult your tax advisor for information on these technical provisions.

(shareholders) and the ability to allocate these losses in different proportions to different individuals are restricted by various technical provisions of the Internal Revenue Code and IRS Regulations. Generally, you can only deduct losses in an S corporation up to the "basis" (tax value) of your stock and of loans made by you to your corporation (however, if these losses cannot be deducted by you in a given year, they can generally be carried forward to and deducted in future tax years if you then have a sufficient basis in your shares). We won't go through the tedious and technical process of explaining how to compute your basis in S corporation stock or specifically mention the grey areas involved in this computation—we'll just oversimply here and say that you start out with a basis in your shares equal to the price you paid for them (or the value of the property contributed for your shares). The important point is this: If you plan to elect S corporation status to pass corporate losses through to you on your individual tax return, make sure you will have sufficient basis in your stock and any indebtedness to allow you to take these losses at the personal level. All corporate tax advisors should be intimately familiar with this issue and able to help you make sure you can deduct S corporation losses on future individual tax returns.

Note on Material Participation: In order to use S corporation losses to offset the active individual income of a shareholder, the shareholders must materially participate in the business of the S corporation. See the accompanying box for a summary of several of the material participation regulations promulgated by the Treasury Department.

What Constitutes Material Participation?

The Treasury Department has issued regulations defining "material participation." Here are a some of the ways in which a business owner (or any taxpayer) can satisfy the IRS under the regulations that the owner materially participates in a business activity during a taxable year:

- The person participates in the business for more than 500 hours during the year;

- The person participates in the business for more than 100 hours during the year, and that participation is not less than any other individual's participation in the business;

- The person participates in the business for more than 100 hours during the year and participates in other activities for more than 100 hours each, for a total of more than 500 hours during the year

- The person's participation in the business for the year constitutes substantially all the participation in the business of all individuals for that year;

- The person materially participated in the business for any five of the last ten taxable years;

- The business involves the performance of personal services in the fields of health, law, engineering, architecture, accounting, actuarial science, performing arts or consulting, and the person materially participated in the business for any three preceding taxable years; or

- The person can show, based upon all facts and circumstances, that he participates in the business on a regular, continuous and substantial basis during the year.

Please Note: This is only a partial explanation of rapidly developing tax rules. Make sure to go over all the material participation regulations with your tax advisor if this is an issue for you (see, Temp. Reg. §§ 1.469-1T, -2T, -3T, -5T and -11T and related regulations issued under Section 469 of the Internal Revenue Code).

- Unlike regular corporations, S corporations must generally choose a calendar-year as their corporate tax year. Exceptions exist under IRS Revenue Procedures which allow S corporations to elect a non-calendar tax year in certain circumstances, including (1) if the S corporation can show a valid business purpose for the non-calendar year or (2) if the non-calendar year results in a deferral of income for 3 months or less and other requirements are met. Please see Section D below for additional information on choosing a corporate tax year.

- S corporations cannot adopt an employee stock ownership plan (although they are permitted to adopt a stock bonus plan).

- S corporations, like partnerships, cannot provide tax deductible fringe benefits to owners (i.e., shareholder-employees owning more than 2% of the S corporation's stock) such as:

  1. Qualified accident and health plans;

  2. Medical expense reimbursement plans;

  3. $50,000 of group term life insurance;

  4. $5,000 death benefit;

  5. Free meals and lodgings furnished for the convenience of the corporation (e.g., furnished on company premises).

1. Qualifying for S Corporation Tax Status

In order for a corporation to qualify for S corporation tax status, it must meet the following small business corporation requirements:

1. It must be a domestic (U.S.) corporation;

2. None of the shareholders may be non-resident aliens;

3. There must be only one class of stock (all shares have equal rights, e.g., dividend, liquidation rights). However, differences as to voting rights are permitted.

4. All shareholders must be individuals or estates or certain trusts;

5. There must be no more than 35 shareholders. Shares which are jointly owned by a husband and wife are considered to be owned by one person;

6. The corporation cannot be a member of a group of affiliated corporations. If your corporation plans to own stock in, or have its stock owned by, another corporation, it might be an affiliate and thus not qualify for S corporation tax treatment.

In the past, some incorporators avoided electing S corporation status since doing so would place restrictions on contributions to their corporate pension and profit-sharing plans. However, these additional restrictions to S corporation retirement plans have, for the most part, been eliminated with S corporations and regular corporations (referred to as "C" corporations in the Internal Revenue Code) now being placed on a relatively equal footing with respect to most corporate plan provisions (however, S corporation plans are still prohibited from lending money to a participant owning more than 5% of the corporation's stock—see Section G2 below for general information on regular corporate pension and profit sharing plans).

2. Electing Federal S Corporation Tax Status

If a corporation wishes to become an S corporation and meets the foregoing requirements, it must make an election by filing Form 2553 with the IRS indicating the consent of all shareholders. The election must be made on or before the 15th day of the third month of the corporation's tax year for which the S status is to be effective, or any time during the preceding tax year. For newly-formed corporations which wish to start off as an S corporation, this means making the election before the 15th day of the third month after the date the corporation's first tax year begins.

For purposes of the S corporation election, the corporation's first tax year begins when it issues stock to shareholders, acquires assets, or begins doing business, whichever occurs first. Generally, your first tax year will begin on the date you file your Articles of Incorporation. Since your S corporation election will be invalid if made at the wrong time, please check with your tax advisor to ensure that you fully understand these election rules and make your election on time (see Chapter 6B1).

The S corporation election must be consented to by all persons who are shareholders at the time it is made, as well as by all persons who were shareholders during the taxable year before the election is made. Their consents should be indicated on the election form when it is mailed to the IRS. If the shares are held jointly (e.g., in joint tenancy), each co-owner must sign the consent form.

3. Revocation or Termination of Federal S Corporation Tax Status

Once your corporation elects to become an S corporation, it continues to be treated as one through later tax years until the status is revoked or terminated. A revocation is made by filing shareholder consents to the revocation. The consent of shareholders who collectively own at least a majority of the stock in the corporation is required to effect a revocation.

S corporation status will be terminated, however, at any time, if the corporation fails to continue to meet all the small business corporation requirements discussed above (e.g., if the corporation issues a second class of shares, issues stock to a 36th shareholder, etc.). Such a termination will be effective as of the date on which the terminating event occurs (not retroactively to the beginning of the tax year).

A termination will also occur in certain situations where the corporation has a specified level of passive investment income. This type of income generally includes royalties, rents, dividends, interest, annuities and gains from the sale or exchange of stock or securities. Many S corporations will not have to be concerned with this type of termination since it also requires that the corporation have "accumulated earnings and profits" from operating previously as a regular C (a non-S) corporation.

Once S status has been revoked or terminated, the corporation may not re-elect S corporation tax status until five years after the termination or revocation. Note that certain inadvertent terminations will be ignored, provided, among other things, that the corporation takes specified corrective action.

D. Corporate Accounting Periods and Tax Years

THE ACCOUNTING PERIOD of the corporation is the period for which the corporation keeps its books and will correspond to the corporation's tax year. Generally, a corporation's accounting period (and its tax year) may be the calendar year from January 1 to December 31 or it may be a fiscal year, consisting of a twelve-month period ending on the last day of any month other than December (for example, from July 1 to June 30). In special situations, a corporation may wish to choose a "52-53 week" year. This is a period which ends on a particular day closest to the end of a month (e.g., "the last Friday of March" or "the Friday nearest to the end of March"). Most corporations will choose either a calendar year or a fiscal year as their accounting period (however, see the "Special Calendar Year Rules for S and Personal Service Corporations" below).

For some corporations, a calendar tax year will prove easiest since it will be the same year as that used by the individual shareholders. Others, because of the particular business cycle

of the corporation or simply because December is a hectic month, may wish to choose a different month to wind up their yearly affairs. Moreover, having the corporation's tax year end after that of the individual shareholders (after December 31), may allow special initial and ongoing tax advantages such as the deferral of income to the employee-shareholders of a small corporation.

You should also realize that choosing a fiscal rather than a calendar year is often in your accountant's interest since she is usually busy preparing and filing individual tax returns after the end of the calendar year. In fact, some accounting firms provide discounts if you choose a fiscal year which ends after the individual tax season (January to April). So if your accountant suggests a fiscal tax year for your corporation, you might suggest a fiscal-year discount on your accounting bill.

Special Calendar Year Rules For S and Personal Service Corporations: If you plan to elect federal S corporation tax status (see Section C above) or if your corporation meets the definition of a "personal service corporation" (defined below), generally, you must choose a calendar year for your corporate tax year (and your accounting period) unless the IRS approves the use of a fiscal year (see the discussion of exceptions to these calendar tax year rules below).

Under provisions of the Internal Revenue Code, a personal service corporation (for purposes of choosing a corporate tax year) is defined as "... a corporation the principal activity of which is the performance of personal services ... [if] such services are substantially performed by employee-owners." Also, "...an employee-owner is any employee of the corporation who owns, on any day during the taxable year, any of the outstanding stock of the personal service corporation."[11] Note that federal S corporations will not be considered personal service corporations (however, as we have indicated, they too are required, generally, to adopt a calendar year as their tax year).

As a result of these special rules, your corporation will be subject to this calendar-year rule if (1) you elect federal S corporation tax status, or (2) you are incorporating a service-only business or profession (for example, lawyers, architects, engineers, business consultants, etc.). Of course, many of these incorporated professions must organize themselves as a New York professional corporations and will not be using this book to form their corporation (see Chapter 2A2(a) for a discussion of professional corporations).

You may need to consult Treasury regulations and other clarifications to determine if your service-based corporation is subject to this calendar year rule for personal service corporations.[12] The main points to keep in mind are the following: If your corporation plans to derive income primarily from the performance of personal services, and if the owner-employees only, or primarily, will perform these services, then your corporation may be required to adopt a calendar year as the tax year of your corporation. Your tax advisor can help you determine if this special personal service corporation rule applies to you.

Exceptions to Special Calendar Year Rules for S and Personal Service Corporations: Despite the above special calendar year rules, IRS procedures provide exceptions which allow certain S corporations and personal service corporations to adopt a non-calendar (fiscal) tax year. Please see the accompanying shaded box for a summary of these rules.

Note: The discussion of special fiscal year rules for S corporations and personal service corporations is intended only to introduce you to some highly technical and rapidly changing tax material. If you wish to elect a non-calendar tax year for your S or personal service corporation, make sure to discuss these and other applicable rules and regulations with your tax advisor and, above all else, be sure to file the required tax year election forms with the IRS on time.

---

[11]See IRC § 269(A)(b)(1)-(2) and § 441(i)(2).

[12]The IRS has issued temporary regulations [starting with Temp. Reg § 1.441-1T] defining the nature and extent of personal service activities which will trigger this calendar year rule for personal service corporations. For example, the regulations state that 1) the fields of health, law, engineering, architecture, accounting, actuarial science, performing arts and consulting are personal services subject to this rule; 2) performing arts services does not include the personal services of managers and promoters; and 3) that consulting does not include the performance of services such as sales or brokerage activities since compensation for these services is contingent on the consummation of the transaction that these services are intended to effect. Again, see your tax advisor for current developments and clarifications.

S and Personal Service Corporation Fiscal Year Rules

25-Percent Test: IRS Revenue Procedure 87-32 allows S corporations and personal service corporations to elect a fiscal year for their corporation if they can show that the fiscal year requested represents the natural business year of the corporation. To make this showing, these corporations must meet the "25% test." Generally, this test is met if 25% or more of the corporation's gross receipts from services or sales have been recognized during the last two months of the requested fiscal year for the past consecutive three years (e.g., if a personal service corporation wishes a fiscal year ending on June 30th, then 25% or more of its receipts from services must have derived during the months of May and June during each of the previous three years). If the corporation has not been in existence for three years, then, generally, the IRS will look at the gross receipts of the pre-existing unincorporated business.

Business Purpose: Even if you cannot meet the 25% test explained above, you may be able to establish another business purpose for your non-calendar tax year (e.g, if the fiscal year requested corresponds to the natural annual business cycle of the corporation)—Revenue Procedure 87-57 contains eight factual examples of valid and invalid business purposes when requesting a fiscal year for an S corporation.

Three-Month Deferral of Income: Under Section 444 of the Internal Revenue Code, S corporations and personal service corporations may be allowed to adopt a non-calendar tax year if the tax year results in a deferral on income of three months or less. For example, if a fiscal year ending September 30th is requested, this tax year will be allowed for the corporation (if other requirements are also met) since this results in a three month deferral of income when compared to the otherwise required calendar year ending December 31st. Please realize that use of this three-month deferral rule comes with a price tag: S corporations using this procedure have to make a "required payment" to the IRS each year; personal service corporations utilizing this election are limited in the amount of corporate deductions which can be taken for payments made to the employee-shareholders unless certain minimum distributions are made to these share-holders before the end of the calendar year and carrybacks of net operating losses of the personal service corporation are restricted.

Important: The procedure for electing a fiscal year varies depending on the basis for the fiscal year request and whether or not you are making a "back-up" election (a back-up election is a way of reserving your right to a fiscal tax year if your primary basis for the fiscal year election is denied). For example, S corporations may be required to elect a fiscal year by making a request on their S corporation election form (by noting their request and using a few "magic words" on IRS Form 2553) or by submitting IRS Form 8716, *Election to Have a Tax Year Other Than a Required Tax Year*.[13] The procedures also vary for personal service corporations. Please make sure to check with your tax advisor and use the right form (and IRS sanctioned wording) when applying for a fiscal tax year for your corporation.

13See Treasury regulations issued under IRC § 444 (starting with Temp. Reg. § 1.444-1T).

E. IRC Section 1244 Ordinary Loss Treatment of Stock Losses

UNDER SECTION 1244 of the Internal Revenue Code, many corporations can provide shareholders with the benefit of treating losses from the sale, exchange, or worthlessness of their stock as "ordinary" rather than "capital" losses on their individual federal tax returns, up to a maximum of $50,000 ($100,000 for a husband and wife filing a joint return) in each tax year. This is a definite advantage since, generally, ordinary losses are fully deductible against individual income, whereas capital losses are only partially deductible (normally the latter can only be used to offset up to $3,000 of individual income in a given tax year). Stock issued by a corporation that qualifies for this federal ordinary loss treatment is known as Section 1244 stock.

To qualify for Section 1244 stock treatment, the following requirements must be met:

- The shares must be issued for money or property (other than corporate securities) and more than 50% of the corporation's gross receipts during the five tax years preceding the year in which the loss occurred must have been derived from sources other than royalties, dividends, interest, rents, annuities, or gains from sales or exchanges in securities or stock. If the corporation has not been in existence for the five tax years preceding the year in which the loss occurred, the five-year period is replaced by the number of tax years the corporation has been in existence prior to the loss.

- The corporation must be a small business corporation as defined in Section 1244 of the Internal Revenue Code. A corporation is a small business corporation under this definition if the total amount of money or the value of property received by the corporation for stock, as a contribution to capital and as paid-in surplus, does not exceed $1 million.

- At the time of loss, the shareholder must submit a timely statement to the IRS electing to take an ordinary loss pursuant to Section 1244.

Note: Ordinary loss treatment for the stock loss is only available to the original owner of the stock.

Corporations formed by using this book should automatically meet most of these requirements. However, if you issue shares in return for cancellation of indebtedness, problems may arise in some situations (e.g., if the notes were secured). Also, if you anticipate problems in being classified as a small business corporation (as defined above), or significant income from passive sources such as dividends or interest, or if you plan to have partnership shareholders, you should check with your tax consultant to make sure you can rely on ordinary loss treatment should a loss occur.

You do not have to file a special election form with the IRS or adopt a formal Section 1244 stock plan to be eligible for this special tax treatment—you simply must meet the requirements indicated above.

Forms Note: The tear-out Minutes, prepared as part of Chapter 5, Step 8, contain a Section 1244 resolution which is used as formal documentation of your intent that future stock losses of your shareholders be eligible for Section 1244 tax treatment. We expect most incorporators will wish to include this resolution in their Minutes. If your corporation does not meet the Section 1244 requirements at the time of a stock loss, the loss will simply be treated as the usual capital loss associated with regular shares of stock. Of course, if Section 1244 treatment of future stock losses is a critical factor in your incorporation, you will want to check with your tax advisor to be sure you will be eligible for this special stock loss treatment should a loss occur.

F. IRC Section 351 Tax-Free Exchange Treatment of Your Incorporation

MANY INCORPORATORS will wish to issue stock in return for the transfer of property to the corporation. If you plan to do this, you should realize that taxes may have to be paid by one or more of the transferors of the property unless special requirements contained in Section 351 of the Internal Revenue Code are met. If all of your shareholders will simply pay cash for their shares, you may ignore this section since an all-cash transaction of this sort is simply a purchase of shares, not a potentially taxable transfer of property to your corporation.

First, let's back up a little. As you know, anytime you sell an asset to someone (in the case of an incorporation, you are "selling" property to the corporation in return for stock), you are normally liable for the payment of taxes on the profit you make from the transaction. In tax terms, the profit is the difference between the selling price and your "adjusted basis" in the property. Without covering all the technicalities, the basic rule for business property is that your adjusted basis in the property will be the original cost of the property minus depreciation plus capital improvements.

Here's a (simplified) example: Assume that your business purchased a building at a cost of $180,000. It has taken $90,000 depreciation on the property and made $20,000 capital improvements to the property since the property was purchased. The adjusted basis of the property is $110,000 (cost of $180,000 - $90,000 depreciation + $20,000 improvements). If the property is sold for $210,000, the taxable gain (profit) is $100,000 ($210,000 - $110,000 adjusted basis). Note that we are ignoring, for purposes of this example, the cost, sales price and basis of the land on which the building is located (land is not depreciable).

Naturally, most incorporators will not wish to pay taxes on the sale of property to their corporation in return for shares of stock. This is particularly true if property which has increased in value (appreciated property) is being transferred to the corporation. For example, if a building which originally cost $60,000 and has been depreciated down to an adjusted basis of $30,000 is being transferred to the corporation for $100,000 (the current appreciated value of the building), the gain on the transfer would be $70,000 ($100,000-$30,000 adjusted basis).

Fortunately, many small corporations will be able to transfer property to their corporation in return for stock in a tax-free exchange without recognizing any gain or loss on the transfer. Specifically, under Section 351 of the Internal Revenue Code, the transfer of property in return for shares of stock (or other securities) will generally be treated as a a tax-free exchange if, immediately after the transfer, the transferors (shareholders) meet certain "control" tests. The tests which must be met are:

1. The transferors, as a group, must own at least 80% of the total combined voting power of all classes of issued stock entitled to vote; and

2. They must also own at least 80% of all other issued classes of stock of the corporation.

Most initial stock issuance transactions of small closely-held corporations using this book should meet these control tests and be eligible for this tax-free exchange treatment since this is your first stock issuance involving one class of common voting shares and you don't need to establish control over previously issued stock or other classes of stock. Also note that cash and intangible types of property such as the goodwill of a business or patents are considered property for purposes of Section 351.

Example: Harvey, Frank and Frances decide to form a corporation. The corporation will issue 500 shares of stock at a price of $100 per share. Harvey will receive 100 shares for a $10,000 cash payment; Frank and Frances will receive 200 shares apiece for their equal interests in the assets of their partnership valued at $40,000. The transaction qualifies for Section 351 tax-free exchange treatment since at least 80% (in this case, 100%) of all shares will be owned by the transferors of money and property after the transfer (Harvey is not personally affected by this tax-free exchange treatment since he is simply purchasing shares for cash; however, Frank and Frances do not want to recognize a taxable gain on the transfer of their partnership assets.) Moreover, even without considering Harvey's permissible transfer of money to the corporation for his shares, Frank and Frances themselves will control the required 80% of the corporation's shares after the transfer of their property (400 out of 500 shares).

Of course, nothing (or next to nothing) is really free under tax statutes and regulations. A tax-free exchange simply defers the payment of taxes until your shares are sold (e.g., when you sell your shares to someone else or your corporation, itself, is sold or liquidated). Technically (and, of course, with some exceptions), the adjusted basis of the property transferred to the corporation is carried over to your shares (the adjusted basis of the shareholder's property becomes the basis of the shareholder's newly-purchased shares).

Example: You transfer property with a fair market value of $20,000 and an adjusted basis of $10,000 to the corporation in a Section 351 tax-free exchange for shares worth $20,000. Your shares will then have a basis of $10,000. If you sell the shares for $30,000, your taxable gain will be $20,000 ($30,000 selling price minus their basis of $10,000). Note also, the corporation's basis in the property received in a tax-free exchange will also generally be the same as the adjusted basis of the transferred property (in this example, the corporation's basis in the property will be $10,000).

Even in a tax-free transaction, the shareholders will be taxed to the extent of any money or property they receive in addition to stock. For example, if you transfer a truck in a tax-free exchange worth $50,000 to the corporation in return for $40,000 worth of shares and a $10,000 cash payment by the corporation, you will have to report the $10,000 as taxable income.

1. Potential Complexities Under IRC Section 351

There are, of course, added complexities which may arise in attempting to qualify an exchange of property for stock in your corporation as a Section 351 tax-free exchange. Let's look at a few of the more common situations which may trigger special rules:

Where shares are issued in return for the performance of services. Although New York law allows stock to be issued for past services performed for the corporation (see Chapter 2F), services are not considered "property" for purposes of Section 351 (remember, stock must be issued in return for property to qualify for this tax-free exchange treatment). Consequently, you cannot normally count shares issued to shareholders for services in calculating the 80% control requirement. Moreover, even if you are able to meet the control test (not counting the stock issued for services), any shareholder who receives stock for services will have to report the value of her shares as taxable income.

Example: Your corporation plans to issue $50,000 worth of shares upon its incorporation to you and the co-founder of your corporation, Fred. You will transfer property worth $30,000 for $30,000 in shares while Fred will receive $10,000 in shares in return for services already performed for the corporation valued at $10,000. The transfer will be taxable to both you and Fred since the basic control test of Section 351 will not have been met: You are the only person who will transfer property in return for stock and you do not meet the control requirement of Section 351 since you will only own 75% of the shares of the corporation.

If the facts in this example are changed so that you receive 80% of the stock in exchange for property (you transfer $40,000 worth of property; Fred still receives $10,000 in shares for his services), the transfer will be tax-free under Section 351, but Fred will have to report the $10,000 in shares as taxable income.

Where the corporation issues notes or other "evidences of indebtedness" in return for the transfer of property to the corporation. (For example, you transfer your unincorporated business to the corporation in return for both shares of stock and a promissory note which will be repaid over time by your corporation—see the Phil Spectrum example in Chapter 2E). The technical issue here is that Section 351 requires that property be transferred in return for "stock or securities" of the corporation.

To begin with, you won't want a loan to be considered "stock" (an equity investment) in your corporation since this will result in your being denied the benefits associated with the loan (the ability of the corporation to deduct interest payments on the note and the shareholder to treat the repayment of principal on the note as a nontaxable return of capital—see Chapter 2E for further details).

This leaves you with the other alternative of making sure that any loans will be seen as "securities" in order to meet the requirements of Section 351 (since we are dealing here with loans, the more exact term is "debt securities"). There are no clear guidelines on this issue in the Internal Revenue Code or IRS regulations. However, court cases have indicated that the critical condition in having your loan treated as a debt security is the length of the note which evidences the loan. Generally, short-term notes and demand notes (payable on demand by the shareholder) will not qualify as debt securities. On the other hand, notes with a term of 10 years or more should qualify. Many accountants are a little less conservative on this issue and feel that a loan term of 7 years or more is sufficient (opinions on this point vary—please check with your tax advisor if this issue arises in your incorporation). Of course, the note should contain all the relevant terms of the loan such as the maturity date, amount of principal to be repaid, a reasonable rate of interest, timing and amount of payments by the corporation under the note, etc.

Where the corporation assumes (agrees to pay) liabilities associated with the transferred property. This technicality typically arises when an existing business is being incorporated (i.e., where the owners of a prior business transfer the assets and liabilities of the prior business to the corporation in return for shares of stock). Under this exception to Section 351 tax-free exchange treatment, the prior business owners will be subject to the payment of taxes if the liabilities assumed by the corporation exceed the basis of the business assets transferred to the corporation.

For example, if you transfer business assets with a basis of $40,000 to your corporation along with $60,000 worth of liabilities, the difference of $20,000 is, as a general rule, taxable to you.

As a conclusion to this discussion, we'll simply note that this federal tax statute and its associated regulations contain many rules and exceptions to rules. As a result, if you will be transferring property to your corporation in return for shares of stock (and, possibly, notes to be repaid by the corporation), an accountant can usually show you how to structure the capitalization of your corporation so as to qualify for tax-free exchange treatment under Section 351 of the Internal Revenue Code.

Recordkeeping Note: Federal income tax regulations require the corporation and each shareholder to file statements with their income tax returns listing specific information concerning the Section 351 tax-free exchange.[14] Permanent records containing the information listed in these statements must also be kept by the corporation and the shareholders.

---

[14]See Treasury Regulation Section 1.351-3.

G. Tax Treatment of Employee Compensation and Benefits

1. Salaries

A corporation may deduct amounts paid to employees as salaries for corporate income tax purposes. To be deductible, salaries must be reasonable and must be paid for services actually performed by the employees. Substantial salary increases or large discretionary lump-sum bonuses paid to shareholder-employees of closely-held corporations may be scrutinized by the IRS, since they can be, and sometimes are, used as a means of paying disguised dividends to the shareholders (i.e., as a return of capital to the shareholder rather than as a bona-fide payment for services rendered by the employee).

If the IRS determines that a salary was not related to bona-fide services actually performed by a shareholder-employee or was paid in an unreasonable amount, it will treat the excess amount as a dividend. This will not have an adverse effect on the shareholder-employee's tax liability because the payment must be included on his individual tax return either way. However, it will prevent the corporation from deducting the disallowed payment as a business expense.

Therefore, try to avoid the payment of large discretionary bonuses and keep any increase in salaries tied to increased corporate productivity related to the employee's performance or the going rate of pay for employees in similar businesses.

Reality Note: In the majority of small corporations, the owner-employees will rarely be in a position to pay themselves unreasonably large salaries (small business owners are notoriously under-compensated, particularly in contrast to their highly-paid publicly-held corporation counterparts).

However, if you do decide to pay yourself a large salary, it may be wise to draw up an employment contract between yourself and your corporation. You may also wish to adopt a board resolution detailing your abilities, qualifications, and responsibilities, showing why you are entitled to the wages the corporation is paying you. In these situations, paying out dividends occasionally (if possible) is also useful since it helps demonstrate to the IRS that you are acting in good faith in not paying as salary what should be going out as dividends.

2. Pension and Profit-Sharing Plans

As with salaries, any benefits paid to shareholders will be presumed to be a payment of a nondeductible dividend unless related to a bona fide employment relationship. Corporations may deduct payments made on behalf of employees to qualified pension or profit-sharing plans. Contributions and accumulated earnings under such plans are not taxed until they are distributed to the employee. This is advantageous because employees generally will be in a lower tax bracket at retirement age, and the funds, while they are held in trust, can be invested and allowed to accumulate with no tax being paid prior to the distribution.

Corporate and non-corporate pension plans for business owners (i.e., Keoghs) are, for the most part, the same with respect to contributions and benefits for participants, integration with social security benefits, and most other plan provisions. There are also strict rules which apply specifically to "top-heavy" plans, whether corporate or non-corporate—those set up primarily to benefit key employees (this is the type of plan you will most likely have if you decide to have one at all).

However, corporate plans still contain a few advantages over non-corporate plans such as allowing loans of $50,000 to be made from the corporate plan to participants. Also, whereas corporate defined contribution plans (which guarantee a specified yearly contribution to the plan on behalf of the participant) and non-corporate Keoghs limit annual contributions for participants to a maximum of $30,000 or 25% of earnings, whichever is less, corporate defined benefit plans (which guarantee a specified benefit upon retirement) allow annual contributions of the lesser of $90,000 or 100% of a participant's average compensation (the cost of administering defined benefit plans is higher however). Further, with respect to non-corporate individual plan arrangements (IRAs) where contributions for an individual are generally limited to $2,000, full or partial deductions for contributions to these plans are only permitted to individuals who are not covered by a company retirement plan or, if they are so covered, to individuals whose adjusted gross income does not exceed certain maximum limits (e.g., $35,000 for an individual; $50,000 for a married couple filing jointly).

Please consult your accountant, tax advisor or plan trustee for more information on these complex federal and state pension and profit-sharing plan rules.

3. Medical Benefits

a. Medical Expense Reimbursement

Amounts paid by a corporation as part of a medical expense reimbursement plan to repay the medical expenses of employees, their spouses and dependents, are deductible by the corporation and are not included in the employee's income for tax purposes.

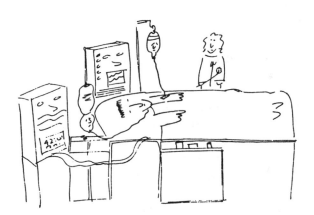

4. Life Insurance

A corporation can also deduct premiums paid on behalf of employees for group-term life insurance. This tax break is available only if the plan does not discriminate in favor of key employees. An employee covered by a qualified group-term insurance plan does not have to count premiums paid by the corporation for up to $50,000 worth of insurance coverage as taxable income. Death proceeds under such insurance are also generally not included in the employee's income for tax purposes if you set up the right kind of plan.

b. Accident and Health Insurance

A corporation may deduct premiums paid by the corporation for accident and health insurance coverage for employees, their spouses and dependents. The premiums paid by the corporation are not included in the employee's income for tax purposes. Similarly, insurance proceeds and benefits are not normally taxable. Coverage need not be part of a group plan, such as Blue Cross. The employee may pick his own policy, pay for it, and obtain reimbursement from the corporation.

Sole Proprietorship and Partnership Tax Note: Unincorporated business owners are allowed to deduct a portion (25%) of the premiums paid for themselves and their spouses for health insurance. These deductions do not, however, reduce the individual's liability for self-employment (social security) taxes; are not available if the individual is eligible to participate in an employer-sponsored plan; and are subject to non-discrimination and other coverage rules (e.g., employees of the unincorporated business must also be provided coverage).

5. Disability Insurance

Premiums paid by a corporation for disability insurance coverage for its employees are deductible by the corporation. Any disability benefits, however, are included in the employee's gross income, subject to a few exceptions involving permanent and total disabilities. If the premiums are paid by the employee, however, all benefits are nontaxable.

H. Corporate Accumulated Earnings Credit

IN THIS SECTION, we discuss a benefit of doing business as a corporation: the federal accumulated earnings credit.

As we've discussed earlier in this book, the decision to incorporate is often based upon the desire of business owners to split business income between themselves and their corporation. The Internal Revenue Code helps corporations do this by allowing them an automatic accumulated earnings credit of

$250,000.[15] What this means is that the IRS will allow you to retain this amount of earnings in your corporation without challenging you for not paying it out to the shareholders as dividends, salaries, or in other ways which would make it subject to taxation on their individual tax returns. Of course, the corporation must pay taxes on these accumulated amounts at the corporate tax rate but this tax rate (particularly on the first $75,000 of taxable corporate income) is often lower than the individual tax rates of the shareholders.[16] Note that federal S corporations do not receive (or need) the benefit of this credit since the undistributed earnings of the corporation pass through to the shareholders of S corporations each year (see Section C above). This accumulated earnings credit is, as we've said, one of the advantages of doing business as a corporation—sole proprietors and partnerships do not enjoy this type of tax flexibility.

Most small corporations will not need (or be able) to accumulate earnings anywhere near this $250,000 credit since salaries, bills and other business expenses will reduce earnings below this amount. If, however, you do need to accumulate income in the corporation above this limit, you may do so, as long as these excess

accumulations are held for the reasonably anticipated needs of the business (not just to shelter income).

I. Personal Holding Company Penalty

IN THIS SECTION we briefly discuss provisions of the federal tax law[17] which some closely-held personal service corporations will need to be aware of: the personal holding company penalty tax. If your corporation does not plan to derive income from passive sources (such as rents, royalties, dividends) or will not derive income from the performance of personal services, you may wish to skip this section.

This tax is a 28% corporate surtax, in addition to regular corporate taxes, on the income of certain types of corporations which receive a significant portion of their adjusted gross income from "passive" sources or from services performed under contract. With a few simple precautions, this tax should not pose a problem for these corporations—the only real danger is inadvertently becoming subject to this tax due to a lack of knowledge of these provisions.

Without discussing all of the technical definitions and exceptions of this federal tax law, the personal holding company tax may apply to a corporation if five or fewer of its shareholders own 50% or more of the corporation's stock and if 60% or more of the corporation's gross income (minus several technical adjustments) for the tax year is from certain types of passive sources

---

[15]Section 535(c)(2)(B) of the Internal Revenue Code limits the amount of this credit to $150,000 for corporations whose principal function is the performance of services in the fields of health, law, engineering, architecture, accounting, actuarial science, performance arts, or consulting. This lesser credit should still be sufficient for most corporations. **Note:** Many of these professional service corporations must incorporate as New York professional corporations (see Chapter 2A2).

[16]Note, however, that the personal service corporations listed in the previous footnote which are only allowed the $150,000 accumulated earnings credit must pay a flat tax of 34% on retained corporate taxable income—see Section B1 above for further information on this special flat-tax provision).

---

[17]Internal Revenue Code Sections 541 through 547.

such as dividends, interest, rents or royalties[18] or is derived from personal service contracts. Although many small corporations will have five or fewer shareholders who own at least half of the corporation's shares, most corporations using this book will derive most of their income from engaging in active business pursuits rather than these types of passive sources. Consequently, the concern here will usually be whether your corporation provides contracted services, and, if so, whether this income is subject to being classified as personal service contract income.

Under Section 543(a)(7) of the Internal Revenue Code, personal service contract income means, generally, "amounts received under a contract under which the corporation is to furnish personal services, if some person other than the corporation has the right to designate (by name or description) the individual who is to perform the services, or if the individual who is to perform the services is designated (by name or description) in the contract." In addition, the individual who is to perform the services, or who may be so designated, must be at least a 25% shareholder.

What does all of this mean? Simply stated, if your corporation is planning to provide services under the terms of a contract, you will want to make sure that the corporation has the right to

designate the individual who will perform the contracted services (not the person or business for whom the services will be performed) and that the name of the individual who is to perform the services does not appear in the contract. By doing this you should be able to stay clear of this personal holding company penalty.

Note When Incorporating a Pre-existing Business: If you are incorporating a personal service business, such as your own computer repair and service corporation, you will not want to assign your individual personal service contracts to your new corporation without checking first with your tax advisor—this could trigger a penalty.

It should be of some comfort to note that the Internal Revenue Code anticipates that corporations will be subject to this penalty tax usually due to an oversight or poor planning and, consequently, allows them to avoid the imposition of this tax, in many cases, by the payout of what is known as a "deficiency dividend." Even under this procedure, however, the corporation is subject to interest and other penalty payments. Nonetheless, if you are incorporating a service business, or if your corporation plans to receive a substantial portion of its income from the type of passive sources which we've mentioned above, please check with your tax specialist to make sure you will not inadvertently run afoul of this penalty tax provision.

J. Tax and Financial Considerations When Incorporating a Prior Business

IN THIS SECTION, we discuss a few key legal and tax issues involving the incorporation of an existing business—for a broader discussion of

---

[18]**Note For Software Developers and Distributors**: We know that many readers of this book will be deriving corporate income from the licensing of software. The Internal Revenue Code contains an important exemption here for software royalties which may be apply to you. Specifically, "active business computer software royalties," defined as those which are "received by the corporation during the taxable year in connection with the licensing of computer software," are not treated as personal holding company income if certain specific technical tests are met—see IRC Section 543(d) and check with your tax advisor for more information.

the basic considerations relevant to your decision to incorporate, please see Chapter 1. If you are simply incorporating a new business, you may wish to skip this section.

1. When Is the Best Time to Incorporate the Prior Business?

You will want to incorporate your prior business at a time which results in the most favorable tax treatment (mostly, this means the time which results in your paying the least amount of taxes).

Example: If you anticipate a loss this year and a healthy profit next year, you may wish to remain unincorporated now and take a personal loss on your individual tax return. Next year you can incorporate and split your business income between yourself and your corporation to reduce your overall tax liability.

2. Special Financial and Tax Considerations

Typically, when incorporating a pre-existing business, all the assets and liabilities of the prior business will be transferred to the new corporation which will then carry on the pre-existing business. Further, as explained in Section F above, most incorporators will want the transfer of the assets of the prior business to the corporation in return for shares of stock to qualify for tax-free exchange treatment under Section 351 of the Internal Revenue Code. In special circumstances, however, some incorporators may not wish to transfer all assets or liabilities of the prior business to the corporation, or, for special reasons, may not wish this transfer to qualify for Section 351 tax-free exchange treatment. We discuss these special circumstances in this subsection.

a. Do you wish to retain (not transfer) some of the assets of the prior business?

In some instances, the prior business owners may not wish to transfer some of the assets of the prior business to their new corporation. For example:

• Sufficient cash should be retained to pay liabilities not assumed by the corporation (such as payroll and other employment taxes).

• You may wish to retain ownership in some of the assets of the prior business. For example, you may wish to continue to own a building in your name and lease it to your corporation. In this way, you can continue to deduct depreciation, mortgage interest payments, and other expenses associated with the property on your individual tax return (the corporation, moreover, can deduct rent payments made under the lease).

b. Do you wish to have the corporation assume some, but not all, of the liabilities of the prior business?

As with the assets of your unincorporated business, you may not wish to transfer (have your corporation assume) all of the liabilities of the prior business. Two considerations relevant to this decision are listed below:

- The assumption of the liabilities of the prior business may, in special situations, result in the recognition of taxable gain by the prior business owners under an exception to the tax-free exchange rule of Section 351 (as discussed in Section F above).

- Payment of liabilities and expenses by the prior business owners, rather than by the corporation, will allow the owners to deduct these expenses on their individual tax returns (to reduce their individual taxable incomes).

c. Is a Section 351 tax-free exchange desirable?

Although not typical, a small number of incorporators may wish to have the transfer of assets of the prior business to the corporation be a taxable exchange. Since the general rule under Section 351 (discussed in Section F above) is that the exchange of property for stock by individuals who will be in control of the corporation after the exchange is a tax-free transfer, oddly enough, you may need to do a little advance tax planning to accomplish this taxable result. Reasons why a few incorporators may wish to be taxed on the transfer of the assets of their prior business to the corporation include the following:

- Some incorporators may wish to recognize taxable gain on the transfer of business assets to increase the corporation's "basis" in these assets. For example, let's assume that you will transfer assets with a fair market value of $50,000 to your corporation. Your basis in these assets is $30,000. If you transfer these assets to the corporation for $50,000 worth of stock in a *taxable* exchange, you will recognize a taxable gain of $20,000. However, the corporation's basis in these assets will be your basis before the sale ($30,000) plus the amount of gain recognized by the transferor (your individual gain of $20,000).

Consequently, the corporation's basis in these assets will be increased to $50,000. This allows the corporation to take additional depreciation in these assets over time and will lower the gain the corporation will have to pay upon a sale of these assets (if the corporation sells the assets for $60,000, the gain will be $10,000—the difference between the corporation's basis and the selling price).

On the other hand, if these assets had been transferred to the corporation in a tax-free exchange, the corporation's basis would be the same as your pre-transfer basis in the property ($30,000) and the gain recognized by the corporation from the sale of these assets would be the higher figure of $30,000 (the difference between the corporation's $30,000 basis and the $60,000 selling price). Of course, whether the advantages of obtaining a higher corporate basis in assets is worth the gain which you, the transferor, will have to pay in a taxable exchange, will be determined by the individual facts of your incorporation (e.g., will you be able to offset this individual gain with losses or deductions on your individual tax return?, etc.). As we've said, normally, you will want to transfer assets to your corporation in a tax-free exchange to avoid the recognition of gain on the transfer.

- Some incorporators may wish to recognize a loss on the transfer of assets to their corporation. If you transfer assets to your corporation under Section 351, you cannot recognize either a gain or a loss on the transfer. If the value of the assets has decreased below your basis in the property, you may wish to take a loss on the transfer. For example, if your basis in a building is $75,000, and, because of market conditions, the current value of the building is now only $60,000, you will need to transfer the building to the corporation in a taxable exchange (and meet other technical requirements) to recognize this loss of $15,000. Again, this is not a typical situation but it may be relevant to some incorporators.

3. Liability for the Debts of the Prior Business

In addition to the above considerations involving the assumption of liabilities of the prior business by your new corporation, legal rules exist concerning the liability of the prior business owners and the corporation for the debts of the prior business.

Note: These rules will have little significance for most newly-formed corporations which will wish, as a matter of course and as a matter of simple good-faith business dealings, to continue to carry on the business and continue to pay all the debts and liabilities associated with the business, whether incurred before or after incorporation. However, to underscore the fact that you cannot incorporate as a means of avoiding the liabilities of the prior business, and by way of briefly mentioning other specific considerations related to this issue, we include the following points:

- If the corporation agrees to assume all of the debts and liabilities of the prior business, it is exempted from most of the provisions of the Bulk Sales Act of the Uniform Commercial Code. This can result in significant reduction in paperwork (see Chapter 5, Step 9).

- Regardless of whether or not the corporation assumes the debts and liabilities of the prior business, the prior owners may also remain personally liable for these debts and liabilities.

- A new corporation is not liable for the debts and liabilities of the prior business unless it specifically agrees to assume them. However, if the transfer is not done in strict compliance with the terms of the Bulk Sales Act, or is in any way fraudulent or done with the intent to frustrate or deceive creditors, the creditors of the prior business can seize the transferred business assets. Similarly, if the corporation does not, in fact, pay the assumed liabilities of the prior business, the transferred assets may be seized by creditors of the prior business.

- If transferred assets are subject to recorded liens (e.g., a mortgage on real property), these liens will survive the transfer and the assets will continue to be subject to these liens.

- The former business owners may be liable for debts incurred after incorporation if credit is extended to the corporation by a creditor who believes that he or she is still dealing with the prior business (e.g., a creditor who has not been notified of the incorporation). See Chapter 6A1 for the steps to take to notify creditors of the prior business of your incorporation.

- The corporation may be liable for delinquent sales, employment or other taxes owed by the prior business.

Chapter 5

STEPS TO FORM YOUR CORPORATION

Chapter 5

STEPS TO FORM YOUR CORPORATION

THIS CHAPTER WILL SHOW YOU, on a step-by-step basis, how to form your New York corporation by preparing and filing a Certificate of Incorporation, preparing your Bylaws and a Statement of Incorporators, preparing Minutes of and holding your first meeting of Directors, selling and issuing your initial shares of stock, and taking care of other essential organizational formalities. You'll see that these steps are really not complicated and involve, for the most part, simply filling in a small number of blanks on the tear-out forms contained in the Appendix at the end of this book. Take your time and relax, you'll be surprised at how easy it all is.

We recommend that before you file your Certificate of Incorporation or sign and file other corporate documents, you have them reviewed by an accountant and a lawyer. This is not required by law and some incorporators may not feel that it is necessary in their situation. Just the same, we feel that it makes excellent sense to consult people who have more experience than you do in the often complicated questions that surround incorporation. An experienced lawyer and accountant are very likely to make helpful suggestions, some of which may save you time and aggravation later on. A consultation with a lawyer and accountant to review the forms and other organizational aspects of your incorporation before you file your Certificate of Incorporation and legally bring your corporation into existence is far different than having them do it all for you. Their job in this context will be to answer your specific, informed questions and to review your papers, not to do all the routine paperwork. Your time with them, for which they receive an agreed upon hourly fee, will be greatly reduced once you have followed the steps in this chapter (see Chapter 7 for information on choosing the right lawyer and accountant).

Step 1. Choose a Corporate Name

A. Introduction

THE FIRST STEP in organizing your corporation is the selection of a corporate name. The name you choose is essentially up to you, provided that it meets the requirements of state law and does not interfere with rights which might be held by other people. As you'll see, the name you choose must be acceptable to the Department of State when you file your Certificate of Incorporation with this office. First, two basic points regarding your choice of a corporate name:

- **Filing Your Corporate Name With The Secretary of State Does Not Guarantee Your Right to Use It.** Contrary to the belief of many people, having your name approved by the New York Department of State when you file your Certificate of Incorporation does not guarantee that you have the absolute right to use it (as explained further below, an unincorporated business may already be using it as their trade name[1] or another business may be using it as a trademark or service mark). Consequently, you may wish to do some checking on your own to be relatively sure that no one else has a prior claim to your proposed corporate name. We discuss special self-help measures you may wish to take prior to deciding on a corporate name in "Perform Your Own Name Search" below.

---

[1] A trade name is simply a name used in conjunction with the operation of a trade or business. It may consist of the real name(s) of the business owners or an assumed name (e.g., Charles Smith may decide to do business under the assumed name of "Chuck's Steak Company"). We discuss special rules associated corporate assumed names in Chapter 6A2.

• **Using A Name Different Than Your Formal Corporate Name Is Allowed.** If you want to adopt a formal corporate name in your Certificate of Incorporation which is different from the one which you have used, or plan to use, locally in your business, you can accomplish this by filing an assumed name statement with the New York Secretary of State (we explain how to prepare and file this statement in Chapter 6A2 below).

Before looking at the specific legal requirements for choosing a corporate name, let's briefly discuss the importance of choosing the right name for your new corporation.The most significant aspect of choosing a name is that it will, to a large degree, identify the "goodwill" of your business. We don't mean this in any strict legal, accounting or tax sense, but simply that the people you do business with, including your customers, clients, other merchants, vendors, independent contractors, lenders, and the business community generally, will identify your business primarily by your name. For this reason, as well as a number of practical reasons such as not wanting to print new stationery, change Yellow Page or advertising copy, create new logos, purchase new signs, etc., you will want to pick a name that you will be happy with for a long time. So pay particular attention to your choice of a corporate name. As a practical matter, it's likely to become one of your most important assets.

Of course, if you are incorporating an existing business, you'll probably wish to use your current name as your corporate name if it has become associated with your products, services, etc. Many businesses do this by simply adding an "Inc." after their old name (e.g., Really Good Widgets decides to incorporate as Really Good Widgets, Inc.). Using your old name is not required, however, and if you have been hankering after a new one, this is your chance to claim it.

B. Legal Limitations

THERE ARE MANY legal limitations which may affect the name you wish to use. They are, for the most part, intended to either make clear to others that they are dealing with a corporation, or to make sure that your corporate name can be distinguished from others on file with the Department of State. A listing of the major restrictions and considerations affecting your choice of corporate name follows:

• Every corporation must have the word "Corporation," "Incorporated," or "Limited," or an abbreviation of one of these words (e.g., Corp., Inc., or Ltd.) in its name.

• The name you choose can't be the same as the name of a corporation presently authorized to do business in New York.

• You can't use a name which has been reserved for use with the Department of State by another proposed corporation or which is not distinguishable from other corporate names on file with the Department of State. (Instructions on how to reserve your name are given below.)

• No word can be used that may mislead anyone into thinking that your corporation has anything to do with the governments of New York or the United States. For example, you should avoid the words "United States,"

"U.S.," "Federal," or "New York" in your name.

- You cannot use words which may mislead the public, generally, or which are against public policy (e.g., obscene words). For example, if you simply list your surname as your corporate name, such as Rosencrantz, Inc., the Department of State may feel that this individual corporate name is misleading and require that you use your full first name (e.g., Ralph Rosencrantz, Inc.) or add a descriptive phrase in the name, such as Rosencrantz Home and Hamlet Renovators, Inc. Avoid generic, non-descriptive names whenever possible—be as specific as you can in choosing a corporate name (for example., by making sure that your corporate name reflects, at least in part, the type of business you are engaged in).

  Examples: Highland Construction Corporation, Last Resort Travel Agencies, Inc. .

- Certain words (or their abbreviations) cannot be used in the name of an ordinary business corporation (the type of corporation we show you how to form). As a general rule, you can't use any word or phrase which implies that your corporation will be engaging in a business which has to be licensed or approved by the state. This includes such professions as lawyer, doctor, dentist, architect, therapist, etc. (see subsection 2e below). Common sense should guide you on this.

  Listed below are specific examples of words or phrases which are either prohibited or restricted and which should not be used as part of your corporate name. If you need to use one of the restricted words in your name, you will need to obtain the prior approval of a state agency and will need to see a lawyer. The lists below are not meant to be all inclusive; rather, they are meant to provide specific examples of

the types of names and activities which are subject to special rules. In other words, if your corporate activities are such that you think one of these restricted words might be appropriate as part of your corporate name, this should be a "red flag" to you, indicating that you are forming a special type of business corporation which requires prior approval or a license from a state agency before you file your Certificate of Incorporation. In this case, you will need to see a lawyer to customize the certificate included in this book before filing it with the Department of State—more on this in Step 2, below.

1. Prohibited Words

board of trade	state trooper
chamber of commerce	tenant relocation
community renewal	urban development
state police	urban relocation

2. Restricted Words

a. Words requiring the approval of either the Department of Insurance or the Department of Banking:

acceptance	indemnity
annuity	insurance
assurance	investment
bank	loan
benefit	mortgage
bond	savings
casualty	surety
endowment	title
fidelity	trust
finance	underwriter
guaranty	

b. Words requiring the approval of the State Board of Standards and Appeals:

council   labor
industrial organization   union

If the context in which the word is used clearly indicates that the corporation is not a labor organization, consultant, advisor, mediator or arbitrator, or involved in any way with labor, then the word can be used, but be cautious.

c. Words requiring approval of the State Department of Social Services:

blind   handicapped

d. The name "exchange" requires the permission of the New York Attorney General.

e. Words related to providing professional services. Here are a few examples:

architect   lawyer
doctor   surveying
engineer

Avoid the use of any word that implies the practice of a licensed profession. If you do, in fact, plan to incorporate the practice of a licensed profession, you will probably need to form a professional service corporation—see Chapter 2A2(a) for further information and a list of professions which must incorporate as professional service corporations.

f. Words related to an educational facility:

academy   school
college   university
education

Words and phrases which indicate an educational purpose may require prior approval or require that you register with the Department of Education.

g. Other restricted words:

cooperative   hospital
court   housing

You should be certain that the above words do not appear in your selected name. If any of them do, your Certificate of Incorporation will be rejected (or you will be required to obtain consent from the appropriate state agency before your certificate is processed).

A few further notes on names:

• Your corporate name may be in a language other than English so long as it is written in the Roman alphabet. For example, Huevos Rancheros, Inc. is a legal corporate name.

• As we've said, approval by the Department of State of your corporate name doesn't necessarily mean that you have the legal right to use this name. It may violate another person's or business's prior rights to the name as a trademark, service mark, or trade name. Generally, whoever first adopts and uses a name has the right to it. If you feel there is any likelihood that your name may be similar to that used by another business, especially if that business is in a similar or related field, you may wish to perform your own name search or consult a lawyer and conduct a state and federal trademark, service mark, and trade name search, and register your name in order to feel a little more comfortable about your right to use it, particularly since your corporate name can be a very valuable business asset. For further information on performing your own name search, see subsection D below.

- You should also realize that you should not rely on being able to use a particular name until your Certificate of Incorporation is actually filed with the Department of State. Consequently, don't order stationery or other documents, records or papers which show your proposed corporate name until your certificate has been filed (this will be done as part of Step 3, below).

C. Name Availability Check

YOU MAY WISH TO CHECK with the Department of State, which has primary responsibility for overseeing business corporations in New York, to see if a specific name is available. This can be done by writing to the Department of State (you cannot check corporate name availability by telephone). A tear-out letter is included in the Appendix for this purpose. Simply fill in the tear-out letter following the sample letter below when filling out this name availability letter.

Note: there is a charge of $5.00 for each name you ask them to check. All checks sent to the Department of State must be certified (unless then are sent by an attorney and have his or her name and business address on them).

√ The parenthetical blanks, i.e., "(_____)," indicate information which you must complete on the tear-out form.

√ We suggest you tear out the form in the Appendix and fill in the blanks (using a typewriter with a black ribbon or printing neatly with a blank ink pen) as you follow the sample form and instructions below.

Warning: Fees are subject to change. If you want to be doubly sure that the above fee amount is current at the time of your incorporation, call the Division of Corporations in Albany at 518-473-2492.

It may take up to 6 weeks (or more) for the Department to respond to your name availability request letter, depending upon the current Department workload. Also, even if your proposed corporate name is available at the time your name availability request is processed, this is not, of course, a guarantee that your name will be available when you file your Certificate of Incorporation. For these reasons, you may wish to dispense with this written name availability check and prefer simply to reserve your corporate name, as explained in Section F below. Moreover, if you are in a rush, you may wish to take your chances and completely bypass these name availability or reservation procedures by simply preparing and submitting your Certificate, showing your proposed name, to the Department of State on a special-handling (24-hour) basis as explained in Step 3 below.

Finally, please realize that the Division of Corporations only checks your proposed corporate name against its own list of corporate names—the Division does not check your proposed name to see if it conflicts with state trademarks or service marks or assumed names which are listed with other offices of the Department of State. We discuss steps you can take to check these other lists in "Perform Your Own Name Search" below.

Sample Request for Name Availability Check

<u>(Your name)</u>
<u>(Address)</u>
<u>(Date)</u>

Department of State
Division of Corporations
162 Washington Avenue
Albany, NY 12231

Division of Corporations:

Please advise if the following name(s) is/are available for corporate use:

<u>(First Choice for Corporate Name)</u>
<u>(Second Choice)</u>
<u>(Etc.)</u>

I am enclosing a certified check in the amount of $<u>   (enclose $5.00 for each name listed)</u> .

Very truly yours,

<u>(signature)</u>
(typed name)

D. Perform Your Own Name Search

AS WE'VE SAID, approval by the Department of State's office of your corporate name doesn't necessarily mean that you have the legal right to use this name. More specifically, acceptance of your name by the Department of State's office simply means that your name does not conflict with that of another corporation already on file with the Department and that you are presumed to have the legal right to the use of this name for your corporation in New York. It is important to realize, however, that other businesses (corporate and non-corporate) may already have the right to use this same name (or one similar to it) as a federal or state trademark or service mark used to identify their goods or services (the Department only checks your proposed corporate names against other corporate names on file—your name is not checked against the Department's separate lists of registered state trademarks and service marks). Also, another business (corporate or non-corporate) may already be presumed to have the legal right to use your name in a particular county if they are using it as a trade name (as the name of their business) and have filed an assumed name statement with the New York Secretary of State (again, this list is separate from the Department of State's list of corporate names and is not checked when you seek approval of your corporate name or file your Certificate of Incorporation).

Without discussing the intricacies of federal and state trademark, service mark and trade name law, the basic rule is that the ultimate right to use a particular business name will usually be decided on the basis of who was first in time to actually use the name in connection with a particular trade or business, service or product. In deciding who has the right to a name, the similarity of the types of businesses and their geographical proximity are usually taken into account. For example, if you plan to operate the "Sears Bar & Grille, Inc.," you probably won't have a problem at least as far as the well-known retail chain is concerned[2] (but you might if there is another bar or restaurant using the same name in your area or perhaps even if they are only currently operating in another part of the

---

[2]Although the law generally affords individuals a preferential right to their names in connection with their businesses, we'll use this opportunity to mention an exception to this rule and to general principles of trademark law under state "dilution of trademark" statutes. Specifically, even if you use your own surname in your corporate name and even though your products, services and geographical area of operation and marketing are unrelated to those of another business, if your corporate name contains a word or phrase which is the same or similar to the name of their mark, they can seek to enjoin (stop) you from using your name on the theory that your use will dilute the value of their mark. Without going into the technicalities here, our best advice, again, is to use common sense. If your proposed corporate name contains a word of phrase which is the same as a known mark, you may wish to add a word or phrase to your corporate name to make it clear that you are unaffiliated with the company that owns the mark (e.g., in the example in the text, the owners might decide to incorporate under the full name of the owner as "John P. Sears Bar & Grille, Inc."). This issue will not arise for most incorporators. If it does, we suggest you check with a trademark lawyer.

country but later expand to your area).[3] Similarly, if you find out that your Buffalo car dealership, Bob's Buicks, Inc., is the same as that of a White Plains car dealer, you're also probably on safe ground since it is unlikely that the public would be deceived as to the origin of any goods or services. However, you could be challenged (probably successfully), if, in these examples, you incorporated as "Sears Merchandising, Inc.," or operated your car dealership in Larchmont. To deal with this rather slippery concept, simply ask yourself whether you, as a hypothetical customer, might reasonably confuse your proposed name with another one that already exists, and thereby deal with the wrong business? If you're honest, you can provide as good a guideline for yourself as any lawyer.

The upshot of this discussion is that it is wise to do a little checking on your own before filing your Certificate of Incorporation to see if another business is already using your name as a trade name, service mark or trademark, particularly in the geographical area in which you plan to operate. Obviously, you will not be able to be 100 percent certain since you can't possibly check all names in use by other businesses. However, you can check obvious sources likely to expose similar names which are not listed as corporate names on the Secretary's list. Here are some suggestions:[4]

- Call the Department of State's Miscellaneous Records office in Albany (this office is responsible for registering New York trademarks and service marks) at (518-474-4770) and see if your proposed name is already registered with them for use by another business. They will check up to two names per day over the phone at no charge. If you wish to check more than two names at once, you can submit your names to them in writing. The fee for checking more than two names in writing is $5 for each additional name (remember, non-lawyers must pay fees with a certified check). Mail your written request to NYS Department of State, Miscellaneous Records, 162 Washington Avenue, Albany, NY 12231.

- Check with the County Clerk in the county or counties in which you plan to do business to see if your name, or one similar to it, has already been registered by another person or business as an assumed name. Most county clerks will require you to come in and check the files yourself—it takes just a few minutes to do this if the county clerk has computerized the assumed names records. If the records are kept manually, you will need to search back through at least a few books (each book usually covers several years of assumed name filings). [5]

- Go to a public library or special business and government library in your area which carries the federal Trademark Register, a

---

[3]Also, in an age where a huge number of service businesses—muffler shops, smog checks, eyeglass stores, house cleaning services, etc.—are being purchased nationally by large franchise chains, service businesses should be careful that their local name is not in conflict with a national name which may later move into their area.

[4]A comprehensive guide on how to search and secure trade names, trademarks and service marks, including a thorough study and explanation of the process of performing an extensive corporate or non-corporate name search, is "Trademarks: How to

Protect Your Business Name, Products and Services," by Stephen Elias (Nolo Press), available Spring 1989.

[5]Unincorporated businesses file assumed name statements (dba's) with the county clerk's office. Also, although corporate assumed name certificates are initially filed in Albany with the Secretary of State (see Chapter 6A2 below), these statements are forwarded to the local county clerk's office.

listing of federal trademark and service mark names broken into categories of goods and services. This aspect of your search is extremely important. If a name is placed on the Principal Register (the primary federal trademark register) you are deemed to know that it exists and is owned by someone else. Then, if you select a business name that is close to this mark and use the name in the marketing of your goods or services, you may be liable for trademark infringement, especially if your goods or services are related to the goods or services carrying the registered mark and you are both marketing in the same part of the country. In that event you will probably have to give up your name and maybe even pay damages to the trademark's owner. The moral? Always check the federal and state registers and stay away from names that might be confused with marks on the Principal federal trademark register.

- To check unregistered trade names (this is true for the majority of names used by unincorporated businesses), use a common sense approach. Check major metropolitan phone book listings, business and trade directories, and other business listings, such as the Dunn & Bradstreet business listing. Larger public libraries have phone directories for many major cities within and outside of New York.

Computer Resource Note: The federal and state registers, along with yellow page listings and other business directory databases, are available as part of various commercial computer databases For example, the federal and state registers can be accessed through TRADEMARKSCAN® which is part of the Dialog℠ database; the federal register is also available through the Compu-Mark® database (for more information, call 800-555-1212 and ask for the company's toll-free number).

If you own, or have access to, a computer and a modem, you may wish to log on to one of these databases and perform a computer search. You should realize that most of these commercial databases charge initial and ongoing access fees which may prove costly, particularly if you are not already familiar with the mechanics of accessing a particular database or performing your own computerized trademark and service mark search.

If you want to check further or don't want to do it all yourself, you can pay a private records search company to check federal and state trademarks and service marks as well as local and state-wide business listings. They can check your proposed name against the sources we've listed above including federal and state trademarks and service mark filings, major business directories, metropolitan phone listings, etc.

Alternatively, or in conjunction with your own efforts or search procedures, you can pay a trademark lawyer to oversee or undertake these searches for you. They will take the responsibility of hiring a private search company.[6] In addition, they may provide a legal opinion on the legal issues surrounding, and the relative legal safety of, your use of your proposed corporate name. This opinion can be valuable if the search discovers several similar, but not identical, names.

Obviously, the amount of checking and consulting you can do is limited only by the amount of effort or money you are willing to devote to the task and by how safe you need to feel about your choice of a corporate name. In most situations, just following the self-help measures listed above, including, if appropriate, the use of a name search service, will be enough

[6]One such company in New York is XL Corporate Services, New York, NY (212) 431-7000.

to reassure most small corporations that their choice of a corporate name is a safe one.

E. Protecting Your Name

ONCE YOU HAVE FILED your Certificate of Incorporation (as explained in Step 3 below), you may wish to take additional steps to protect your name. Specifically, if your name is also used to identify products which you sell or services that you provide, you may wish to register it with the Department of State of New York[7] and the United States Patent and Trademark Office as a trademark or service mark (registration in other states may also be appropriate). While the application procedures are relatively simple and inexpensive, state and federal trademark and service mark law, as well as trade name law generally, are complex areas and are beyond the scope of this book [again, for detailed information on securing federal and state trademarks and service marks, see "Trademarks: How to Protect Your Business Name, Products and Services," by Elias (Nolo Press), available Spring 1989].

F. Reservation of Corporate Name

ONCE YOU HAVE DECIDED on a corporate name (and established that it is available for use with the New York Department of State and/or after taking additional self-help measures as discussed in the "Perform Your Own Name Search" section below), it makes sense to reserve it with the Department of State (unless you will be filing your Certificate immediately or you feel your name is so fanciful that no one else is likely to choose it before you file your Certificate). By

doing this, you will be assured of being able to use your name in your Certificate of Incorporation—at least for a period of sixty days from the date it is reserved.

To reserve your proposed corporate name, simply fill in the tear-out Reservation of Corporate name letter included in the Appendix and mail it, together with the required filing fee, to the Albany office of the Department of State. The letter should be signed by one of the persons who will formally act as your incorporator (one of the persons who will form your corporation by signing the Certificate of Incorporation as part of Step 2, below). Again, processing time for your reservation of name request will vary and may take up to six weeks.

Below is a sample corporate name reservation letter with instructions.

√ The parenthetical blanks, i.e., "(_____)," indicate information which you must complete on the tear-out form.

√ We suggest you tear out the form in the Appendix and fill in the blanks (using a typewriter with a black ribbon or printing neatly with a blank ink pen) as you follow the sample form and instructions below.

---

[7]New York trademark and service mark applications are available from the Miscellaneous Records office of the Department of State in Albany.

Sample Application for Reservation of Corporate Name

(Name of Incorporator)_____
(Address)_____
(Date)_____

Department of State
Division of Corporations
162 Washington Avenue
Albany, NY 12231

Division of Corporations:

The undersigned is applying for reservation of a corporate name for a period of 60 days pursuant to the provisions of Section 303 of the Business Corporation Law.

The application is made by the undersigned, **(name of incorporator)**, whose address is **(street address of incorporator)**, **(type the word "City" or "Town" or "Village")** of **(name of city, town or village)**, County of **(county)**, State of New York. It is made with the intention of forming a domestic corporation which will be engaged in the business of **(state general nature of business, e.g., "computer sales and service," "manufacturing", etc.)**.

The name wished to be reserved is **(proposed name of corporation)**. Enclosed please find a certified check, payable to the Department of State, in the amount of $20.00.

Very truly yours,

(signature of incorporator)_____
(typed name)

Remember: all checks must be certified

If there are no difficulties with the name you have selected, you will receive back a Certificate of Reservation. You must now file your Certificate of Incorporation within 60 days of the date written on the Certificate of Reservation. If for some reason you can't do this, you may be able to reserve the name you have chosen for up to two additional 60-day periods (or a total of 120 extra days) by filing a request for extension of your corporate name reservation, together with a copy of your original Certificate of Reservation before the end of each 60-day period (the fee for each extension is $20). We assume you will file your Certificate of Incorporation within the first 60-day period and will not need to follow these extra formalities if you reserve a name.

Step 2. Prepare Your Certificate of Incorporation

The next step in organizing your corporation is the preparation and filing of your Certificate of Incorporation. The Department of State must file your papers if they conform to law and the proper fees are paid. You will find a ready-to-use, tear-out Certificate of Incorporation in the Appendix at the back of this book.

There is nothing difficult about preparing your Certificate of Incorporation. Relax, take your time and read the special instructions carefully. You will be surprised at how easy it is.

√ The parenthetical blanks, i.e., "(_____)," indicate information which you must complete on the tear-out form.

√ Each circled number (e.g., ①) refers to a special instruction which provides specific information to help you complete an item. The special instructions immediately follow the sample form.

√ We suggest you tear out the form in the Appendix and fill in the blanks (using a typewriter with a black ribbon) as you follow the sample form and instructions below.

■

Sample Certificate of Incorporation

OF

__(name of corporation)__ ①

UNDER SECTION 402 OF THE BUSINESS CORPORATION LAW

The undersigned, in order to form and organize a corporation under Section 402 of the Business Corporation Law of the State of New York, hereby certify that:

1. The name of such corporation shall be __(name of corporation)__ .①

2. The purposes of this corporation shall be to engage in any lawful act or activity for which corporations may be organized under the Business Corporation Law. The corporation is not formed to engage in any act or activity requiring the consent or approval of any state official, department, board, agency or other body without such consent or approval first being obtained.②

3. A director of the corporation shall not be liable to the corporation or its shareholders for damages for any breach of duty in such capacity except for:

(a) liability if a judgment or other final adjudication adverse to a director establishes that his or her acts or omissions were in bad faith or involved intentional misconduct or a knowing violation of law or that the director personally gained in fact a financial profit or other advantage to which he or she was not legally entitled or that the director's acts violated BCL Section 719, or

(b) liability for any act or omission prior to the adoption of this provision.③

4. The aggregate number of shares which the corporation shall have the authority to issue is __(total number of authorized shares, e.g., "TWO HUNDRED (200)")__ ④ shares, all of which are to be common shares without par value.

5. The office of the corporation is to be located in __(county)__ ⑤ County, State of New York.

6. The Secretary of State of the State of New York is hereby designated as agent of the corporation upon whom process against it may be served. The post office address to which the Secretary of State shall mail a copy of any process against the corporation served upon him is:⑥

_____(street address)_____

___(city, town, or village)___

_____(state)_____

The undersigned incorporator, or each of them if there are more than one, is of the age of eighteen years or over.

IN WITNESS WHEREOF, this certificate has been subscribed this _____ day of _____, 19___, by the undersigned who affirm(s) that the statements made herein are true under the penalties of perjury.

_____　　_____⑦

Type name of incorporator　　Signature

_____

Address

_____　　_____

Type name of incorporator　　Signature

_____

Address

_____　　_____

Type name of incorporator　　Signature

_____

Address

SPECIAL INSTRUCTIONS

① Type in the name of the corporation in both blanks, keeping in mind the limitations discussed in Step 1, above. If you have previously reserved a name, be sure to indicate the exact name which you have reserved.

② We have included this standard paragraph relating to the general purposes of your corporation based on the assumption that your corporation will not be operating a business which requires licensing or permission from a state agency. (As we mention in Step 1, above, certain words in the corporation's name will require such approval and others may imply that approval is needed.)

As further mentioned in Step 1, if your corporation is going to engage in a business that requires state approval, you cannot use this paragraph. Instead, the Certificate of Incorporation will have to list the specific purposes of the corporation and you will have to obtain any necessary state approval before you file your certificate. Failure to obtain such consent prior to filing your Certificate of Incorporation (or the use of any of the prohibited or restricted words listed in Step 1, above, in your corporate name) are the two major reasons for rejection of Certificates of Incorporation by the Department of State. Consequently, if your corporation plans to engage in a business which requires state approval, you cannot use this paragraph in your Certificate of Incorporation and will need to consult a lawyer to include the appropriate language in this part of your certificate and to obtain state approval from the appropriate agency before filing your certificate.

③ This paragraph contains language allowed under Section 402(b) of the Business Corporation Law to eliminate the personal liability of the corporation's directors for breach of their duty to the corporation or shareholders. See the shaded box titled *New York Director Immunity and Indemnification Rules* in Chapter 2D2 for an explanation of these special director immunity provisions.

④ State the number of authorized shares of your corporation as shown on the sample certificate. Authorized shares are simply those which the corporation can later sell to shareholders, at which time they are referred to as issued shares. Many incorporators will specify 200 as the number of authorized shares—this is the maximum number of authorized no-par shares for the smallest initial filing fee (see Step 3, below). Also keep in mind that the number of authorized shares must be sufficient to provide for your initial stock issuance (see Chapter 2G4). For example, if the incorporators have agreed to divide 100 shares between them, then the Certificate of Incorporation must authorize the issuance of at least 100 shares (you can still show a larger amount here, such as 200). In this paragraph we have indicated that there will be only one class of shares (common shares) which will have no par value. This is common practice and will be appropriate for most small corporations—see Chapter 2G. Consult your attorney and accountant if you wish to issue different classes of stock or shares with a designated par value.

⑤ Type in the county where the corporation will maintain its main office, e.g., "Putnam County, State of New York." If your corporate office is in a borough of New York City, make sure to show the correct county, e.g., Kings County for Brooklyn, Richmond County for Staten Island, New York County for Manhattan, etc.

⑥ In paragraph 6 of the Certificate of Incorporation, the Secretary of State is named as agent for service of process. This means that if any legal papers have to be served on the corporation, they can be given to the Secretary of State. That office will forward them to your corporation. You should indicate an actual mailing address here. It should either be the address of the corporation or, if the corporation does not yet have an address, you should use the address of someone who can be trusted to forward mail, such as the address of one of the incorporators who sign the certificate (see special instruction 7, below). **Note:** Regardless of which address you use, if it ever changes, you will have to amend the Certificate of Incorporation.

⑦ The incorporators must date and sign the Certificate of Incorporation in these blanks and type in their names and addresses on the appropriate lines. **Important:** Make sure that one of the persons who signs here is the same person who applied for and obtained a reservation of name for the corporation (if you reserved a name as discussed in Step 1, above). You should realize that you only need one person to sign your certificate since the law only requires that you have one incorporator. Again, if you reserved a name, and if you do only select one person to sign here, make sure this person is the one who reserved your corporate name.

This is all you are required to do. Your basic Certificate of Incorporation is now complete. In special situations, as we have previously discussed in Chapter 3B, you may wish to add additional provisions to meet special circumstances which may arise within the context of a small corporation. The following clauses are examples of the type of language you might use in your certificate to implement these special provisions. The section numbers relate to the Business Corporation Law. If you want to add one or more of these clauses to your certificate, you will need to consult a lawyer. Again, most incorporators will not need these complex provisions.

1. Section 620. "The business of the corporation and the conduct of its affairs shall be managed by its shareholders."

2. Section 616. "At least ____% of all the shareholders of the corporation shall be required to constitute a quorum for the transaction of any business and the affirmative vote of ____% of all the outstanding shares entitled to vote shall be required to approve any corporate action."[8]

3. Section 709. "At least ____% of the directors of the corporation shall be required to constitute a quorum for the transaction of any business and the affirmative vote of ____% of all the directors present shall be required to approve any corporate action."[9]

Step 3. File Your Certificate of Incorporation

Your Certificate of Incorporation should now be complete. If you have chosen to type your own Certificate of Incorporation (as opposed to filling in the one at the back of this book), make sure that you use letter size paper and type on one side only.

Make Three Copies of the Certificate of Incorporation

Six copies should be enough for your immediate purposes—one for inclusion in your records book and two as extra copies for

---

[8]The Business Corporation Law normally requires only a majority. This is the proportion we have provided in the Bylaws. You can require any proportion greater than a majority, but can't permit less than one-third of the shares entitled to vote (in your case, all the issued shares) to constitute a quorum (see BCL § 608).

[9]The same restrictions discussed in the previous footnote apply to Section 709 (see BCL § 707).

business purposes (e.g., bank transactions, licenses, etc.). The original certificate you send to the Department of State will not be returned to you; you will only receive a filing receipt.[10] So it's essential that you make copies and keep them in a safe place (e.g., your corporate records book).

Prepare a Backing Sheet

The Department of State requires that your original Certificate of Incorporation, submitted for filing, be accompanied by a backing sheet showing the name of the corporation and the person filing the certificate. We have included a tear-out backing sheet in the Appendix for this purpose. Simply tear it out and type in the blanks as follows:

a. Indicate the name of your corporation, exactly as shown on your Certificate of Incorporation, on the first blank line.

b. Type in the name and mailing address of the person who is submitting the Certificate for filing on the remaining lines. For your purposes, you will show the name and address of one of your incorporators (one of the persons who signed the certificate) on these lines.

Pay Fees

You'll have to pay the following fees when filing the Certificate of Incorporation:

a. $100 for filing the Certificate of Incorporation; and

b. Organization tax: $.05 per share for each authorized share with no par value (we assume you are issuing no-par shares).[11] The minimum fee is $10. For example, if paragraph 3 of your Certificate of Incorporation authorizes 200 no-par shares (most incorporators will authorize 200 no-par shares), the fee will be the minimum of $10 (this is the largest number of authorized no-par shares for the minimum fee). If your corporation authorizes 500 no-par shares, the fee will be $25, etc.

Total fees will therefore be no less than $110. Remember, all checks must be certified (unless they are an attorney's checks) and made payable to the Department of State.

Warning: Fees are subject to change. If you want to be doubly sure that the above fee amounts are current at the time of your incorporation, call the Division of Corporations in Albany at 518-473-2492.

Prepare a Cover Letter

Prepare a cover letter to the Department of Corporations. We have included a tear-out cover letter in the Appendix. It should be signed by, and show the name and mailing address of, the incorporator whose name and address are given on the backing sheet which you've just prepared. A sample cover letter with instructions is included below.

√ The parenthetical blanks, i.e., "(_____)," indicate information which you must complete on the tear-out form.

√ Each circled number (e.g., ①) refers to a special instruction which provides specific information to help you complete an item. The special instructions immediately follow the sample form.

---

[10]Make sure you don't lose this receipt; you will need it later.

[11]The organization tax for par value shares is 1/20 of one per cent of the amount of the par value of all shares [see § 180(1), New York Tax Law].

√ We suggest you tear out the form in the Appendix and fill in the blanks (using a typewriter with a black ribbon or printing neatly with a blank ink pen) as you follow the sample form and instructions below.

Sample Cover Letter to Department of State

(Name of Incorporator)
(Address)
(Date)

Department of State
Division of Corporations
162 Washington Avenue
Albany, NY 12231

RE: _(name of corporation)_

Division of Corporations:

Enclosed please find the proposed Certificate of Incorporation of _(name of corporation)_ together with its backing sheet [as well as the Certificate of Reservation previously received]. Also enclosed is a certified check in the amount of $_(total fees)_ to cover payment of the following fees:

Filing of Certificate of Incorporation $ 100

Organization tax on _(number)_ ① no par value authorized shares $ ___

                                       Total $ ___ ②

Please file the enclosed Certificate of Incorporation and return the receipt indicating filing of this document to the above address.

["I am also enclosing a copy of a Certificate of Reservation for the above corporate name."]③

Very truly yours,

(signature of incorporator)
(typed name)

SPECIAL INSTRUCTIONS

① Indicate the number of shares authorized in paragraph 4 of your Certificate of Incorporation.

② Type in the amount of organization tax you are required to pay (most incorporators will pay the minimum amount of $10—see the previous subsection) and the total fee amount in the two "total" blanks indicated (the total for most corporations will be $110).

③ If you have reserved your corporate name with the Department of State (as explained in Step 1 above, type this sentence as the last paragraph on your tear-out cover letter.

Send Certificate, Backing Sheet, Cover Letter and Fees to the Department of State

Send your incorporation papers by first class mail to the Department of State, Division of Corporations, 162 Washington Avenue, Albany, NY 12231. Enclose:

1. The original Certificate of Incorporation;

2. Your backing sheet for the certificate;

3. A copy of your Certificate of Reservation (if you have reserved a name—see Step 1, above); and

4. Your certified check.

You should staple your certificate pages and your backing sheet together, with the backing sheet attached to the back of the last page of the certificate. Make sure the text side of the backing sheet faces outward from the back (blank side) of the last page of your certificate.

Special Handling: The time necessary for the Department of State to process and file your Certificate varies and may be up to 6 weeks (or more) depending on their workload. You can reduce this processing time to one day by requesting special handling for an additional $10 fee. Note: Although your Certificate will be filed within one day under this procedure, you may still have to wait up to 2 to 3 weeks before you receive a response (filing receipt) from the Department. To do this:

- Enclose a separate check for $10 payable to the Department of State;

- Include a P.S. at the bottom of your cover letter stating, "I am enclosing a separate check in the amount of $10 for special (24 hour) handling of my Certificate of Incorporation."

- Clearly mark your mailing envelope with the words, "SPECIAL HANDLING."

If Your Certificate Is Returned: If you have not reserved your name and your Certificate is returned because your proposed corporate name is not available for your use, your papers and check will be returned to you by the Department of State (they will, however, keep and cash your separate $10 check if you have requested special handling). To resubmit your Certificate showing a different corporate name, you do not have to retype your Certificate in full. The common practice in this situation is to simply white-out the (unavailable) corporate name on your Certificate (in the heading and in the first paragraph) and on your backing sheet, type in your new choice for a corporate name in these blanks, make copies for your records and resubmit the Certificate and backing sheet with a new cover letter to the Department (again, using the $10 special handling procedure if you wish to speed things up).

Note: Keep all copies of your Certificate of Incorporation and Certificate of Reservation in a safe place (see Step 5, below, on setting up a corporate records book).

Step 4. File Your Stock Registration Certificate

Every corporation which has a principal place of business in New York State or which has an office in New York State where it sells or transfers its stock must file a registration certificate with the State Tax Commission in Albany, New York. The Appendix contains a tear-out form which can be sent to the State Tax Commission for this purpose. This form must be mailed within *ten* business days after you receive notice from the Department of State that your Certificate of Incorporation has been accepted and filed. **Note:** You can also obtain a pre-printed stock registration form to use for this purpose from the Tax Commission by calling their office in Albany at (518) 457-4265.

Because of this ten-day deadline, we include this step here, just after the filing of your Certificate of Incorporation. Note, however, that the language of this form assumes that you have held the first meeting of the board of directors and that your corporation has elected a president (you will hold this meeting and elect officers as part of Step 9, below) at the time of preparation of this form. These steps are not difficult and you should have time to accomplish them before preparing this form— make sure to send this form to the Tax Commission on time. We include a sample registration certificate and special instructions below.

SPECIAL INSTRUCTIONS

① Indicate the number of shares authorized in paragraph 4 of your Certificate of Incorporation.

② Type in the president's name here.

③ You must include the street name and number in the address of the corporation. This should be the same address where the corporate records are kept. In almost every case, this will be the same address as the principal place of business of the corporation.

④ The date the corporation was incorporated will be indicated on the filing receipt which you received from the Department of State.

⑤ The president must date and sign this form in the presence of a notary. The acknowledgement below the form must show the name of the president. The notary will complete the rest of the acknowledgement.

⑥ Make a copy of the original notarized form. You should attach this copy to the minutes of your first board meeting (Step 8, below).

⑦ Mail the Stock Registration Certificate to:

Stock Transfer Tax Division, Room 409
Building No. 9
State Campus
Albany, NY 12227

Sample Stock Registration Certificate
Under Section 275-a Tax Law

(Name of Corporation)
(Address of Corporation)

Number of shares authorized: Common Stock: _____① shares

I, _____ ② the President of _____ (name of
corporation)_____, do hereby certify that this corporation keeps a place for the sale,
transfer, or delivery of its stock at _____ (street address)_____ ③ , in the
___ ("City," "Town," or "Village")___ of _____, County of
_____, State of New York.

I further certify that this corporation was incorporated on the _____ of _____ ④,
19___, pursuant to the laws of the State of New York.

Date:_____   _____ (signature)_____
                                                      , President

County of _____   )
) ss
State of New York   )

On this _____ day of _____ ⑤ , 19___, before me personally came
_____ to me known, and who being by me duly sworn, did
depose and say that s/he is the President of the corporation above named and that s/he
executed the foregoing certificate on behalf of the above corporation pursuant to authority
vested in him/her by a vote of the board of directors of said corporation.

                                    _____
                                    Notary Public

The purpose of the Certificate of Registration is to inform the Tax Commission of the existence of your corporation since New York State collects a tax every time shares of stock are transferred (with some exceptions). The most notable, and for your purposes the most important, exception is that *there is no transfer tax due the first time your corporation issues its shares,* so you do not need to pay any tax when you mail this stock registration certificate to the Tax Commission. All other transfers, even if shares are returned to the corporation, are subject to the transfer tax.[12] Typically, the transfers you will most likely be involved with are gifts of your stock to your spouse or children, or the sale of your stock to a third person. Both of these transactions are taxable.

If you do transfer shares at a later date, both the person transferring the stock and the person receiving the stock will be responsible for seeing that the tax is paid, so you will want to make sure that it is clear who will pay the tax. Every time stock is transferred, the corporation must be notified.

The amount of tax on future transfers is not excessive, and varies with the amount of the transaction. The general rate schedule is as follows:

- If the price is less than $5/share....................1-1/4 cents/share

- Between $5 and $10/share..........................2-1/2 cents/share

- Between $10 and $20/share ....3-3/4 cents/share

- More than $20/share..................... 5 cents/share

- Generally, the maximum tax for one transfer of one class of shares is limited to $350.

By the way, if you do pay stock transfer taxes in the future, don't be surprised if you receive a rebate claim form back from the Stock Transfer Tax Division. The transfer tax is used to fund state Municipal Assistance Corporate bonds. Often the funding is not needed and you will be allowed to claim a 100% refund of any stock transfer taxes paid.

Caution: A few words of caution may be advisable at this point. Shares of stock in a corporation are quite valuable in non-monetary terms. Among other things, they give you the ability to influence the activities of your corporation. They should not be viewed as a type of "legal tender" and transferred freely.[13] Also, as discussed in Chapter 3, shareholders may enter into an agreement not to transfer their shares. This avoids a situation where the initial shareholders are faced with being in business with a stranger.

---

[12]There are some transfers which are exempt from this tax, too many in fact for us to be able to list here. These exemptions can be found in Sections 270(5), 270-b, and 270-c of the New York Tax Law.

---

[13]Remember: future stock transfers should be reviewed by an attorney to ensure compliance with the state and federal securities laws.

Step 5. Set Up Your Corporate Records Book

You will need a corporate records book to keep all your papers in an orderly fashion (Certificate of Incorporation, Stock Registration Certificate, Bylaws, Statement of Incorporators, Minutes of your first board meeting, stock certificates and stubs, minutes of ongoing director and shareholder meetings, etc.). Setting up and maintaining a neat, well-organized records book is one of your most important tasks—it will serve as a repository for corporate documents and as a formal "paper trail" documenting organizational and ongoing corporate formalities. You should keep your corporate records book at the principal office of your corporation at all times.

To set up a corporate records book, you can simply place all your incorporation documents in a three-ring binder. If you prefer, however, you can order a custom designed corporate records book as part of one of the corporate kits offered by Nolo Press (described below). You do not need to order a corporate kit, but many people find it convenient to do so.

Important Note: Before ordering any material on which the name of your corporation will appear (corporate kit or specially ordered corporate seal or stock certificates), wait until you have received your Certificate of Incorporation filing receipt.

A. Nolo Corporate Kits

If you wish to order one of the corporate kits offered by Nolo Press,[14] you can do so by completing the order form contained at the back of this book. Each Nolo corporate kit includes:

- A corporate records book (see descriptions below) with index dividers for Certificate of Incorporation, Bylaws, Minutes and Stock Certificates and minute paper;

- A metal corporate seal designed to emboss your corporate name and year of incorporation on important corporate documents;

- 20 lithographed green and black stock certificates (with full-page stock stubs)—the name of your corporation is printed on the face of each certificate; and

- A separately bound Share Transfer Ledger to keep a consolidated record of the names and addresses of of your shareholders.[15]

The basic difference between the three kits offered is the style of the corporate records binder itself: Each higher-priced kit contains a better quality corporate records binder. Here is a brief description of each:

---

[14]The corporate kits described here are offered by Nolo Press in conjunction with Julius Blumberg, Inc.

[15]Legal stationers and suppliers also sell corporate kits containing bylaws, minutes of the first meeting, printed stock certificates, as well as a corporate seal and a three-ring binder bearing the corporate name. These forms contain blanks which you must type in yourself. This book includes tear-out bylaws and minutes as well as other essential incorporation documents (cover letters, Certificate of Incorporation, Statement of Incorporators, etc.). Consequently, the less expensive kits advertised at the back of the book contain all the "extras" you should need. Also, you should realize that the bylaws and minutes contained in these other kits are often generic or minimal in nature and will not correspond to our forms or the specific instructions contained in this book.

The Black Beauty®

features a 3-ring black looseleaf vinyl binder with your corporate name on a label attached to the spine.

The Ex Libris®

features a high quality vinyl binder with your corporate name embossed on the spine.

The Portfolio

features a handcrafted, simulated red and black leather binder with your corporate name on a gold label attached to the spine. If you are willing to pay for an extra touch of class, this kit is worth it.

For further information, please see the corporate kit order coupon at the back of the book.

Black Beauty and Ex Libris are registered trademarks of Julius Blumberg, Inc. Portfolio is our name for the Syndicate® kit, a registered trademark of Julius Blumberg, Inc.

B. Corporate Seals

A CORPORATE SEAL is used to indicate that a given document is the duly authorized act of the corporation. While the Business Corporation Law does not specifically require that a corporation have a seal, we suggest you get one for several reasons. The primary reason is that the use of a seal on a corporate document creates a presumption that the document is valid and properly authorized. For this reason, banks and other companies frequently require that a seal be used on certain corporate documents. Also, certain corporate actions traditionally require a seal. To avoid delays and complications later on, it is better to get a seal now. It isn't normally used on everyday business documents such as invoices, purchase orders, etc., but is used on more formal documents such as leases, stock

certificates, mortgages, loan documents and the like.

As indicated above, a good quality, a metal pocket seal is included in each corporate kit offered by Nolo Press. Embossed and stamped seals are also available separately through legal stationers for approximately $40. Most seals are circular in form and contain the name of the corporation, the state, and year of incorporation.

C. Stock Certificates

THIS BOOK PROVIDES YOU with 10 black and white certificates printed on book quality paper; the corporate kits described above contain 20 lithographed certificates with green borders with your corporate name printed on each. If you wish to order stock certificates separately, legal stationers will sell you printed stock certificates containing the name of your corporation and any stock certificate legends which you select (more on this below).

Any extra words (called legends) which the stock certificates will bear depends entirely on the type of stock which you issue. The stock certificates used in this book are for no par value stock of one class only with no special legends and are keyed to the tear-out Certificate of Incorporation contained in this book. If you wish to issue stock with a par value or wish to issue different classes of stock, you should consult an attorney. For a further discussion on stock certificate legends, see Step 9, below.

Step 6. Prepare Your Bylaws

After you have received a filing receipt from the Department of State, your corporation is legally able to do business. However, to make rules for the management and operation of the corporation, it's essential that you prepare Bylaws. There's not much to this since there are only a few blanks which must be filled in on the tear-out Bylaws we've included in the Appendix at the back of this book. Read the Bylaws carefully to understand their purpose and effect. Many provisions in the bylaws have been discussed in some detail in Chapters 2 and 3 and you may wish to refer back to these chapters at this point.

These Bylaws have been carefully drafted and compiled to serve a few important purposes. First, they reflect specific information central to the organization of your particular corporation (i.e., the number of directors, dates of meetings, location of principal office, etc.). Second, they restate the most significant provisions of the New York Business Corporation Law which apply to your corporation. Third, they provide a practical, yet formal, set of rules for the operation of your corporation.

It should be noted that several alternative models were considered before deciding on provisions relating to the operating formalities of your corporation. Ultimately, we determined to prepare sample Bylaws which conform with the basic requirements of the Business Corporation Law of New York rather than attempting to consider every possibility. These Bylaws are sufficient to meet the requirements of the ordinary small business and present a set of rules to resolve disputes, provide certainty regarding procedures, and insure control over corporate operations.

You may want to modify these Bylaws to meet your specific needs. Some of the reasons why you may wish to do so are discussed in Chapter 3B. If you want to make changes, consult an attorney—otherwise, some changes you make may be in violation of the Business Corporation Law and may therefore be invalid and/or not binding upon future shareholders of the corporation.

Technical Note on Indemnification of Directors and Officers: We've already summarized New York's director and officer indemnification rules (see the shaded box titled *New York Director Immunity and Indemnification Rules* in Chapter 2D2). To repeat: we assume most small New York corporations will be content with New York's statutory indemnification rules and will not wish to provide for special non-statutory indemnification of directors and officers. In case you do wish to go beyond the statutory indemnification rules, however, Article X of the tear-out Bylaws in this book authorizes you to do so under the provisions of Section 721 of the Business Corporation Law—this bylaw repeats some of the provisions of Section 721 and allows the corporation to provide for non-statutory indemnification for directors and officers in director or shareholder resolutions or in an indemnification agreement). Remember, even under Section 721, indemnification is not allowed in a few circumstances (again, see Chapter 2D2). A reminder: if you wish to prepare special indemnification documents of this sort, or, in any case, if the general issue of indemnification is important to you, please see a lawyer—indemnification provisions can be tricky and this is simply our best attempt to authorize additional indemnification under this relatively recent section of the BCL).

The Bylaws are contained in the Appendix. Because there are so few blanks to fill in, we don't reprint them here. Simply tear them about and fill them in according to the Special Instructions immediately below.

SPECIAL INSTRUCTIONS

① HEADING; ARTICLE I, SECTION 1. Insert the name of the corporation exactly as it appears on the Certificate of Incorporation (Step 2) and the filing receipt you have received from the Department of State (Step 3).

② ARTICLE I, SECTION 2. Indicate the street address (not a post office box number) of the principal office of the corporation (i.e., street address; city, town or village; and county). This address should be the place where the corporation receives mail.

③ ARTICLE II, SECTION 2. Indicate the date on which the annual shareholders' meeting will be held. It must be held every year on the same date. Typically, the date will be set shortly before or after the end of the corporation's tax year so that the previous year's business can be discussed and the next year's business planned. It is suggested that you designate a specific date (e.g., the second Monday of a particular month)

to avoid a planned meeting falling on a weekend.

④ ARTICLE II, SECTION 3. Indicate the number or percentage of shareholders required to call a special meeting of shareholders. The Business Corporation Law does not require a minimum number. We suggest, however, that you require at least a majority of the outstanding shares.

⑤ ARTICLE II, SECTION 9. Indicate the number of days before a meeting by which the list of shareholders must be prepared. We suggest that at least one week be allowed so that the list may be reviewed by other shareholders, if they desire.

⑥ ARTICLE III, SECTION 1. Indicate the number of authorized directors. By law, each corporation must have at least three directors if there are three or more shareholders (see Chapter 3A). If there are fewer than three shareholders, then the number of directors must be at least equal to the number of shareholders. For example, if your corporation only has two shareholders, then only two directors are required (although you can have more since a director does not have to be a shareholder). Similarly, if there is only one shareholder, there need be only one director.

The Bylaws state that the directors shall be elected by a plurality vote. What this means, simply, is that the candidates who receive the highest number of votes are elected. For example, suppose your corporation has a total of 300 shares issued among ten shareholders and is electing four directors from seven candidates. If three candidates receive seventy votes each, one receives thirty votes and the other three receive twenty votes each, then the candidates who received seventy votes and the one who received thirty votes are the new directors.

⑦ ARTICLE III, SECTION 3. Indicate the number of directors required to call a special meeting of the board of directors. We suggest that a majority be required. Also, indicate how soon the meeting must take place after it is called. This can be as soon as you wish, but keep in mind that some directors may have to travel to the place of the meeting, so give them at least a few days to get there.

⑧ ARTICLE III, SECTION 4. Indicate the minimum amount of time to give directors notice of a special board meeting. One week is usually an adequate amount of time. Keep in mind that the time given for holding the meeting (Article III, Section 3) must be at least as long as the period of notice required here.

⑨ ARTICLE III, SECTION 8. Indicate how soon a vacancy on the board must be filled. We suggest that it be done as quickly as possible. Unless a regular meeting of the board is scheduled soon after a vacancy occurs, a special meeting will be needed. Therefore, make this time consistent with the timing required for special meetings. For example, if a special meeting must take place within two weeks after it is called and directors must be given at least one week's notice, you might require a vacancy be filled within two weeks after it occurs.

⑩ ARTICLE IV, SECTION 2. Indicate the period of the terms of office for the officers. Officers can be elected for any convenient or practical period of time. For consistency and convenience, you should have their terms end on the date of the annual directors' meeting so officers can be elected (or re-elected) by the board of directors at that time. For example, officers should be elected for terms which are multiples of one year (e.g., "annually," "for a term of five years," etc.).

⑪ ARTICLE IV, SECTION 5. Indicate how soon an office must be filled. Follow the suggestions in 9, above.

⑫ ARTICLE V, SECTION 1. An imprint of the corporate seal, once approved by the board at their first meeting (Step 9, below), should be placed here.

⑬ ARTICLE VIII, SECTION 1. Indicate the ending date (month and day) of your corporation's tax year in this blank (your corporate tax year should be the same as your corporation's accounting period—see Chapter 4D for a discussion of the rules which apply to selecting a corporate accounting period and tax year). For example, if you choose a calendar tax year for your corporation, type the ending date as "December 31."

You should realize that the IRS and the state Department of Taxation and Finance will look to your initial tax returns to determine the ending date of your corporate tax year: If your first corporate tax returns are submitted for a period ending on July 30th, this date will be taken as the end date of your corporate tax year. In other words, you are not bound by this initial minute resolution (although your response here should reflect your current expectations for your ultimate corporate tax year and accounting period).

After you file your initial returns, you will usually need the consent of the IRS and the Department of Taxation and Finance to change your tax year. For further information on filing initial corporate tax returns, see Chapter 6B8.

⑭ Do not fill in the blanks in the last paragraph of the bylaws or fill in the date or signature lines yet. This portion of the bylaws— the Certification—will be completed after the incorporators prepare a statement ratifying the bylaws (Step 8, below) and after the directors hold their first meeting and elect a secretary (Step 9). You will come back and fill in these blanks as part of Step 9, below.

Step 7. Prepare Statement of Incorporators

Your next step in perfecting the organization of your corporation is to have the incorporator(s) (the person or persons who signed your Certificate of Incorporation as part of Step 2, above) adopt the Bylaws and elect the directors of the corporation. Since the corporation can be legally managed only by the board of directors, this election is required before the corporation can begin to operate. There are two ways to do this: by a formal meeting or by a statement signed by the incorporators. We show you how to use the latter procedure since it avoids extra paperwork.

In the Appendix you will find a tear-out "Statement of Incorporators[17] in Lieu of Organization Meeting." Tear it out and type in the blanks, showing the name of the corporation and the date of filing of your Certificate of Incorporation by the Department of State (this date is indicated on the filing receipt which you received from the Department). Also indicate the full names of the initial directors of the corporation under paragraph 3 of the form. Then have all of your incorporators sign this document at the bottom, showing the date of their signature. Remember—the incorporators are the people who signed your certificate in Step 2, above (again, you may have only one incorporator). Finally, attach a copy of your Certificate of Incorporation, the Department of State's filing receipt, and a copy of your Bylaws to the Statement and place these documents in your corporate records book.

---

[17]Don't let the word "Incorporators" concern you—this is the standard title for this form. Your corporation can have one (or more than one) person act as incorporator.

Step 8. Prepare the Minutes of the First Meeting of the Board of Directors

Now that the Certificate of Incorporation has been filed, the Bylaws adopted and the directors elected by the incorporators, the corporation is legally in business. At this point the first meeting of directors should be held.

The business to be conducted at this first meeting of the directors is to elect officers, adopt resolutions which are needed to start corporate operations, approve the issuance of stock, and take care of any other business which they feel are necessary or appropriate.

You should hold the meeting by preparing the tear-out Minutes contained in the Appendix. These minutes, when completed, reflect the business transacted at this meeting.

Some of the resolutions contained in the minutes will be used by all corporations. Other resolutions, which have been printed on separate pages, will be used only if they specifically apply to your corporation. Tear the minutes out of the appendix and prepare the appropriate pages and resolutions according to the instructions below. There is nothing hard here, but there are a lot of details, so be careful and work slowly.

A. Waiver of Notice of Directors' Meeting

SINCE THE FIRST MEETING of the board of directors will typically be held immediately after the signing of the Statement of Incorporators in Lieu of the Organization Meeting, it is not practical to provide notice of the directors' meeting. Therefore, your should have all of the directors complete the Waiver of Notice of Directors' Meeting which appears at the beginning of the minutes in the Appendix. Indicate the name of the corporation, the place where the meeting is held (street address, city, town or village, and county) and the time of the meeting.

B. Minutes of the Meeting of the Board of Directors

FILL IN ALL OF THE BLANKS on the first two pages of the minutes. Indicate the name of the corporation, the names of the directors who were present and absent, and the names of the two persons temporarily elected chairperson and secretary.

Indicate, in the appropriate blanks, the period for which the officers are elected and the names of each person elected to each office. The term of office should correspond to the term indicated in Article IV, Section 2 of the Bylaws which you've prepared. Finally, indicate, in the two places provided, the date on which the Statement of Incorporators was signed (Step 8). You should attach the Statement to these minutes.

1. Resolutions

Corporate Seal Resolution: Make an impression of your corporate seal in the space provided to the right of the resolution.

Stock Certificate Resolution: Attach a copy of the stock certificate of your corporation to the minutes. Use either one of the tear-out certificates included in the Appendix of this book or one of those which you've ordered separately, such as those included as part of the corporate kits discussed in Step 5 above (also see order coupon at back of book). Mark it with the word "SAMPLE" prominently across its face in capital letters.

Registration of Stock Resolution: Attach a copy of the Stock Registration Certificate, prepared as indicated in Step 4, above. If you have completed a pre-printed form which you've obtained from the State Tax Commission, attach a completed copy of this alternative form to your minutes.

Accounting Period Resolution: Put in the ending date of the corporation's accounting period. This should be the same date as that given in Article VIII of the Bylaws which you've prepared.

Principal Office Resolution: Fill in the street address of the principal office of the corporation. This should be the same address as the one given in Article I, Section 2 of the Bylaws.

Bank Account Resolution: Indicate the name and address of the bank where the corporation will maintain accounts. The banking resolution referred to here will be provided by your local bank, and a copy should be attached to the minutes. Indicate the number and title of the officers permitted to sign checks and other such documents. Typically, two signatures are needed to sign corporate checks, etc. The tear-out Bylaws in this book indicate that the president and treasurer can perform this function. If you choose other officers or employees to do this, you must change the Bylaws to authorize them to take this action.

Payment and Deduction of Expenses Resolution: Many incorporators will wish to include this resolution in their minutes to allow the corporation to reimburse the incorporators for, and have the corporation pay and deduct over a period of time, the expenses incurred in organizing the corporation under Section 248 of the Internal Revenue Code (without a specific election to deduct these expenses over a specified period of time, such a deduction is normally not possible). Note that you must implement this federal tax election by attaching a statement to your first federal corporate income tax return indicating that you are choosing to amortize organization expenses, providing a description of the expenses together with other required details. Check with your tax advisor for help in deciding whether to use this resolution (and for help in preparing the statement to send to the IRS).

Issuance of Stock Resolution: Fill in the amount of shares the corporation is authorized to issue. This is the number that appears in paragraph 4 of the Certificate of Incorporation.

Allocation to Surplus Resolution: This resolution relates to the portion of the value of each no par share to be allocated to surplus. You may, or may not, wish to use this resolution. For reasons of financial flexibility and accounting methods, some corporations allocate a portion of the value of each no par share to surplus, with the remainder going to the stated capital account. The question here is a technical one, governed by special rules contained in Section 506 of the Business Corporation Law—see the discussion in Chapter 2E. The decision as to whether to use this resolution at all, or the actual dollar figure to indicate as going to your surplus account, should be made by your accountant (as indicated in the resolution). If you do not wish to

use this resolution, simply leave it out of your minutes.

The following resolutions concern the issuance of stock in the corporation. You may need to use one or more of these different resolutions, depending on, and according to, the types of payment to be made by your initial shareholders.

Under New York law, a corporation can only issue its stock in return for cash, cancellation of indebtedness, property actually received, work and services actually performed for the corporation, or the assets of an existing business. A promise to perform work, deliver property or pay cash to the corporation in the future is not sufficient to pay for stock (see Chapter 2F). All shares which are initially issued should be sold for the same price per share. Therefore, in preparing these resolutions, make sure this is the case.

Note: These resolutions do not result in the issuance of shares—they simply authorize the appropriate corporate officers to issue shares to the shareholders at a later time under the terms specified in these resolutions. Shares will actually be issued as part of Step 9, below.

Review Notes

Before filling in the blanks in your stock issuance resolution, we suggest that you re-read Chapter 3, Sections D and E to make sure you understand the requirements for issuing your shares in compliance with the New York and federal securities laws. Let's review a few points mentioned in earlier chapters regarding the issuance of your shares:

- Make sure that the total number of shares to be issued to all shareholders is not greater than the number of shares authorized to be issued in paragraph 4 of your Certificate of Incorporation—paragraph 4 places an upper limit on the number of shares which you can actually issue (see Step 2, instruction 4).

- Under New York law generally, you may issue shares for any legal consideration which includes:
  - money
  - labor done or services actually rendered to, or for the benefit of, the corporation
  - cancelled debts, and
  - tangible or intangible property actually received by the corporation

If shares are sold for other than money, the board of directors should state, by resolution at a meeting, the fair market value of the services, property, or other form of payment given for the shares. Shares cannot be given in return for promissory notes of the purchaser or in return for the performance of future services. In practice, most small corporations will not be in a position to issue shares for labor done or services rendered since they are just getting started. See Chapter 2, Sections F and G for further information on authorizing and issuing shares of stock.

- As a matter of common sense, and to avoid unfairness or fraud, issue your shares for the same price per share to all initial shareholders. Make sure to place a fair value on the assets or other property or services being given in return for the shares. If you are transferring the assets of an existing business to your corporation in return for shares (if you are incorporating a prior business), we suggest that you have an accountant or other qualified appraiser make a written determination of the value of these assets. You may also wish to have a balance sheet prepared for the prior business, showing the assets and liabilities being transferred to your corporation (you can attach this balance sheet to the Bill of Sale which you can prepare as part of Step 9 below to document this type of transfer). Be realistic in your determination of fair value of all non-cash payments for shares, particularly if you will be issuing shares in return for speculative or intangible property such as the goodwill of a business, copyrights, patents, etc. You don't want to "short-change" other shareholders who have put up cash or tangible property of determinative value.

Issuance of Stock in Exchange for Cash Resolution: Fill in the blanks, indicating the name of the purchaser, the number of shares being purchased by that person, and the total amount of money he is paying.

Issuance of Stock in Exchange for Cancellation of Indebtedness Resolution: If the shares are to be sold in return for cancellation of indebtedness owed by the corporation, a full description of the note, etc. should be given (ideally, a copy of the document evidencing the note should be attached to the minutes). The amount of money owed should equal the remaining unpaid principal amount plus accrued interest.

Issuance of Stock in Exchange for Property Actually Received Resolution: If one or more shareholders will transfer specific items of property to the corporation in return for shares, show the name of each shareholder, the number of shares she will receive, and provide a brief description of the property (e.g., if a vehicle, a description and registration number; if land, a legal description, etc.) and its fair market value (e.g., for a vehicle, bluebook value is a good measure). You must be sure that the property is actually given to the corporation before the certificates are issued (Step 9). This means the offerer must sign all papers giving full ownership to the corporation. This resolution should not be used if you are transferring the assets of a pre-existing business to the corporation in return for shares. A resolution for this special case is included elsewhere in the minutes and is discussed below. Here, we are only discussing property owned by individuals such as a computer system, truck, patent or copyright, etc., and not the assets of an existing business.

Issuance of Stock in Exchange for Services Actually Rendered Resolution: Indicate the name of the person who has performed the services. The amount due for such services and a description of them should be contained in a bill which should be attached to the minutes. Fill in the amount of shares to be issued to the person. Make sure that before the certificate is issued (Step 9, below), the person marks the bill "Paid in Full." Remember, you can't issue shares for services which have not yet been performed.

Issuance of Stock in Exchange for Assets of a Business Resolution: Use this resolution if a shareholder will transfer his part, or full, interest in a prior business to the corporation in return for shares (e.g., if you are incorporating a prior business).

Fill in the blanks indicated, providing a description of each shareholder's interest in the business being transferred and the value each interest in the column titled "Description and Dollar Value of Property Offered."

Example: If two business owners will be incorporating their pre-existing partnership, "Just Partners," the following simple description would be appropriate for each shareholder (each prior business owner):

"One-half interest in assets of the partnership 'Just Partners,' as more fully described in a Bill of Sale to be prepared and attached to these minutes."

This Bill of Sale can be prepared as part of Step 9 below. Each partner can show one-half of the appraised value of the business (e.g., 1/2 of the book value of the prior business' assets as reflected on a current balance sheet) as the dollar value of the property offered.

Federal S Corporation Tax Treatment: The decision to include this resolution in your minutes involves several tax factors discussed in Chapter 4C—please review this material. If you decide to elect federal S corporation tax status, include this resolution in your minutes.

New York Tax Note: You may also wish wish to elect New York state S corporation tax status (you do not need, and we do not include, a separate minute resolution for this purpose). See Chapter 4C for further information on this separate state tax election.

IRC Section 1244 Stock Resolution: Most incorporators will wish to have their stock treated as Section 1244 stock (so that any future stock losses may be deductible as "ordinary losses"—see Chapter 4E for a further discussion of this special provision of the Internal Revenue Code). If you do wish this tax treatment, include this resolution in your minutes. Note the necessity of keeping ongoing records to insure that you will be able to meet the requirements of Section 1244—your tax advisor can help you maintain these records.

Compensation for Officers Resolution: If you will provide for officer salaries, you should determine the salaries which will be paid to each officer now—it may avoid disputes later (among the officers or with the IRS). Indicate whatever salaries you decide on next to each officer's name. If a position is not filled or if you do not wish to provide for a particular officer's salary, simply indicate "None" opposite the appropriate officer title.

Reality Note: Many smaller corporations will not wish to provide for officer salaries (and will not fill in these blanks) because the individuals who will actively work for the corporation, whether they are also directors, officers or shareholders, will not be paid a salary as an officer, per se, but in some other capacity related to the particular business of the corporation.

Example: Betty Bidecker is a 75% shareholder and the President and Treasurer of her incorporated software publishing company. Bix Bidecker, her spouse, is a 25% shareholder and the Vice President and Secretary of the corporation. Rather than being paid for serving in any officer capacity, both are paid annual salaries as executive employees of the corporation: Betty as the Publisher, Bix as the Associate Publisher.

If you do provide for officer salaries, remember, salaries should be reasonable in view of the actual duties performed by the officer and should be comparable to compensation paid for similar skills in similar businesses (see Chapter 2D3 for a further discussion of this issue). Don't be overly concerned here: If you are active in your business and can afford to pay yourself a large salary because of the profitability of your corporation, your salary will most likely be reasonable in view of your material participation in your corporation's productivity and, generally, in view of the trend towards paying higher corporate salaries in most key corporate positions these days.

Certificate of Assumed Name: If you plan to operate the corporation under an assumed name (skip ahead, at this point, and read the discussion in Chapter 6A2, below), include this resolution in your minutes. Indicate in the blank the assumed name which you plan to use. This resolution allows the president to file a Certificate of Assumed Name with the Secretary of State. After the Certificate of Assumed Name is completed (as part of Chapter 6A2, below), a copy of the certificate should be attached to these minutes.

C. Consolidate Your Papers

YOU ARE NOW DONE with the minutes. make sure to do the following before going on to Step 9 below:

- Have your newly-elected corporate Secretary sign the last page of the minutes on the line indicated.

- Go back and have the newly elected corporate Secretary sign and date the certification section at the end of the Bylaws showing the name of the corporation and the date of signing of the Statement of Incorporators (prepared in Step 8) in the text of the certification paragraph.

- Now that you have officially adopted a corporate seal, impress the seal in the space provided in Article V of the Bylaws.

- Place the signed Waiver of Notice of Meeting page before the minutes of this meeting.

- All documents referred to in the minutes of the directors' meeting should be attached to the minutes. These include:

Bills
Certificate of Assumed Name
Receipts
Sample Stock Certificate
Standard Bank Resolution
Statement of Incorporators
Stock Registration Certificate
Title documents

- Set up a corporate records book with (at least) the following four sections:

Certificate of Incorporation
Bylaws
Minutes of Meetings
Stock Certificates

You can use a simple three-ring binder for this purpose. If you have ordered a Nolo Press corporate kit as explained in Step 3 above, it will include a corporate records book divided into these sections. You should keep the corporate records at the corporation's principal office at all times.

- Keep your corporate records book at the corporation's principal office at all times. It is a vital part of the corporation, and its loss can be very costly.

- An important part of corporate life is keeping your records properly, so be sure to document future corporate transactions (by preparing standard minutes of annual director and shareholder meetings) and place copies of corporate minutes and other documents in your corporate records book.

Congratulations! You have now completed the Minutes of your first meeting. We explain how to accomplish your last major organizational task, issuing your shares, in Step 9 below. Stay with us, you're just one step away from completing your incorporation.

Step 9. Issue Shares of Stock

After the first meeting of the directors of the corporation, stock certificates should be issued in return for cash, the cancellation of indebtedness, past services rendered, property transferred to the corporation, or for the assets of a pre-existing business. Issuing shares of stock is an essential step in your incorporation process and, as a general (and we think important) rule, you should not begin doing business as a corporation until you have completed this step (see Chapter 2).

A Few Reminders

- Your corporation cannot issue more shares than the amount of shares authorized by your Certificate of Incorporation. As we've said in Step 2 above, it's common for corporations to authorize more shares in their Certificate than they will actually issue here.

- Stock certificates should be issued to only those persons who have been listed in the minutes of the first directors' meeting.

- All of your initial shares should be sold for the same price per share. For example, if someone pays the corporation $1,000 cash for 10 shares, then another person selling the corporation a machine worth $10,000 should receive 100 shares.

- Of course, by now you know that you must issue your initial shares in compliance with New York and federal securities laws. See Chapter 3, Sections D and E to refresh yourself on these rules.

A. If Applicable, Comply with the Provisions of the Bulk Sales Act

BEFORE DISCUSSING THE DETAILS of your stock issuance, we must make a slight detour to mention a pre-stock issuance formality which may apply to some readers—compliance with New York's Bulk Transfer Law. This formality only applies to you if one or more of your prospective shareholders will be transferring the assets of a prior business to your new corporation in return for shares. If you do not plan to do this, you can ignore this section and go on to Section B below. If one or more of your shareholders will be transferring a prior business to the corporation in return for shares, then you will want to read the following material.

The purpose of the Bulk Sales Act is to prevent business owners from secretly transferring the "bulk" of the assets of their business to another person or entity in an attempt to avoid creditors and to prevent schemes whereby the prior business owners "sell out" (usually to a relative at bargain prices) and come back into the business through a back door later on. The great majority of incorporators of their own business are simply changing the form of their business, not trying to convince others that they are disassociated from their prior business (and its debts) and should, therefore, be complying with the Bulk Sales Act procedures discussed below only as a formality. If, on the other hand, your unincorporated business will have debts outstanding at the time of your incorporation and your corporation is not going to assume and pay these debts as they become due, then the publication and filing of this notice is more than a mere formality and you must see a lawyer.

More specifically, the Bulk Sales Act is designed to protect the creditors of a business which is being sold by requiring that they be notified of the sale. The protection consists mainly of giving notice to the creditors of the fact of the sale, where the goods are going, details of the financial aspects of the sale, and similar information. Almost every type of business is subject to the provisions of this Act. Specifically, the law includes all enterprises whose principal business is the sale or rental of merchandise from stock, including manufacturers of merchandise and all restaurants and other food dispensing establishments.

Compliance with the provisions of the Bulk Sales Act can cause delay and expense since first, there are a number of forms which have to be filled out and mailed, and second, no action can be taken until the statutory waiting periods elapse. Fortunately, there are exemptions available for the type of transaction you are very likely planning, that is, transferring all the assets of an existing business to a corporation formed for the purpose of receiving them. These exemptions apply to the more cumbersome formalities of the Act—you will still have to follow some formalities, as explained below. But before you are entitled to these exemptions, you must meet certain requirements of the law. Otherwise all of the provisions of the Act will apply to you.

Forms Note: We have included several sample forms, below, which you may wish to use. Alternatively, you can obtain pre-printed versions of these standard Bulk Sales Act forms from a local newspaper or from a legal forms supplier, since this may be more convenient than typing these forms out yourself.

1. Transfers Exempted from the Bulk Sales Act

In the case where you are merely transferring your assets to a new corporation which was formed to receive them, the formalities are much easier than they otherwise would be under the Bulk Sales Act. A transfer is exempt from most of the formalities if:

- the transfer of assets is to a new business enterprise (e.g., a new corporation) organized to take over and continue the business,

- public notice is given,

- the new enterprise agrees to assume (pay) the seller's business debts, and

- the seller does not receive anything other than shares of stock in the new corporation and these shares do not entitle the seller to any rights to receive profits or corporate property which are greater than the rights of the creditors of the prior business. In other words, if your old business owed any money, you can't sell it to a new corporation and receive any money or other property either in addition to or instead of shares of the corporation, or any shares which give you a preference to the financial assets of the corporation.

If you meet these initial requirements, simply comply with the following procedures:

- Make sure that the new corporation agrees to assume all of the prior business's debts (see the Bill of Sale for Assets of a Business, Step 9 below).

- If you were the owner of the business whose assets are being transferred, don't accept anything for them other than shares of stock in the new corporation.

- Give notice of the transfer and the assumption of the debts to all creditors of the prior business. To do this, you must publish a notice of bulk sale at least once a week for two consecutive weeks in a newspaper of general circulation in the place where the transferor (that is, the person whose business it was) had his principal place of business. This notice must include (1) the name and address of both the transferor and the transferee; (2) the effective date of the transfer (that is, the date on which the corporation will receive the assets); and (3) the fact that the corporation has agreed to assume all of the liabilities and debts of the transferor.

Your local newspaper, if it is published at least once a week, is a newspaper of general circulation. As we've said, these newspapers or legal forms suppliers can usually supply you with standard pre-printed Bulk Sales Act forms. Here is a sample form which you may use for this purpose, if you wish, followed by special instructions.

■

Notice of Bulk Sale

NOTICE IS HEREBY GIVEN, pursuant to Section 6-103 of the Uniform Commercial Code, that all of the right, title and interest in the business, inventory, fixtures, goods, supplies and merchandise of _____ ① with a former address at _____ ,② have been sold, transferred, delivered and assigned to _____ ,③ a New York corporation with an address at _____ .④ The effective date of the transfer shall be _____ , 19___ .⑤ The _____ has agreed to assume and pay all debts and liabilities of _____ .①

■

SPECIAL INSTRUCTIONS

① Insert the name of the transferor. This should be the name under which he or she was doing business.

② Put in the street address of the transferor. This should be the address at which the business received its bills.

③ Insert the name of the corporation. This should be the same name as appears in the Certificate of Incorporation.

④ Put in the address of the corporation. This should be the same address as that which appears in Article I, Section 2 of the Bylaws.

⑤ Indicate the date on which the assets will be transferred. The transfer date must be at least two weeks after the date this notice is first published (since it must be published for two weeks).

Note Regarding Seizure of Assets: If you qualify under this exemption of the Bulk Sales Act, you must remember that the property which the corporation receives is still subject to

the debts of the former business. This means that if these debts are not, or cannot, be paid by the corporation, the property may be taken away by the creditors of the former business.

2. Transactions Not Exempted Under the Bulk Sales Act

If you can't, or choose not to, be exempted from the requirements of the Bulk Sales Act (because, for example, the corporation will not be assuming all of the liabilities of the prior business or because you will be receiving money as well as shares of stock), then you must follow the procedures discussed below. Again, it is important that you follow these procedures if they apply to you. If you don't, the sale of the assets is not effective against any of the creditors of the former business (this means that they can disregard the sale and attempt to seize the assets transferred). This procedure for non-exempt transactions requires the preparation of several forms as well as providing additional notices. Remember, a local newspaper or legal forms supplier should have pre-printed standard forms which you may wish to use as a more convenient alternative to preparing these forms yourself.

Note: For the sake of convenience, we will first describe the five tasks you must complete if you are not exempt from the Bulk Sales Act. Immediately following this description you will find the sample forms with special instructions necessary to complete each of them.

The procedure, which involves five major tasks, is as follows:

1. The corporation must get the transferor to give it a list of all of the creditors of the business. The list must include the names and addresses of the creditors and the amounts owed to each. Also, if anyone is asserting any claim against the transferor (for example, if the business of the transferor is being sued), these persons must also be included in the list. The transferor must swear, in front of a notary, as to the accuracy of the list. A sample form for such a list, entitled List of Creditors, is provided below.

2. A schedule of all of the property being transferred must be prepared by the transferor and given to the corporation. The property must be described in detail (for instance, with model or serial numbers), and the quantity of each item listed and its location must be given. A sample Schedule of Property form is provided below.

3. The corporation must send a notice to each and every one of the persons named on the List of Creditors. This notice must be either delivered personally to the creditor or sent by registered mail at least ten (10) days before the corporation issues stock in exchange for the assets of the transferor or makes any other type of payment for them. The notice must contain the following information:

a. That a bulk transfer is about to be made. A bulk transfer includes the transfer of a major portion of the merchandise and/or inventory of a business.

b. The name and address (principal place of business) of both the corporation and the transferor. Also, all other names and addresses used by the transferor within the past three years must be listed if they are known to the corporation.

c. Whether or not the corporation will be paying all of the debts of the transferor in full as they become due, and, if all are to be paid, the address to which creditors should send their bills.

d. If the debts are not going to be paid in full by the corporation as they become due, then the notice must state:

   (1) the location and description of the property being transferred;

   (2) the address where the List of Creditors and the Schedule of Property can be inspected (see 4, below);

   (3) an estimated total of the transferor's debts (which will be found on the List of Creditors);

   (4) whether the transferor is going to pay some of the existing debts, and, if so, how much and to whom;

   (5) whether the corporation is going to give money or property to the transferor and if so, how much and when.

We provide sample Notice forms, below.

4. The corporation must save the List of Creditors and the Schedule of Property for at least six months after the date of transfer of the property and allow any of the transferor's creditors to inspect them during this period.

5. The corporation must send a Notice of Bulk Sale to the State Sales Tax Bureau at least ten days before the corporation takes possession of the business assets (see Section C of this step, below).

List of Creditors

The undersigned hereby swears and affirms that the following is a true and accurate list of his or her creditors, compiled in accordance with the requirements of Section 6-104 of the Uniform Commercial Code.

Name of Creditor   Business Address   Amount Owed

_____ _____ _____ ①

_____ _____ _____

_____ _____ _____

CLAIMS IN DISPUTE

Name of Creditor   Business Address   Amount Claimed

_____ _____ _____ ②

_____ _____ _____

_____ _____ _____

_____ ③
Seller

State of New York   )

County of _____)

_____, being sworn, deposes and says: I am the person who signed the foregoing list of creditors pursuant to the requirements of Section 6-104 of the Uniform Commercial Code. The foregoing is a complete and accurate list of all of the creditors and claims against me, known to me to the best of my knowledge.

_____ ③
Seller

Subscribed and sworn to before me this _____ day of _____, 19___.

_____ ③
Notary Public

SPECIAL INSTRUCTIONS

① List the names and business addresses of creditors and the amounts owed to each.

② List the names and business addresses of any creditors whose bills are in dispute, and the amount of these disputed bills. For example, you should include here the amounts claimed by any persons who are suing the business.

③ The transferor should sign these lines in the presence of a notary.

Schedule of Property

The following is a schedule of property to be transferred, sold, assigned and delivered by

_____,① transferor, to _____,②

on or after _____:③

Description	Quantity	Location
_____	_____	_____④
_____	_____	_____
_____	_____	_____

The corporation agrees to retain this schedule at its principal place of business at

_____,⑤ and make it available for inspection and/or reproduction by any creditor of the transferor for a period of six months following the date of transfer of the above-mentioned property.

Dated:_____   _____⑥
                                                                    Seller

---

SPECIAL INSTRUCTIONS

① Indicate the business name of the transferor.

② Show the name of the corporation, exactly as it appears in the Certificate of Incorporation.

③ Indicate the date the transfer is to be made. This date should be at least ten (10) days after the date of signing this agreement.

④ A complete list of the assets to be transferred should be given here, together with an accurate description of each asset, its quantity, and location. Provide model or serial numbers of assets when describing them if you can.

⑤ Show the principal place of business of the corporation (from Article I, Section 2 of your Bylaws).

⑥ The transferor should sign and date the form.

There are two forms of notice that must be sent to creditors. The first covers the case where the corporation will be paying all of the debts of the transferor as they become due even though the corporation has not specifically or legally assumed the debts or liabilities of the prior business. The second covers the case where the corporation will not be paying the transferor's debts. Again, for convenience, you may wish to

obtain pre-printed versions of these notice forms from a local newspaper or legal forms supplier. Below are samples of these two notice forms, followed by special instructions:

■　　　　　　　　　　　　　　　　　　　　　　　　　　　　■

Notice If Debts Will Be Paid as They Come Due

To _____:①

A bulk transfer under Article 6 of the Uniform Commercial Code will be made on or after _____, 19___.② The transferor is _____,③ with a current address of _____.④ For the past three years, the transferor has had the following other business addresses and operated its business under the following names:

⑤

All debts of the transferor will be paid in full as they fall due. Statements should be sent to the purchaser, _____,⑥ at its principal place of business at _____.⑦

Dated: _____ ⑨　　　　　____(name of corporation)____

　　　　　　　　　　　　　　　　　　_____⑧
　　　　　　　　　　　　　　　　　　, President

■　　　　　　　　　　　　　　　　　　　　　　　　　　　　■

SPECIAL INSTRUCTIONS

① Put in the name of the creditor to whom this notice is being sent.

② Put in the date that the assets will be transferred. This date must be at least ten (10) days after the date this notice is mailed.

③ **and** ④. Put in the name and current business address of the transferor.

⑤ Put in all of the names and addresses used by the transferor within the past three years that you know of. If there aren't any, type the word "NONE" in this space.

⑥ **and** ⑦. Put in the name of your corporation and the address of its principal place of business.

⑧ The president should sign this notice, on behalf of the corporation.

⑨ Indicate the date the notice is sent.

Notice If Debts Are Not Going to Be Paid in Full

To _____:①

A bulk transfer under Article 6 of the Uniform Commercial Code will be made on or after
_____, 19___.② The transferor is _____,③
with a business address at _____.④ The
transferee is _____,⑤ with a principal place of business at
_____.⑥

The transferor has used the following names and addresses in its business within the past
three years:

⑦

The transferee is not going to pay all of the debts of the transferor in full.

The location of the property to be transferred is _____.⑧

A general description of the property which will be transferred is:

⑨

The estimated total of the debts of the transferor is $_____.⑩ The schedule
of property being transferred and the list of the transferor's creditors can be inspected at
_____.⑪

The transfer of these assets is not to pay all existing debts of the transferor, but the
following debts will be paid:

⑫

The transferor will be paid the sum of $_____⑬ on _____, 19___.⑭

Dated: _____⑰   _____(name of corporation)_____⑮

_____⑯
, President

SPECIAL INSTRUCTIONS

① Put in the name of the creditor to whom this notice is being sent.

② Put in the date of the transfer of the assets. It must be at least ten (10) days after the date this notice is mailed.

③ **and** ④. Put in the name and current address of the transferor.

⑤ **and** ⑥. Put in the name and principal place of business of the corporation.

⑦ Put in any other names and addresses used by the transferor that you know of. If there aren't any, indicate "NONE."

⑧ Put in the address where the property that is going to be transferred is located as of the date of the notice.

⑨ Describe the property. This should be the same description that is contained in the Schedule of Property prepared earlier.

⑩ Put in the total amount of money owed by the transferor. This should be the same amount as shown in the List of Creditors prepared earlier.

⑪ List the address where your corporation will be keeping the Schedule of Property and the List of Creditors for the next six months (e.g., the corporation's principal place of business).

⑫ List any debts which will be paid. If none will be paid, put the word "NONE" in this space.

⑬ **and** ⑭ State how much money or other property will be paid to the transferor and when it will be paid. If you are going to receive shares of stock in the new corporation, state how many shares you will receive and the percentage of the total issued shares your shares represent. This stock information should be obtained from the stock issuance resolutions in your minutes.

⑮ Type in name of corporation.

⑯ The president should sign this notice, on behalf of the corporation.

⑰ Put in the date on which the notice is mailed.

3. Mail Notice of Bulk Sales to the Tax Bureau

The Sales and Use Tax Law of New York requires that in the event of a bulk sale, it is the responsibility of the transferee (that is, in this case, the corporation) to notify the Tax Commission by registered mail that the sale is taking place, and the price, terms and conditions of the sale. This requirement applies to all bulk sales, regardless of whether or not you are exempt from particular provisions of the Bulk Sales Act as discussed above under Sections A and B of this step, and regardless of whether or not the transferor owes any taxes. This must be done at least ten (10) days before your corporation takes possession of the property.

A standard Notice of Bulk Sales form is available for this purpose, Form AU-196.10, and can be obtained from most local State Tax offices or by calling the State Tax Bureau in Albany at

800-342-3536 (ask for "Sales Tax"). Obtain two copies of this form—the original will be filed in triplicate with the State Sales Tax Bureau and you will want to keep one copy for your corporate records.

Fill in this standard form as indicated, providing the Certificate of Authority Identification Numbers (sales tax number) of both the purchaser (corporation) and the seller (prior business). Note, most businesses, including your new corporation, must have a sales tax number. Apply for one now, if you haven't done so already (see Chapter 6, Section C9).

This notice form requires specific financial information related to the transfer of the prior business to the corporation. Since you will be consulting an accountant for other reasons, we suggest you have her help you with the sales price figures and the description of the terms of the sale requested on the form.

Make sure you send this Notice of Bulk Sales form, in triplicate, at least 10 days before the date on which the corporation will take possession of the property, by registered mail, to the State Sales Tax Bureau at the address indicated on the form. Again, keep a copy for your corporate records.

B. The Form of Your Stock Certificate

Ten blank, ready-to-use stock certificates are included in the Appendix at the back of this book. They are designed for corporations issuing initial common shares without par value with no special legends and are keyed to the tear-out Certificate of Incorporation and procedures contained in this book. If you want to order specially printed certificates for your corporation, you can do so by ordering one of the corporate kits offered by Nolo Press (see the order form at the back of the book). Each kit contains 20 custom-printed stock certificates. For a further discussion on choosing the right certificates, see Step 5D above.

In Chapter 3B and Chapter 5, Step 2, we discussed other provisions which you might want to include in the Certificate of Incorporation for purposes of special voting and quorum rules or shareholder control. If these provisions are adopted, then you must state that fact on your stock certificates. Samples of the legends[18] which would be used if these (and other) special provisions were included in your Certificate of Incorporation are given below, with the section numbers indicating the appropriate sections of the Business Corporation Law upon which they are based:

1. Section 620

"Paragraph ___ of the Certificate of Incorporation restricts the discretion or the powers of the Board of Directors in its management of the business affairs of this Corporation, pursuant to Section 620 of the Business Corporation Law."

2. Section 616

"Paragraph ___ of the Certificate of Incorporation provides that the proportion of shares needed to constitute a quorum or to

---

[18]A legend is merely a statement on the stock certificate which indicates special privileges or restrictions associated with the shares represented by the certificate. Stock legends must generally be printed conspicuously on the front or back of the stock certificate (certain corporations with stock registered with the SEC are exempt from some of the legend requirements discussed in this section).

approve corporate action is greater than[19] that required by the Business Corporation Law."

3. Section 709

"Paragraph ___ of the Certificate of Incorporation provides that the number of directors needed to constitute a quorum or to approve corporate action is greater than[20] that required by the Business Corporation Law."

4. Section 1002

"Paragraph ___ of the Certificate of Incorporation provides that this corporation may be dissolved upon the occurrence of the event or events stated in said paragraph, and/or upon the vote of ____% of the shareholders of the corporation."

5. Other Legends

Additional restrictive legends that may be required, depending on your individual case, are:

"The transfer of shares is restricted in accordance with Paragraph _____ of the Certificate of Incorporation."

or

"The transfer of shares is restricted in accordance with a shareholder agreement dated _____."

Important Note: The above provisions are provided by way of example only, to give you an idea of the types of legends you would be required to use if you adopted these special

provisions in your Certificate of Incorporation. If you use the forms included in this book, you will not be adopting these special provisions or using these stock legends. If you do wish to use them, you should consult an attorney.

C. Taking Title to Stock

IN THE NEXT SECTION you will actually fill out your stock certificates. Before you do, however, a few words about how to take title to your shares are in order.

Taking title to stock means no more than putting your name on the ownership line, and having the secretary of the corporation register your name and stock holdings on the corporate books. Occasionally, shareholders will hold stock jointly (for example, "as tenants by the entirety," "as joint tenants with right of survivorship," or "as tenants in common"). If shares are owned jointly, the ownership line of the stock certificate should indicate this fact (e.g., "Henry Dexter and Henrietta Dexter, as tenants by the entirety," or "Reuben Ruiz and Herman Grizwold, as tenants in common").

"Tenancy by the entirety," a form of joint ownership for spouses, provides each spouse with a "right of survivorship," so that a

---

[19]If the Certificate of Incorporation requires less than a majority, you would substitute "less than" for "greater than."

[20]Or "less than" (see previous footnote).

surviving spouse, for instance, can obtain full title to the shares upon the death of the other spouse without the need for the shares to go through probate. During the life of each owner, the shares will be considered to be owned 50/50. The tenancy by the entirety will end, however, upon the dissolution of the marriage.

Non-married co-owners can own shares jointly with a right of survivorship by specifically taking title "as joint tenants with right of survivorship." The joint tenancy will terminate, however, upon the sale by any joint tenant of his or her interest in the shares.

If shares or other property are owned jointly by two people "as tenants in common," each co-owner receives an interest in the shares but does not receive a right of survivorship—this interest may be willed to someone other than the other co-tenant.

Note that this is just a preliminary and partial discussion of the issue of joint ownership of shares. Since there are important legal, tax and financial implications to joint ownership of any kind (for example, if the property of one spouse is used to purchase jointly held shares, a gift to the other spouse may have been made and gift taxes may have to be paid), we suggest that you consult your lawyer or accountant before deciding on the best way to take title to joint shares.

Estate Planning Note: As an estate planning measure, the use of an intervivos trust (living trust) allows the beneficiary of the trust to receive title to the shares upon the death of the shareholder and also keeps the shares outside of probate. In other words, a shareholder may wish to transfer shares to this type of trust for the benefit of another person rather than taking title to their shares jointly with another person. If you do transfer your shares to a trust, you will need to make out new share certificates showing the trust as the owner of the transferred shares.

D. Fill Out Your Stock Certificates and Stubs

Issue stock by filling in the blanks on the tear-out stock certificates contained in the Appendix at the back of the book (or on the specially printed certificates you have ordered—see Step 5). The appropriate information on the stock certificate stubs should also be completed. Simply follow the directions on the sample stock certificate which we provide here. The circled numbers in the blanks on the sample certificate refer to the special instructions which immediately follow the sample.

Each stock certificate should represent the number of shares the corporation is issuing to a particular shareholder (or, if issuing joint shares, to the joint owners of the shares). If shares are owned jointly, only fill out one stock certificate for the joint owners, showing both names and the manner of taking title to the shares on the ownership line (as explained below).

Certificate Number ①

For _____ **Shares**
(number of)

Issued To:
_____
(name of shareholder)

_____ 19 __
(date of issuance)

Dated _____

From Whom Transferred ⑩

Dated _____ 19 __

No. Original Shares	No. Original Certificate	No. of Shares Transferred

---

Received Certificate No. _____

For _____ **Shares**
(number of)

This _____ day of
(date of issuance)

_____ 19 __

_____
(signature of shareholder)

NUMBER ①

SHARES ②

INCORPORATED UNDER THE LAWS OF THE STATE OF NEW YORK

_____
(name of corporation) ③

The Corporation is authorized to issue ④ _____ **Common Shares without par value, of one class**

This Certifies that _____ is
(name of shareholder) ⑤

the owner of _____ fully
(number of shares) ⑥

paid and non-assessable Shares of the above Corporation transferable only on the books of the Corporation by the holder hereof in person or by duly authorized Attorney upon surrender of this Certificate properly endorsed.

In Witness Whereof, the said Corporation has caused this Certificate to be signed by its duly authorized officers and to be sealed with the Seal of the Corporation.

Dated _____ ⑦
(date of issuance)

_____
(signature of President) ⑧ , *President*

_____
(signature of Secretary) ⑧ , *Secretary*

⑨

SPECIAL INSTRUCTIONS

① Fill out the left and right portions of the stub as indicated on the sample stub.

Note: The date of issuance and shareholder signature lines on the stubs will be filled out when you distribute your stock certificates (Section E below). If you've ordered one of corporate kits offered by Nolo Press, fill out each separate stub page in your kit in the same manner (these stub pages are already numbered).

Number each certificate and its associated stub. Each person you issue stock to gets one certificate no matter how many shares she purchases (joint owners of shares, of course, get one certificate for their jointly owned shares). The stock certificates issued by the corporation should be consecutively numbered, and should be issued in consecutive order. This is important since it enables the corporation to keep track of who owns its shares.

Example: If you plan to issue stock to four people (no matter how many shares each person will receive), the certificates should be numbered 1 through 4. Thus, if Jack pays $10,000, Sam $5,000, Julie $2,500 and Ted transfers a computer with a fair market value of $1,000 for their shares, assuming the price of the shares is established at $100 per share, Jack receives a certificate for 100 shares, Sam receives one for 50 shares, Julie one for 25 shares and Ted a certificate for 10 shares. Obviously this means you should issue four certificates numbered 1 through 4 (it doesn't matter who gets the certificate numbered #1, #2, etc.).

② Type in the number of shares which each certificate represents. The number of shares each person is entitled to receive is indicated in the stock issuance resolutions of the Minutes of the First Directors' Meeting.

③ Put in the name of the corporation just as it appears on the Certificate of Incorporation.

④ In this blank indicate the total number of shares which the corporation is authorized to issue. Obtain this information from paragraph 4 of your Certificate of Incorporation. Remember, if you have decided to authorize par value shares instead, you cannot use the tear-out certificates at the back of this book (see Step 2, Special Instruction 4).

⑤ Type the name of the shareholder. If the stock certificate is being held by two or more persons, put in the relationship they bear to one another (e.g., "as tenants by the entirety," "as joint tenants with right of survivorship," or "as tenants in common"). As we've said, ownership of shares by two or more persons presents legal and tax questions which should be discussed with an attorney or accountant.

⑥ Spell out the number of shares the certificate represents, then provide the figure in parentheses [e.g., "ONE HUNDRED (100)"]. It should be the same number that you indicated in 2, above.

⑦ Indicate the day, month and year on which the certificate is issued. This date must be the same day or later than the day of payment, delivery or performance of the cash, property or services for which the shares are issued. It cannot be earlier than these dates. To avoid confusion and possible future controversy (and to qualify for the available exemptions under New York Securities Law discussed in Chapter 3D), we strongly suggest that you issue all of your initial shares on the same day.

⑧ The appropriate officers should sign the certificates. The tear-out bylaws included in the Appendix of this book state that the president and the secretary are the only authorized signers.

⑨ An impression of the corporate seal should be placed on the bottom left portion of the stock certificate. It can, however, be placed anywhere on the certificate, if you wish.

⑩ The transfer sections (both here, on the stub, and on the back of the certificate) should be left blank. They are to be used only if and when the stock certificates are transferred by the original shareholders—with the aid of an attorney. If you've ordered a corporate kit from the back of this book, this also applies to the transfer sections on the separate stub pages and on the back of the printed stock certificates which are included as part of the kit.

After filling out the stock certificates and stubs, place the completed stubs in consecutive order in the stock certificate section of your corporate records book. These stubs represent your corporation's share register. If you have ordered a corporate kit from the back of this book, leave the completed stub pages in the stock certificate section of your corporate kit.

Note: You'll need to neatly cut the stub away from the top of the stock certificate (along the dotted line) if you are using the certificates provided in the Appendix at the back of this book. It's easier to do this if you first tear out the entire page.

If you've ordered a corporate kit from Nolo Press, do not detach the completed stub pages in the stock certificate section of your corporate kit. Each kit contains a separate "Stock Transfer Ledger (Share Register)." Fill out one line on the left side of each page for each shareholder in the appropriate alphabetical box (the columns at the extreme right are used for transfers of the original shares).

E. Complete Your Stock Ledger Sheet

The Appendix contains a blank Stock Ledger Sheet. This one sheet should be sufficient for your initial issuance since each line on the sheet is devoted to a particular shareholder (the corporate kits advertised at the back of the book contain a multi-paged, alphabetized ledger). The Stock Ledger Sheet contains the same basic information as the stock certificate stubs, except, due to space constraints and for purposes of clarity, we haven't included columns to document future transfers of shares. You will want to document future transfers by adding your own page with the appropriate transfer information as discussed further, below (or by using the two-page ledger sheets which come with the corporate kits shown at the back of the book). However, since it is important for the corporation to know who owns its shares, we suggest that you put this information on this form, as well. Fill out the Stock Ledger Sheet by referring to the sample below and the Special Instructions which follow it.

Stock Ledger Sheet

① Name of Stockholder	② Address	③ Date of Ownership	Certificates Issued		⑥ Transferor	⑦ Amount Paid
			④ Certificate Number	⑤ Number Shares		

SPECIAL INSTRUCTIONS

① Type in the name of each shareholder to whom the certificate has been issued. Each name should be exactly as spelled on the certificate.

② The current address of each shareholder should be placed in this column. Make sure it is accurate. It is to this address that all notices required under the Bylaws will be sent.

③ Indicate the exact date the certificate was issued. Again, we suggest that this be the same date that the corporation receives the money or property for the shares it is issuing (legally, you can't issue the certificates at an earlier date) and that this be the same day for each shareholder.

④ Put in the number of the certificate (not the number of shares it represents). The first entry in this column should be number 1.

⑤ Put in the number of shares represented by each certificate. This number should be the same as the number which appears on each certificate.

⑥ Indicate the name of the transferor. In this case, it will be the name of the corporation [you can indicate, "*Original Issue by (name of corporation)*"]. If the shares are later sold by the shareholder, his name will appear here. Also, remember from our discussion in Step 4, above, that a tax will usually have to be paid in connection with any future transfers. Since the transfer of shares, and possibly their later reissue by the corporation, involves financial and legal questions outside the scope of this book, you should consult an attorney before doing so. This first issuance of shares by the corporation is relatively trouble-free if you follow the procedures contained in this book.

⑦ Indicate the amount paid by each shareholder for her shares according to the information contained in the stock issuance resolutions of your minutes (prepared in Step 9).

Note: If you transfer shares at a later date (with the help of a lawyer), you will need to add another page to your stock ledger sheet, with columns indicating the following information: the date of transfer, to whom the shares are transferred, the numbers of the surrendered certificates and the shares represented thereby, the number of shares held in balance, and the value of the transferred shares. As we've said, the corporate kit stock ledger sheets already contain columns for this information.

F. Prepare a Bill of Sale and/or Receipts For Your Shareholders

AFTER FILLING OUT YOUR STOCK certificates, you may wish to prepare receipts and, if incorporating a prior business, a bill of sale for your shareholders before actually distributing your stock certificates. You are not legally required to prepare these forms but we think it's generally good business to do so (and a sensible precaution to avoid later confusion as to who paid what for shares in your corporation).

A tear-out Bill of Sale and separate receipts are contained in the Appendix to this book. This paperwork allows the corporation and each shareholder to have a written statement of the details of each person's stock issuance transaction. Simply tear out the appropriate forms from the Appendix, make copies, and prepare these forms according to the sample forms and instructions below.

1. Prepare a Bill of Sale for Assets of a Business (If Incorporating a Prior Business)

If you are incorporating a prior business (you are transferring the assets of an unincorporated business to your corporation in return for the issuance of shares to the prior owners), you may wish to prepare the tear-out Bill of Sale in the the Appendix. If not, skip to Section F2 below.

Note on the Transfer of Real Property or Leases: If you are transferring real property or a lease to your corporation, you will have to prepare and execute new corporate ownership papers, such as deeds, leases, assignments of leases, etc. (the assignment of a lease will usually only occur as part of the transfer of a pre-existing business to the corporation). If the property is rental property, you should talk to the landlord about having a new lease prepared showing the corporation as the new tenant. (An alternative is to have the prior tenants assign the lease to the corporation; however, read your lease before doing this as many leases are not assignable without the landlord's permission.)

If the property being transferred is mortgaged, then you will most likely need the permission of the lender to transfer the property. If your real property note agreement contains a "due on sale or transfer" clause, you may even be required to refinance your deed of trust (mortgage) if rates have gone up substantially since the existing deed of trust was executed. This, of course, may be so undesirable that you decide not to transfer the real property to the corporation, preferring to keep it in the name of the original owner and lease it to the corporation.

Prepare and execute these new ownership papers, lease documents, etc., before you give the prior property owners their shares (this will be done as part of Section F below).

Below is a sample of the tear-out Bill of Sale form with instructions.

√ The parenthetical blanks, i.e., "(_____)," indicate information which you must complete on the tear-out form.

√ Each circled number (e.g., ①) refers to a special instruction which provides specific information to help you complete an item. The special instructions immediately follow the sample form.

√ We suggest you tear out the form in the Appendix and fill in the blanks as you follow the sample form and instructions below.

As indicated in the form, attach to the Bill of Sale an inventory of the assets of the prior business which will be transferred to the corporation. If you have any questions, your tax advisor can help you with the preparation of this inventory and in arriving at a fair appraisal figure for the assets of the pre-existing business.

Sample Bill of Sale for Assets of a Business

This is an agreement between:

_____**(name of prior business owner)**_____ ①

_____**(name of prior business owner)**_____ ①

herein called "transferor(s)," and _____**(name of corporation)**_____,② a New York corporation, herein called "the corporation."

In return for the issuance of _____**(number of shares)**_____ ③ shares of stock of the corporation, transferor(s) hereby sell(s), assign(s), and transfer(s) to the corporation all right, title, and interest in the following property:

All the tangible assets listed on the inventory attached to this Bill of Sale and all stock in trade, goodwill, leasehold interests, trade names, and other intangible assets [except _____**(any nontransferred assets shown here)**_____ ④] of _____**(name of prior business)**_____ ⑤, located at _____**(address of prior business)**_____ ⑥.

In return for the transfer of the above property to it, the corporation hereby agrees to assume, pay, and discharge all debts, duties, and obligations that appear on the date of this agreement, on the books and owed on account of said business [except _____**(any unassumed liabilities shown here)**_____ ⑦]. The corporation agrees to indemnify and hold the transferor(s) of said business and their property free from any liability for any such debt, duty, or obligation and from any suits, actions, or legal proceedings brought to enforce or collect any such debt, duty, or obligation.

⑧ The transferor(s) hereby appoint(s) the corporation as representative to demand, receive, and collect for itself any and all debts and obligations now owing to said business and hereby assumed by the corporation. The transferor(s) further authorize(s) the corporation to do all things allowed by law to recover and collect any such debts and obligations and to use the transferor's(s') name(s) in such manner as it considers necessary for the collection and recovery of such debts and obligations, provided, however, without cost, expense, or damage to the transferor(s).

Dated:_____**(date)**_____ ⑨   _____**(signature of prior business owner)**_____ ⑨
                                        (typed name), Transferor

                                        _____**(signature of prior business owner)**_____ ⑨
                                        (typed name), Transferor

                                        _____**(signature of prior business owner)**_____ ⑨
                                        (typed name), Transferor

Dated:_____**(date)**_____   _____**(name of corporation)**_____ ⑨
                                   Name of Corporation

                          By: _____**(signature of President)**_____ ⑨
                               (typed name), President

                               _____**(signature of Treasurer)**_____ ⑨
                               (typed name), Treasurer

SPECIAL INSTRUCTIONS

① Type (or print) the names of the prior business owners.

② Show the name of your corporation.

③ Enter the total number of shares to be issued to all prior owners of the business in return for the transfer of the business to the corporation.

Example: If Patricia and Kathleen will each receive 100 shares in return for their respective half-interests in their pre-existing partnership (which they are now incorporating), they would indicate 200 shares here.

④ Use this line to show any assets of the prior business that are not being transferred to the corporation (e.g., you may wish to continue to personally own real property associated with your business and lease it to your new corporation). For most businesses being incorporated, all prior business assets will be transferred to the corporation and you should type "No Exceptions" here.

Note: As indicated in this paragraph of the bill of sale, you should attach a current inventory showing the assets of the prior business transferred to the corporation.

⑤ Indicate the name of the prior business being transferred to the corporation. For sole proprietorships and partnerships not operating under a fictitious business name, the name(s) of the prior owners may simply be given here (e.g., "Heather Langsley and Chester Treacher").

⑥ Show the full address of the prior business.

⑦ This paragraph indicates that your corporation will assume the liabilities of the prior business. This will be appropriate for the incorporation of most small businesses. Remember—if the corporation doesn't assume all of the liabilities, you do not qualify for the Bulk Sales Act exemption and must complete the extra forms shown in Step 9A2 of this chapter. If your corporation will not assume any of the liabilities of the prior business, then you will need to re-type the tear-out Bill of Sale, omitting this paragraph.

In the blank in this paragraph, list any liabilities of the prior business which will not be assumed by the corporation. Again, most corporations will assume all liabilities of the prior business and will indicate "No Exceptions" here.

⑧ This paragraph is included in the tear-out Bill of Sale to indicate that your corporation is appointed to collect for itself any debts and obligations (accounts receivable) owed to the prior business which are being transferred to the corporation.

⑨ Type the name of the corporation on the line indicated. Don't fill out the other blanks yet. You should date the form and have the prior business owners (transferors) and the President and Treasurer of the corporation sign the Bill of Sale when you distribute the stock certificates to the prior business owners (as explained in Section G below).

2. Prepare Receipts for Your Shareholders

You may wish to prepare one or more receipts for your shareholders (for preparing a bill of sale to document the transfer of the assets of a business in return for shares, see the previous subsection). In the Appendix we have included tear-out receipts for the following types of payment made by a shareholder:

• Cash
• Cancellation of Indebtedness
• Specific Items of Property
• Services Rendered the Corporation

Let's look at each of these transactions and the associated receipt form below. Obviously, you will need to make copies of each receipt to be prepared for more than one shareholder (e.g., you will want to make two additional copies of the cash receipt form if you will be issuing shares in return for cash payments to be made by three shareholders).

√ The parenthetical blanks, i.e., "(_____),"
indicate information which you must complete on the tear-out receipts.

√ Each circled number (e.g., ①) refers to a special instruction which provides specific information to help you complete an item. The special instructions immediately follow the sample receipt forms.

√ We suggest you tear out the receipt in the Appendix and fill in the blanks as you follow the sample form and instructions below.

Dating and Signing the Receipts: Fill in the date and signature lines on your receipts when you distribute your stock certificates in return for the payments made by each of your shareholders (Section G below).

Joint Shareholder and Joint Payments Note: If you will issue shares to joint owners (see Section B above), you may, if you wish, show the names of both joint owners on the signature line in the sample receipt forms below (although a receipt showing the name of just one of the joint owners is sufficient). Again, this issue of whether a shareholder will take title to shares individually or jointly with another shareholder is primarily the concern of the shareholder, not the corporation. Of course, if two shareholders jointly contribute an item of property in return for the issuance of two separate blocks of individually owned shares, then you will wish to prepare a separate receipt for each of these shareholders. The particular details of each transaction will usually determine the most appropriate way to prepare the receipt form (normally, you will wish to make out the receipt in the name of the shareholder making the payment).

Example 1: Teresa and Vernon Miller will pay $1,000 for 100 shares which they will take title to as tenants by the entirety. You make out a receipt in the name of the shareholder who writes the check (if the funds are written from a joint checking account, you will naturally make the receipt form in the name of both spouses).

Example 2: Mike and his brother, Burt, transfer a jointly owned lathe with a value of $5,000. Each will receive 50 shares. You make out a separate receipt for each brother, with each receipt showing the transfer of a one-half interest in the lathe in return for the issuance of 50 shares.

a. Receipt for Cash Payment

If shares are issued for cash, it is best to pay with a personal check (made payable by the shareholder to the corporation) since the shareholder's cancelled check can serve as an additional proof of payment. Here is a sample of the tear-out cash receipt form.

Sample Receipt for Cash Payment

Receipt of $ __(amount of cash payment)__ ① from __(name of shareholder)__ ② representing payment in full for __(number of shares)__ ③ shares of the stock of this corporation is hereby acknowledged.

Dated: __(date of payment)__ ④

Name of Corporation: __(name of corporation)__ ⑤

By: __(signature of Treasurer)__ ⑥

(typed name), Treasurer ⑦

SPECIAL INSTRUCTIONS

① Fill in the amount of cash being paid by the shareholder in this blank.

②, ③, ⑤ **and** ⑦ Type the name of the shareholder, the number of shares which will be issued to this shareholder, the name of your corporation and the name of your Treasurer in the appropriate blank as shown on the sample form.

④ **and** ⑥ After receiving payment from the shareholder (Section G below), your Treasurer should date and sign each cash receipt on the lines indicated.

b. Receipt for Cancellation of Indebtedness

If shares are issued in return for the cancellation of indebtedness owed by the corporation to a shareholder (as we've said, this is not a common means of payment for newly-formed corporations), you can prepare this tear-out receipt form shown below to document this type of stock issuance transaction. Attach a photocopy of the cancelled debt instrument (if you have one such as a promissory note, written loan agreement, etc.) to the receipt.

Sample Form for Cancellation of Indebtedness

The receipt of _____(number of shares)_____ ① shares of this corporation to ____(name of shareholder)____ ② for the cancellation by ____(name of shareholder)____ ② of a current loan outstanding to this corporation, dated _____(date of loan)_____ ③, with a remaining unpaid principal amount and unpaid accrued interest, if any, totalling $_____(loan balance)_____ ④ is hereby acknowledged.

Dated: ____(date of cancellation of loan)____ ⑤

_____(signature of shareholder)_____ ⑥
(name of shareholder)②

SPECIAL INSTRUCTIONS

① **and** ② Insert the number of shares being issued to this shareholder and the name of the shareholder in these blanks.

③ Indicate the date of the original loan made by the shareholder to the corporation.

④ Show the total of the outstanding principal amount and accrued and unpaid interest (if any) owed on the loan in this blank.

⑤ **and** ⑥ Indicate the date of cancellation of the note in the date line on the receipt—this will be the date you actually distribute the shares. Provide this date and have the shareholder sign the receipt as part of Section G below.

c. Receipt For Specific Items of Property

If specific items of property are being transferred to the corporation by a shareholder (other than the assets of an existing business—in this latter case, see Section F1 above), you may wish to prepare a receipt (bill of sale) for the property before issuing shares to the shareholder. Make sure that the property has first been delivered to the corporation and that any ownership papers ("pink slip" for a vehicle) have been signed over to the corporation. If you are transferring real property interests to your corporation, see the "Note on the Transfer of Real Property or Leases" in Section E1 above.

Below is a sample receipt (bill of sale) to document this type of stock transaction for one or more of your shareholders.

Sample Bill of Sale for Items of Property

In consideration of the issuance of _____(number of shares)_____ ① shares of stock in and by ___(name of corporation)___,② ___(name of shareholder)___ ③ hereby sells, assigns, conveys, transfers, and delivers to the corporation all right, title and interest in and to the following property:

(Description of Property) ④

Dated: ___(date of sale)___ ⑤

_____(signature of shareholder)_____ ⑥
(name of shareholder)③, Transferor

SPECIAL INSTRUCTIONS

①, ② and ③ Show the number of shares being issued to this shareholder, the name of the corporation and the name of the shareholder in these blanks.

④ Provide a short description in this space of the property being transferred to the corporation by this shareholder. This description should be brief but specific (e.g., make, model, and serial numbers of the property, vehicle ID and registration number for vehicles, etc.).

⑤ and ⑥ The date of the sale will be the date you distribute the stock certificate in return for the delivery of the property to the corporation. Complete this date line and have the shareholder (the transferor of the property) sign the receipt when you distribute your shares as part of Section G below.

d. Receipt for Services Rendered the Corporation

If you are transferring shares in return for past services performed by a shareholder for the corporation (remember, you cannot issue shares in return for the performance of services which will be performed in the future by a shareholder—see Chapter 2F), prepare the tear-out form as explained below and have the shareholder date and sign a bill for these services as "Paid in Full" showing the date of payment (the date you distribute the shares in return for these services—Section F below).

Note: As we've said, this is not a common type of stock issuance transaction for newly-formed corporations since (1) most work done for the corporation will occur after your stock issuance and (2) most contractors or other professionals who have performed services will want cash (not shares of stock) as payment for their services. However, if one of the principals of your closely-held corporation has performed services for the corporation prior to your stock issuance, this type of stock issuance transaction may make sense. Of, course, to avoid unfairness to your other stockholders, you will want to make sure that the shareholder charges no more than the prevailing rate for the services performed.

Sample Receipt for Services Rendered

In consideration of the performance of the following services actually rendered to, or labor done for, _____**(name of corporation)**_____ ①, _____**(name of shareholder)**_____ ②, the provider of such services or labor done, hereby acknowledges the receipt of _____**(number of shares)**_____ ③ shares of stock in _____**(name of corporation)**_____ ① as payment in full for these services:

(Description of Past Services) ④

Dated: _____**(date of issuance)**_____ ⑤

_____**(signature of shareholder)**_____ ⑥
(name of shareholder)②

SPECIAL INSTRUCTIONS

①, ② **and** ③ Show the name of the corporation, the name of the shareholder and the number of shares this person will receive in the blanks.

④ Provide a short description in this space of the past services performed by the shareholder [e.g., the date(s), description and value of (amount billed for) past services performed by the shareholder].

⑤ **and** ⑥ When you distribute the shares in return for the past services (Section G below), provide the date of issuance of the shares and have the shareholder sign the receipt on the lines indicated above.

G. Distribute Your Stock Certificates

NOW THAT YOU'VE FILLED IN your stock certificates and prepared receipts for your shareholders (and a bill of sale if you are incorporating a prior business), issue your shares by distributing your stock certificates to your shareholders. Distribute your shares after receiving payment from each shareholder. When completing this step, make sure to do the following:

• Have each shareholder (or, if two persons take title to the shares, the joint shareholders) sign their stock certificate stub. Indicate the date of stock issuance on each stub.

• Date each stock certificate and have your President and Secretary sign each one (impress your corporate seal in the circular space at the bottom of each certificate). If you have ordered a corporate kit from Nolo Press, write the date of issuance in the "Time Became Owner" column for each shareholder

in the Stock Transfer Ledger (Share Register) included with each kit.

• Complete the date and signature lines on your receipts (and bill of sale for the assets of a business if you have prepared this form) as explained in Section F above. Give each shareholder a copy of her receipt(s) and/or a copy of the bill of sale (if you have prepared one to document the transfer of the assets of a business to the corporation).

• Make sure to place all your completed stock stubs and completed copies of all receipts, bills of sale, and any attachments (inventory of assets of the prior business, cancelled notes, paid-in-full bill for services, etc.) in your corporate records book.

A Suggestion: If you have stock certificates left over after filling out the certificates for your initial stock issuance, we suggest that you tear them up and throw them away. Remember, future stock issuances or transfers must be done in full compliance with the prospectus, registration and other requirements of New York (and federal) securities laws. We do not show you how to accomplish future issuances or transfers of your shares in this book—you will need to consult a lawyer first.

CONGRATULATIONS!

You have now completed your last incorporation step! There is one last point we wish to make which is central to the operation of your newly-formed corporation. One of the reasons you decided to form a corporation was to limit your personal liability in business affairs. So, from now on, whenever you sign a document on behalf of the corporation, be certain to do so in the following manner:

_____(name of corporation)_____

By: ____(signature of corporate officer)____
     (name), (corporate title, e.g., President)

If you fail to sign documents this way (on behalf of the corporation in your capacity as a corporate officer or director), you may be leaving yourself open to personal liability for corporate obligations. This is but one example designed to illustrate a basic premise of corporate life: From now on, it is extremely important for you to maintain the distinction between the corporation which you've organized and yourself (and the other principals of the corporation). As we've said, the corporation is a separate legal "person" and you want to make sure that other people, businesses, the IRS and the courts respect this distinction (see Chapter 2I for a further discussion).

Post-Incorporation Procedures: Please read and follow the post-incorporation procedures contained in Chapter 6.

AFTER YOUR CORPORATION IS ORGANIZED

Chapter 6

AFTER YOUR CORPORATION IS ORGANIZED

AT THIS POINT the organization of your corporation should be complete. As you know, operating any business, regardless of its size, involves paying attention to paperwork. In this chapter, we show you how to take a few final necessary steps associated with organizing your corporation and how to comply with the various ongoing state and federal tax requirements which may apply to your corporation. We also discuss other formalities related to hiring employees and conducting corporate business. Due to the individual nature of each corporation and its business, it is not possible to discuss every tax for which your corporation may be liable. Rather, this discussion is intended to be a general guide to routine tax obligations that every corporation faces. Most of the tax forms we discuss below can be obtained from the IRS or New York agencies mentioned in this chapter (or from your tax advisor).

A. Final Formalities After Forming Your Corporation

1. Notify Creditors and Others of Dissolution of Prior Business

If you have incorporated a prior business or transferred its assets to the corporation, you will have complied with New York's Bulk Sales Act (see Chapter 5, Step 9) and will have met the legal requirements of notifying creditors of the change in business ownership. Although there is no legal requirement to do so, as a matter of good business practice, we suggest you send a short, personal letter to your your creditors and other interested parties (suppliers, others with whom you have open book accounts or lines of credit, customers, etc.) informing them that your prior business has been dissolved and that you are now doing business as a corporation, under your new corporate name. You should, of course, inform them of your new corporate address (if you have changed the location of your principal place of business). Sending a personal notice letter of this type is not just a matter of courtesy; it will also help avoid confusion later (and help limit your personal exposure future transactions) by letting outsiders know that they are now dealing with an incorporated entity, not with you personally (see Chapter 2). Place a copy of each letter in your corporate records book.

2. Prepare and File an Assumed Name Certificate (if necessary)

Most corporations do business under the name given in their Certificate of Incorporation.[1] However, if you wish, you can operate under a name that is different from the one used in your Certificate of Incorporation. This second name is

---

[1]If a corporation wishes to change its formal corporate name (the name indicated in the Certificate of Incorporation), it must file an amended Certificate of Incorporation with the Department of State. The new name shown on the amended Certificate must, of course, be acceptable to the Department and be available for use by the corporation (see Chapter 5, Step 1).

For More Information

A truly excellent source of information on starting a small business generally, as well as a source of financial ledgers, worksheets, etc. is *Small Time Operator*, by Kamaroff (Bell Springs Publishing)—see order information at the back of the this book.

We suggest all incorporators obtain IRS Publication 509, *Tax Calendars*, prior to the beginning of each year. This pamphlet contains tax calendars showing the dates for corporate and payroll filings during the year.

Further information on withholding, depositing, reporting and paying federal employment taxes can be found in IRS Publication 15, *Circular E, Employer's Tax Guide* and the Publication 15 Supplement, as well as IRS Publication 539, *Employment Taxes*. Further federal tax information can be found in IRS Publication 542, *Tax Information on Corporations* and Publication 334, *Tax Guide for Small Business*.

Helpful information on accounting methods and bookkeeping procedures is contained in IRS Publication 538, *Accounting Period and Methods* and Publication 583, *Information for Business Taxpayers*. These publications can be picked up at your local IRS office (or ordered by phone—call your local IRS office or try the toll-free IRS forms and publications request telephone number 1-800-424-FORM).

For information on New York corporate taxes together with corporate forms and instructions, obtain the following publications from the New York State Department of Taxation and Finance:

• CT-2 package, *Corporation Franchise Tax Reports and Instructions*

• CT-3S package and CT-6 Election form (New York S corporation tax forms)

• Publication 902, *New York State Business Tax Reform Package*

These and the other Department of Taxation and Finance forms mentioned in this chapter can be ordered by calling the Department's toll-free forms number (from within New York): 1-800-462-8100.

known as an assumed name (or, more colloquially, as a "dba," an acronym for "doing business as …"). There is nothing underhanded about doing business under an assumed name; it is done frequently, for a variety of reasons. For example, your corporate name may be Aardvark Business Computer Services, Inc., and you may plan to use ABC Services, Inc. on your stationery and advertising.

Reality Note: Most small corporations will wish to use their formal corporate name in all business dealings and will not wish to adopt an assumed corporate name. We explain these corporate assumed name procedures mostly to let you know that they are available to you and can be undertaken without difficulty should you wish to operate under an assumed name.

To use an assumed corporate name, there are several legal requirements which you must meet and fees you must pay. Before using an assumed name, you must do the following:

File a certificate (we provide a sample below) with the Office of the Secretary of State indicating that you want to do business under an assumed name. It must include:

- the assumed name you are going to use;

- your actual corporate name;

- the full address of the corporation's principal place of business;

- the name of each county in which the corporation does, or intends to do, business under the assumed name;

- the full address of each place from which the corporation will conduct its business under an assumed name;

- the signature and acknowledgement of the certificate by an officer of the corporation.

There are a few restrictions which you should be aware of:

- You can't use a name which may be misleading or use an assumed name with the intent to deceive others.

- You generally can't use the names of people in the assumed name, although there are exceptions to this rule. The most notable are: (1) you can use the name of any person involved in the conduct of the corporation's business, and (2) you can use the name if it has a secondary historical meaning (e.g., the Julius Caesar Flower Company) and is followed by the abbreviation, "a.n." (i.e., Julius Caesar Flower Company, a.n.). The secondary meaning of such a name, however, must be stated in the certificate you file (that is, you must explain its historical significance or fame).

- You can't use words in the assumed name that you are not permitted to use in the corporate name (see Chapter 5, Step 1).

- If any of the facts contained in your assumed name certificate change, it must be amended within 30 days.

- A certified copy of the certificate must be prominently displayed at each place of business.

There are several fees involved in this procedure. First, you must pay an initial fee of $25 to the Secretary of State (as before, this must be a certified check). Second, you must pay fees to the Secretary of State which will be forwarded to the county clerk in each county in which you will be doing business under an assumed name. The fee is $25 extra for *each* county.

Below is a sample form of the certificate which should be typed and sent to the Office of the Secretary of State if you wish to use an assumed name. The circled numbers refer to special instructions which follow the sample form.

Assumed Name Certificate

The undersigned does hereby certify, pursuant to Section 130 of the General Business Law of the State of New York, that:

l. He/she is the president of __(name of corporation)__ ,① formed under the Business Corporation Law of the State of New York.

2. __(name of corporation)__ ① does or intends to carry on, conduct and transact business in New York State under the assumed name of __(assumed name)__ ② at each of the following locations:

__(street address and county of each location)__ ③

_____

_____

3. The real name of the corporation is __(name of corporation)__ ,① and it has a principal place of business at __(complete street address)__ ③ and intends to do business under such assumed name in the following county or counties:

_____ __(county or counties)__ _____ ⑤

_____

_____

IN WITNESS WHEREOF, I have signed this certificate this _____ day of _____ , 19___.

                              __(signature of president)__ ⑥
                              (typed name) , President

State of New York

County of _____

On this _____ day of _____ , 19___, before me personally came __(name of president)__ , to me known who, being by me duly sworn, did depose and say that he/she is the President of the Corporation above named, and acknowledged that he/she executed the foregoing instrument on behalf of the above Corporation pursuant to authority vested in him/her by a vote of the Board of Directors of such Corporation.

                              _____
                              , Notary Public

SPECIAL INSTRUCTIONS

① Type in the name of the corporation exactly as it appears on the Certificate of Incorporation.

② Insert the assumed name that you wish to use in the appropriate blanks.

③ Put in the street address and county location of all places where the corporation is, or will be, doing business under this assumed name. Show a complete address, including the street, city, county, state and zip code.

④ Put in the principal place of business of the corporation. This location should be the same as the address indicated in Article I, Section 2 of your Bylaws and should also show the street, city, county, state and zip code.

⑤ Put in the name of each county in New York where the corporation plans to conduct business under the assumed name.

⑥ The president should sign and date the form *in the presence of a notary*. The blank in the notary statement should show the president's name.

Next, you should prepare a cover letter, following the sample letter and special instructions below.

<u>(Name of corporation)</u> ①
<u>(Address)</u>
<u>(Date)</u>

Office of the Secretary of State
162 Washington Avenue
Albany, NY 12231

Office of the Secretary of State:

RE: <u>(name of corporation)</u> ①
<u>(assumed name)</u>

Enclosed please find an original and _____ copy/copies of a Certificate of Assumed Name, signed by the President of the above named corporation.

Also enclosed please find a certified check in the amount of $_____ representing payment of the following fees:

1. $25.00 for the Office of the Secretary of State;

2. $_____ representing county fees for the counties in which the corporation will be using an assumed name; and

3. $_____ for the cost of _____ certified copy/copies.

Please return the receipt and certified copy/copies of the Certificate of Assumed Name to the undersigned.

Sincerely,

<u>(signature of president)</u>
<u>(typed name)</u> , President

<u>(name of corporation)</u> ①

SPECIAL INSTRUCTIONS

① The amount of the check, which should be made payable to the "Secretary of State, New York," will vary depending on the number of counties you will be doing business in under an assumed name. You must automatically pay $25 in all cases, plus $25 for each county in which you will be doing business under an assumed name. Consequently, if you are filing a certificate to use an assumed name in one county, you will have to pay $50 ($25 as the basic fee and $25 as the county fee). You will also need to pay a fee for each copy which you send to the Secretary of State for certification—remember, you will need to display a certified copy at each place of business. The fee for each certified copy is $10. Make sure you indicate how many copies you are enclosing on the cover letter and indicate the total fee for certifying these copies. Remember, you must enclose a certified check.

Warning: Fees are subject to change. If you want to be doubly sure that the above fee amounts are current at the time of your incorporation, call the Division of Corporations in Albany at 518-473-2492.

You must prepare a backing sheet for your Assumed Name Certificate. To do this, simply type the following information on a blank 8-1/2" x 11" (letter size) sheet of paper:

Certificate of Assumed Name

of

<u>(name of corporation)</u>

Filed by

<u>(name of president)</u>

For an example of the general layout of a backing sheet, see the backing sheet for the Certificate of Incorporation in the Appendix.

Staple the pages of the original Certificate of Assumed Name to the backing sheet, making sure that this sheet is stapled to the back of the last page of the original certificate with the text of the backing sheet facing outwards. Enclose the original certificate and backing sheet, stapled copies of your certificate, your cover letter and check in an envelope and send it to the Secretary of State at the address indicated on the sample letter. You should receive a receipt for filing of the original certificate and your certified copies back from the Secretary of State's office shortly thereafter.

B. Tax Forms—Federal

1. S Corporation Tax Election

If you have decided to elect federal S corporation tax status, and have included an authorizing resolution in your minutes, you must make a timely election by filing IRS form 2553 and the consents of the shareholders (see Chapter 4C). If you haven't made your election yet (and haven't consulted a tax advisor as to the timing of the election—see Chapter 7B), call your accountant now and make sure the election form is sent in on time—you don't want to miss the deadline for this election.

New York S Corporation Election: If you wish to elect S corporation status at the state level as well, make sure to file form CT-6 with the state Department of Taxation and Finance within the required time limit (see Chapter 4A3).

Tax Year Note: Remember, S corporations must generally select a calendar tax year unless they are eligible to elect a fiscal tax year under IRS rules and regulations (see Chapter 4). You will want to check with your tax advisor at this time and, if appropriate, make a timely election of a corporate fiscal tax year as well.

2. Federal Employer Identification Number

As soon as possible after the Certificate of Incorporation is filed, your corporation must apply for a Federal Employer Identification Number by filling out IRS Form SS-4 and sending it to the nearest Service Center of the IRS. If you are incorporating a pre-existing sole proprietorship or partnership, you will need to apply for a new Employer Identification Number. This number is needed for the employment tax returns and deposits discussed below.

3. Employee's Withholding Certificates

Each employee of the corporation must fill out and furnish the corporation with an Employee's Withholding Exemption Certificate (IRS Form W-4) on or before commencing employment. Obtain the most recent version of Form W-4. This form is used in determining the amount of income taxes to be withheld from the employee's wages.

Generally, any individual who receives compensation for services rendered the corporation, subject to the control of the corporation both as to what shall be done and how it should be done, is considered an employee. All shareholders of the corporation who receive salaries or wages for services as directors, officers, or nontitled personnel are considered employees of the corporation and must furnish a W-4.[2] Be careful of trying to avoid the payment of employment taxes by classifying people as independent contractors. The law in this area is fuzzy, and the IRS and the state are often obstinate. For more information, see IRS Publication 539.

4. Income and Social Security Tax Withholding

The corporation must withhold federal income tax and Social Security tax (FICA) from wages paid to each employee. These, as well as other employment taxes, are withheld and reported on a calendar-year basis, regardless of the tax year

---

[2]Directors, with certain exceptions, aren't considered employees if they are only paid for attending Board meetings. If, however, they are paid for other services or are salaried employees of the corporation, they will be considered employees whose wages are subject to the employment taxes discussed below—check with the IRS.

of the corporation, with returns and deposits being submitted on a quarterly or more frequent basis.

The amount of federal income tax withheld is based upon the employee's wage level, marital status, and the number of allowances claimed on the employee's W-4.

Social Security taxes are withheld at a specific rate on an employee's wage base (the rate and wage base figures change constantly). The corporation is required to make matching Social Security tax contributions for each employee.

5. Quarterly Withholding Returns and Deposits

The corporation is required to prepare and file a Withholding Return (IRS Form 941) for each quarter of the calendar year showing all income and social security taxes withheld from employees' wages as well as matching corporation social security tax contributions.

The corporation is required to deposit federal income and social security taxes on a monthly (or more frequent) basis in an authorized commercial or federal reserve bank. Payment for undeposited taxes owed at the end of a calendar quarter must be submitted with the quarterly return. Consult IRS Publication 15 for specifics.

6. Annual Wage and Tax Statement

The corporation is required to furnish two copies of the Wage and Tax Statement (IRS Form W-2) to each employee from whom income tax has been withheld or would have been withheld if the employee had claimed no more than one withholding exemption on his W-4. This form must show total wages paid and amounts deducted for income and Social Security tax. W-2s must be furnished to employees no later than

January 31 following the close of the calendar year.

The corporation must submit the original of each employee's previous year's W-2 form and an annual Transmittal of Income and Tax Statement (Form W-3) to the Social Security Administration on or before the last day of February following the close of the calendar year.

7. Federal Unemployment Tax

Most corporations are subject to the federal unemployment tax provisions. Under the tax statutes, your corporation is subject to paying Federal Unemployment Tax (FUTA) if, during the current or preceding calendar year, the corporation:

1. Paid wages of $1,500 or more during any calendar quarter, or

2. Had one or more employees for some portion of at least one day during each of twenty different calendar weeks. These twenty weeks do not have to be consecutive.

FUTA taxes are paid by the corporation and are not deducted from employees' wages. The FUTA tax is determined by the current rate and employee wage base and is paid by the corporation (as usual, rates and wage-base figures are subject to change). The corporation receives a credit for a percentage of this tax for New York unemployment taxes paid or for having been granted a favorable experience rating by the state.

Generally, the corporation must deposit the tax in an authorized commercial or federal reserve bank within one month following the close of the quarter. For help in computing your quarterly FUTA tax liability, see instructions in IRS Publication 15. An annual FUTA return (IRS Form 940) must be filed by the corporation with the nearest IRS center by January 31 following the close of the calendar year for which the tax is due. Any tax still due is payable with the return.

8. Corporate Income Tax Return

A regular for-profit corporation must file an annual Corporation Income Tax Return (IRS Form 1120) on or before the fifteenth day of the third month following the close of its tax year. A two-page Short-Form Corporation Income Tax Return (IRS Form 1120-A) is available for use by smaller corporations with gross receipts, total income and total assets of $250,000 or less. The corporation's tax year must correspond with the corporation's accounting period (the period for which corporate books are kept as specified in your Minutes) and is established by the first income tax return filed by the corporation. For a discussion of special corporate tax year requirements for S corporations and personal service corporations, see Chapter 4D.

Your first corporate first tax year may be a short year of less than twelve months. For example, if the corporate accounting period selected in the Minutes is the calendar year, January 1 to December 31, and the corporate existence began on March 13 (the date the Certificate of Incorporation was filed), the corporation would establish its calendar tax year and report income for its first tax year by filing its first annual return on or before March 15 of the following year.

Note that this first return would be for the short year, March 13 to December 31. If the Minutes select a fiscal tax year, say from July 1 to June 30, and the corporate existence begins on May 1, the first return would be filed on or before August 15 for the first short year of May 1 to June 30.

9. S Corporation Income Tax Return

Even though federal S corporations are, for the most part, not subject to the payment of corporate income taxes, such corporations must file an annual U.S. Small Business Corporation Income Tax Return (IRS Form 1120S) on or before the fifteenth day of the third month following the close of the tax year for which the S corporation election is effective.

10. Corporate Employee and Shareholder Returns

Corporate employees and shareholders report employment and dividend income on their annual individual income tax returns (IRS Form 1040). S corporation shareholders report their pro rata share of undistributed corporate taxable income on Form 1040, Schedule E (as noted in Chapter 4C, S corporation shareholders may be required to estimate and pay taxes on this undistributed taxable income during the year).

11. Estimated Corporate Income Tax Payments

Corporations that expect to owe federal corporate income taxes at the end of their tax year (and most will), are required to make estimated tax payments. Estimated tax payments must be deposited in an authorized commercial or federal reserve bank. Both the due date and amount of each installment are computed by a formula based upon the corporation's income tax liability.

To determine corporate estimated tax liability and the date and amount of deposits, obtain IRS Form 1120-W. This form is to be used for computational purposes only and should not be filed with the IRS.

C. Tax Forms—State

I. Election of Accounting Period

Shortly after you file your Certificate of Incorporation, you will receive a Request for New Account Information (form CT-411) from the New York Department of State. Complete this form by providing your federal identification number, your corporation's accounting period and the other information requested. File the form with the state and keep one copy to place in your corporate records book.

2. Corporate Estimated Tax Return

As already mentioned, a New York for-profit corporation is required to pay an annual franchise tax based upon its net income from its previous year's operations and other money it receives each year (see Chapter 4A1). This is similar to the income tax which you pay on your personal income, although there are significant differences. In operation, it works like this:[3]

a. On the date on which you file the franchise tax return (see Section 3, below), you are required to pay 25% of the total of the amount of the previous year's tax. This is the first estimated tax payment you will make for the year.

b. On the 15th day of the sixth month of your corporation's tax year (June 15 if your corporations has a calendar tax year), you must submit an Estimated Tax Payment Form (Form CT-400) in which you estimate what your corporation's total tax liability will be for the year. When you file this form you must also pay one-third of the remainder of the estimated liability (remember you have already paid 25% of it).

c. On the 15th day of the ninth and twelfth months (September 15 and December 15 if you are on a calendar year) you pay one-third of the remaining estimated tax liability.

So, in short, you pay in installments of 25%, and then three equal payments of the balance of 75%.

Example: Assume your corporation has a calendar tax year and in the previous year it had paid taxes of $10,000. Assume further that you estimate your business will be about the same in the coming year. You would pay estimated taxes as follows:

---

[3]If your estimated tax liability (that is, the amount of tax you will have to pay) is less than $1,000, then you will not normally have to comply with the provisions discussed in this section. Further information and appropriate forms are contained in a "CT-2 Package" which should automatically be sent to your corporation after you submit your CT-411 form discussed in the previous subsection. To order this package, call Taxpayers Assistance at (800) 342-3536.

March 15	$2,500 (25% of the total due of $10,000 of estimated taxes)
June 15	$2,500 (33% of the balance of $7,500) (also file form CT-400)
September 15	$2,500 (33% of the $7,500 balance)
December 15	$2,500 (the remainder due)

Keep in mind that there are penalties if you deliberately underestimate the amount of your corporate taxes. Generally you will not have to worry about this if you pay at least as much estimated tax as your previous year's tax liability. However, if you know that your corporate income will be significantly greater, or if during the year, your business is ahead of the previous year, you should increase the amount of estimated tax you pay. If you underestimate your tax liability and pay too little during the year, you will be charged interest on the amount of the underpayment, whether or not it was deliberate. Additional penalties apply if the underestimation was deliberate.

3. Annual Corporate Franchise Tax Return

Regular business corporations must submit an annual *Corporate Franchise Tax Report* (Form CT-3).[4] This return is due on March 15 if your corporation has a calendar tax year or within 2-1/2 months of the end of your fiscal year. With this report, you must pay any portion of the taxes due for that year which were not previously paid. So, if you underestimated your tax liability on Form CT-400, you will have to pay the difference with this return, plus interest and possible penalties.

---

[4]If your tax liability is $1,000 or less, you can file a simplified CT-4 short-form instead.

New York S Corporation Note: New York S corporations (see Chapter 4A3) file form CT-3S, *S Corporation Information Report*, instead of the regular corporate franchise tax report mentioned above.

4. State Withholding Allowance Certificate

Although the corporation can use the information from the federal W-4 form to compute the amount of tax it should withhold from each employee's salary, an employee may want a different amount withheld from his or her state taxes. To do this, the employee must fill out form IT-2104 which is supplied by the employer. The use of this form is optional on the part of the employee. If it isn't used, the corporation should withhold personal income tax from the employee's wages based upon the information contained in federal form W-4.

5. Personal Income Tax Withholding

Every corporation which has salaried employees must file an Employer's Return of Tax Withholding (Form IT-2101). By law, each employer must withhold from an employee's salary a portion of his wages and pay this money periodically to the state. The intervals at which these payments to the state must be made depend on the amount of taxes withheld. They can range from quarterly to twice a month.

The amount withheld by the corporation from employee wages for the purposes of state personal income tax is based upon tax tables which take into account marital status, claimed allowances, and the wages of the employee.

Two things to remember: first, each time you file Form IT-2101 you must also send in the amount of taxes you have withheld for the period covered by the form; second (and this applies to most employment related taxes), no matter what your corporation's tax year is, the filing dates are based upon a calendar year.

The corporation must give each of its employees an Employee Wage and Tax Statement (Form IT-2102) on or before February 15 each year. This form shows the employee how much tax has been withheld from his or her wages during the past year. It is the equivalent of the federal W-2 form.

6. Annual Reconciliation Return

On or before February 28 of each year, the corporation must file an annual Reconciliation Return (Form IT-2103) with the State Tax Commission. This form requires that the corporation total up all taxes withheld from its employee's wages during the year (and sent in with Form IT-2101 discussed in Section 5).

7. Unemployment Insurance

Your corporation must register with the New York State Unemployment Insurance Office. This is entirely separate from your dealings with the Tax Commission. The forms required for your business can be obtained by writing to:

New York State Department of Labor
Unemployment Insurance Department
State Office Building Campus
Albany, NY 12240

There may be a local office where you can drop in and pick up the forms. Check the telephone directory.

Once you have registered with this office, you will receive an identification number which should be used on all further correspondence with this office.

Every three months (that is, quarterly), you will have to file an Employer's Report of Contributions (Form IA-5). The amount you will have to pay when you file this form is based upon a percentage of the wages your corporation pays to its employees. This is adjusted by an "experience rating" which is based upon the number of former employees of the corporation who have received unemployment insurance. Obviously, the larger this number is, the more you will pay.

A more complete explanation of your obligations and responsibilities as an employer is contained in the "Handbook for Employers" issued by the New York State Department of Labor.

8. Disability and Workers' Compensation

With some exceptions, all employees of a corporation, whether officers or otherwise, are required to be covered by Workers' Compensation Insurance. Rates vary depending on the salary level and risk associated with an employee's job. This insurance coverage can be obtained through private insurance carriers. In addition, there is a New York State Insurance Fund set up to provide this sort of coverage. Check with the local office of the Department of Labor for more details.

In addition, both employers and employees must contribute, in most cases, to the cost of disability benefits to cover disabilities arising in non-work related circumstances. The employer is entitled to collect the employee's portion through payroll deductions.

9. Sales Tax Forms

With few exceptions, each business which sells goods or services is required to collect sales tax on the amount of each sale made. The rate of sales tax changes periodically and varies with locality (due to local sales taxes). Therefore you should check to see what your local sales tax rate is.

Within 20 days of the date on which your corporation starts doing business, you must file a Certificate of Registration with the Tax Commission. This certificate can be picked up at a local office of the Tax Commission or from your tax advisor. Within five days after you submit this Certificate, the Tax Commission will send you a Certificate of Authority (and as many duplicates as you have business outlets). This gives you the authority to collect sales taxes. This Certificate of Authority must be prominently displayed at each business location.

For the purposes of sales tax reporting, the year begins on June 1 and ends on May 31. Depending on the amount of sales tax your corporation collects, you will have to file an annual report (Form ST-101), a monthly return (ST-809) or a weekly return (Form ST-100).

10. Local Taxes

Besides the state taxes that you are required to pay, there may be local taxes which apply to the operation of your business. Obviously, we are not able to cover all of these local taxes in this book, but you should be aware of them—they can add up to a significant amount of money and may have penalties associated with them for nonpayment. For example, New York City has its own franchise tax.

Your tax advisor should be able to inform you of local taxes for which your corporation may be liable.

Obviously this entire area of ongoing tax compliance is quite cumbersome, not to mention tricky, and requires specific expertise and experience in corporate taxation as well as in business tax reporting generally. Besides the calculations and record keeping involved, there are numerous deadlines which must constantly be kept in mind. Since missed deadlines or miscalculations can cost you time and money, it might be easier and more cost effective to retain a bookkeeper or accountant to take care of these matters (see Chapter 8B).

D. Licenses, Permits and Final Returns for Prior Business

MANY BUSINESSES, whether operating as corporations or not, are required to obtain state licenses or permits before commencing business. We've already discussed the need, in special situations, for obtaining state approval or consent before engaging in certain businesses as a corporation in Chapter 5, Step 2. Your corporation should obtain all proper licenses before commencing corporate operations. Even if you are incorporating an already licensed business, you must comply with any corporate license requirement in your field. Some businesses must obtain licenses in the name of the corporation, while others must obtain them in the name of supervisory corporate personnel. Make sure you comply with local licensing and permit requirements, as well, before beginning corporate operations.

Final Returns for Prior Business: If you have incorporated an existing business, make sure to file all papers needed to terminate the prior business. Among these will be a final Sales Tax Return and Business Income Tax Return.

E. Private Insurance Coverage

CORPORATIONS, LIKE OTHER BUSINESSES, should carry the usual kinds of insurance to prevent undue loss in the event of an accident, fire, theft, etc. Although the corporate form may insulate shareholders from personal loss, it won't prevent corporate assets from being jeopardized by such eventualities. Basic commercial coverage should be obtained and often includes coverage for autos, inventory, personal injuries on premises, etc. Additional coverage for product liability, directors' and officers' liability and other specialized types of insurance may also be appropriate (of course, these policies may be more difficult—more costly—for a closely-held corporation to obtain). Many smaller companies elect to have a large deductible to keep premium payments down. Obviously, there are a number of options to consider when putting together your corporate insurance package. The best advice we can offer here is to talk to a few experienced commercial insurance brokers and compare rates and areas and extent of coverage before deciding. Look for someone who suggests ways to get essential coverage for an amount you can live with—not someone who wants to sell you a policy that will protect you from all possible risks. In the first place, this type of policy really doesn't exist. Secondly, even if it did, you probably wouldn't want to pay the price.

LAWYERS AND ACCOUNTANTS

Chapter 7

LAWYERS AND ACCOUNTANTS

A. Lawyers

AS WE'VE MENTIONED PREVIOUSLY, we recommend that you arrange for a consultation with a lawyer to review the forms and organizational aspects of your incorporation before filing your Certificate of Incorporation. This consultation process is quite different than having him or her do all the work for you. Your lawyer should be answering specific, informed questions which you ask, and reviewing or customizing, not rewriting, the forms which you have prepared.

There are many reasons why it is impractical, not to mention unrealistic, to write a book on the complexities of incorporating without reference to the need for you to consult an attorney. Foremost among these is that the law is constantly changing. While we update this book at regular intervals, changes in the law will inevitably occur between printings. These changes may be critical to your individual situation. Also, the circumstances, desires, and requirements of your particular incorporation can, and inevitably will, be quite different from those of others. The Business Corporation Law provides you with a number of options and alternatives to meet your individual needs. A face-to-face visit with an attorney will allow you to discuss and choose any specialized provisions which your incorporation requires. Finally, even attorneys have documents which they have prepared reviewed by other attorneys—there is no reason why you should not take the same precautions.

Throughout this book, we have indicated areas and issues which you should, or may wish to, go over with an attorney. The following is a list of questions you may wish to discuss with a lawyer, with references to specific sections of the book. This list is fairly exhaustive and many incorporators will find only one or two questions that are of significance to them. A number of these questions can be referred to your accountant (see Section B, below) since they involve financial and tax issues.

- How should you capitalize your corporation? Chapter 2E

- Should you issue more than one class of stock? Should you issue stock with or without par value? Chapter 2G

- Do you need a shareholders agreement and, if so, what provisions should it contain? Chapter 3B4

- Do you need subscription agreements? Chapter 3C

- Is your stock issuance exempt from the intrastate prospectus requirements of the Martin Act? Chapter 3D2

- Is your corporation going to have to register as a securities dealer under the provisions of the Martin Act? Chapter 3D3

- Is your stock issuance exempt from the provisions of the Federal Securities Laws? Chapter 3E

- Should you elect S corporation tax status? Chapter 4C

- Is Section 1244 stock treatment important to you and, if so, will you be able to meet the initial and ongoing requirements? Chapter 4D

- Is your Certificate of Incorporation sufficient to meet your needs or will additional clauses be necessary? Chapter 5, Step 2

- Are state approvals or consents required before incorporating your business? If so, you will need to obtain these consents before incorporating and will need to use a specific purpose clause in your certificate. Chapter 5, Step 2.

- Do the Bylaws meet your requirements? Chapter 5, Step 7

- Are the resolutions contained in the First Meeting of the Board of Directors adequate in view of your requirements and have you selected the proper ones? Chapter 5, Step 9

- Do your stock certificates require special legends? Chapter 5, Step 9

- Have you properly considered the implications of joint ownership of stock? Chapter 5, Step 9

The following questions relate to additional issues involved when incorporating a pre-existing business:

- Will you be eligible for tax-free exchange treatment under IRC Section 351 or do you want your incorporation to be a taxable exchange? Chapter 4

- Will your corporation be adequately protected against claims or liabilities of the prior business? (various steps in Chapter 5)

- Is your Bill of Sale in order? Chapter 5, Step 9

- Have you complied with the provisions of the Bulk Sales Act? Chapter 5, Step 9A

- Have you prepared new leases, deeds, etc.? Chapter 5, Step 9

The next question is, "What type of lawyer should I consult?" The best lawyer to choose is someone whom you personally know and trust. The next best is someone whom a reliable friend recommends. You will want to find a lawyer who is familiar with corporate law and who maintains an active business law practice. It's a good idea to phone a lawyer first and give him or her an idea of the types of questions you will need answered and the type of service you will need performed (review of papers, drafting special documents, etc.). Be sure to get the hourly rate the lawyer charges set in advance.

Looking Up the Law Yourself: Many incorporators may wish to research legal information not covered in this book on their own. County law libraries are open to the public and are not difficult to use once you understand how the information is categorized and stored. They are an invaluable source of corporate and general business forms, corporate tax procedures and information, etc. Research librarians will usually go out of their way to help you find the right statute, form or background reading on any corporate or tax issue. If you are interested in doing self-help legal research, an excellent source of information on how to break the code of the law libraries is *Legal Research: How to Find and Understand the Law* by Elias (Nolo Press).

B. Accountants and Tax Advisors

AS YOU CAN SEE, organizing and operating a corporation involves a significant amount of financial and tax work, and many important decisions need to be made. Refer to the questions listed in Section A, above, which relate to the financial and tax aspects of your incorporation as well as other areas flagged throughout the book with respect to which you should, or may need to, consult an accountant or other tax advisor. For instance, you may need to talk with an accountant regarding:

- the best time to incorporate

- method of capitalization

- the capital allocation of the money or property received for no-par shares

- whether to elect federal (and state) S corporation tax status and the manner and timing of making these elections

- qualifying for Section 1244 stock treatment

- assistance with the Bill of Sale (including an inventory and appraisal of the prior business assets)

- qualifying for tax-free exchange treatment under IRS Section 351

- potential problems with personal holding company penalties

- establishing qualified fringe benefit packages

- selecting your corporate tax year and, if an S or personal service corporation, the manner and timing of electing a fiscal tax year if appropriate

- setting up double-entry corporate books, payroll system, etc.

Generally, although we tend to use the terms tax advisor and accountant interchangeably, you will probably wish to refer these initial incorporation considerations to an accountant with corporate experience. Don't forget, as mentioned in the introduction to Chapter 5, that you should consult an accountant about these questions before incorporating. Once all these initial questions have been answered, your corporation has been set up, and your books have been established, you may want to have routine tax filings and bookkeeping tasks performed by corporate personnel who have been trained in bookkeeping and tax matters (in many instances trained by the accountant you

are using). Of course, many corporations will turn most of the ongoing form preparation and filing work over to the accountant.

For future financial advice, you may wish to contact an officer in the corporate department of the bank where you keep your corporate account(s). Banks are an excellent source of financial advice, particularly if they will be corporate creditors—after all, they will have a stake in the success of your corporation. Further, the Small Business Administration can prove to be an ideal source of financial and tax information and resources (as well as financing in some cases).

Whatever arrangements you make for financial or tax advice and assistance, you may wish to order the IRS publications listed in the "For More Information" box in Chapter 6 to familiarize yourself with some of the tax and bookkeeping aspects of operating a corporation.[1]

When you select an accountant, bookkeeper, financial advisor, etc., the same considerations apply as when selecting a lawyer. Choose someone you know or whom a friend with business experience recommends. Be as specific as you can regarding the services you wish performed and find someone with experience in corporate taxation and with corporate and employee tax returns and requirements.

---

[1]Two excellent self-help sources, referred to earlier in this manual, are: *Nolo's Small Business Start-Up Plan* by McKeever and *Small Time Operator* by Kamaroff, available from Nolo Press.

Appendix

TEAR-OUT FORMS

Request for Name Availability Check

Application for Reservation of Corporate Name

Cover Letter to Department of State

Notice of Bulk Sale

List of Creditors

Schedule of Property

Notice If Debts Will Be Paid as They Come Due

Notice If Debts Are Not Going to Be Paid in Full

Bill of Sale for Assets of a Business

Receipt for Cash Payment

Form for Cancellation of Indebtedness

Bill of Sale for Items of Property

Receipt for Services Rendered

Certificate of Incorporation

Stock Registration Certificate Under Section 275-a Tax Law

Statement of Incorporators in Lieu of Organization Meeting

Bylaws

Minutes of First Meeting of the Board of Directors

Share Certificates

Stock Ledger sheet

te use:

NOLO PRESS - Self-Help Legal Books & Software

We would like to hear from you.

Please help us provide you with top quality self-help materials by filling out this card. To thank you for your trouble we will give you a FREE one year subscription to the Nolo News, our quarterly self-help legal newspaper which contains interesting articles and updates on a number of legal topics.

Name _____

Address _____

City _____ State _____ Zip _____

Your occupation _____

Did you incorporate using the book? ____ Yes, ____ No

If yes, was it easy for you to do?

(quite easy) 1   2   3   4   5   (very difficult)

Did you consult a lawyer? ____ Yes, ____ No

Did you find the information in the book helpful?

(extremely helpful) 1   2   3   4   5   (not at all)

Where did you hear about the book? _____

Have you used other Nolo books? ____ Yes, ____ No

Where did you buy the book? _____

Comments: _____

NY CORP

Application for Reservation of Corporate Name

Department of State
Division of Corporations
162 Washington Avenue
Albany, NY 12231

Division of Corporations:

The undersigned is applying for reservation of a corporate name for a period of 60 days pursuant to the provisions of Section 303 of the Business Corporation Law.

The application is made by the undersigned, _____
_____, whose address is _____
_____, _____ of
_____, County of _____, State of New York. It is made with the intention of forming a domestic corporation which will be engaged in the business of _____.

The name wished to be reserved is _____.
Enclosed please find a certified check, payable to the Department of State, in the amount of $20.00.

Very truly yours,

Cover Letter to Department of State

Department of State
Division of Corporations
162 Washington Avenue
Albany, NY 12231

RE: _____

Division of Corporations:

Enclosed please find the proposed Certificate of Incorporation of _____
_____
together with its backing sheet. Also enclosed is a certified check in the amount of
$_____ to cover payment of the following fees:

Filing of Certificate of Incorporation	$	100
Organization tax on _____ no par value authorized shares	$ _____	
Total	$ _____	

Please file the enclosed Certificate of Incorporation and return the receipt indicating filing of this document to the above address.

Very truly yours,

Notice of Bulk Sale

NOTICE IS HEREBY GIVEN, pursuant to Section 6-103 of the Uniform Commercial

Code, that all of the right, title and interest in the business, inventory, fixtures, goods,

supplies and merchandise of _____

with a former address at _____,

_____ have been sold, transferred,

delivered and assigned to _____

_____, a New York corporation with an address at

_____.

The effective date of the transfer shall be _____, 19___. The

_____ has agreed to assume

and pay all debts and liabilities of _____.

List of Creditors

The undersigned hereby swears and affirms that the following is a true and accurate list of his or her creditors, compiled in accordance with the requirements of Section 6-104 of the Uniform Commercial Code.

Name of Creditor	Business Address	Amount Owed
_____	_____	_____
_____	_____	_____
_____	_____	_____

Claims in Dispute

Name of Creditor	Business Address	Amount Claimed
_____	_____	_____
_____	_____	_____
_____	_____	_____

_____

Seller

State of New York   )
County of _____)

_____, being sworn, deposes and says: I am the person who signed the foregoing list of creditors pursuant to the requirements of Section 6-104 of the Uniform Commercial Code. The foregoing is a complete and accurate list of all of the creditors and claims against me, known to me to the best of my knowledge.

_____

Seller

Subscribed and sworn to before me this _____ day of _____, 19___.

_____

Notary Public

Schedule of Property

The following is a schedule of property to be transferred, sold, assigned and delivered by
_____, transferor,
to _____, on or after
_____:

Description   Quantity   Location

_____   _____   _____

_____   _____   _____

_____   _____   _____

_____   _____   _____

_____   _____   _____

_____   _____   _____

_____   _____   _____

_____   _____   _____

_____   _____   _____

The corporation agrees to retain this schedule at its principal place of business at
_____,
and make it available for inspection and/or reproduction by any creditor of the transferor
for a period of six months following the date of transfer of the above-mentioned property.

Dated:_____   _____
                                                       , Seller

Notice If Debts Will Be Paid as They Come Due

To _____:

A bulk transfer under Article 6 of the Uniform Commercial Code will be made on or after
_____, 19___. The transferor is _____,
with a current address of _____. For the past three years,
the transferor has had the following other business addresses and operated its business
under the following names:

All debts of the transferor will be paid in full as they fall due. Statements should be sent
to the purchaser, _____, at its
principal place of business at _____
_____.

Dated: _____   _____

                                _____
                                                    , President

Notice If Debts Are Not Going to Be Paid in Full

To _____:

A bulk transfer under Article 6 of the Uniform Commercial Code will be made on or after _____, 19___. The transferor is _____, with a business address at _____.
The transferee is _____, with a principal place of business at _____.

The transferor has used the following names and addresses in its business within the past three years:

The transferee is not going to pay all of the debts of the transferor in full.

The location of the property to be transferred is _____
_____.

A general description of the property which will be transferred is:

The estimated total of the debts of the transferor is $_____. The schedule of property being transferred and the list of the transferor's creditors can be inspected at _____.

The transfer of these assets is not to pay all existing debts of the transferor, but the following debts will be paid:

The transferor will be paid the sum of $_____ on _____, 19___.

Dated: _____   _____

                                 _____
                                                        , President

Bill of Sale for Assets of a Business

This is an agreement between _____
_____ herein called "transferor(s)," and _____
_____ a New York corporation, herein called "the corporation."

In return for the issuance of _____ shares of stock of the corporation, transferor(s) hereby sell(s), assign(s), and transfer(s) to the corporation all right, title, and interest in the following property:

All the tangible assets listed on the inventory attached to this Bill of Sale and all stock in trade, goodwill, leasehold interests, trade names, and other intangible assets except _____ of _____, located at _____.

In return for the transfer of the above property to it, the corporation hereby agrees to assume, pay, and discharge all debts, duties, and obligations that appear on the date of this agreement, on the books and owed on account of said business except _____ _____. The corporation agrees to indemnify and hold the transferor(s) of said business and their property free from any liability for any such debt, duty, or obligation and from any suits, actions, or legal proceedings brought to enforce or collect any such debt, duty, or obligation.

The transferor(s) hereby appoint(s) the corporation as representative to demand, receive, and collect for itself any and all debts and obligations now owing to said business and hereby assumed by the corporation. The transferor(s) further authorize(s) the corporation to do all things allowed by law to recover and collect any such debts and obligations and to use the transferor's(s') name(s) in such manner as it considers necessary for the collection and recovery of such debts and obligations, provided, however, without cost, expense, or damage to the transferor(s).

Dated:_____   _____
                                                            , Transferor

                              _____
                                                            , Transferor

                              _____
                                                            , Transferor

Dated:_____   _____
                              Name of Corporation

                              By: _____
                                                            , President

                              _____
                                                            , Treasurer

Receipt for Cash Payment

Receipt of $_____ from _____

representing payment in full for _____ shares of the stock of

this corporation is hereby acknowledged.

Dated: _____

    Name of Corporation: _____

        By: _____
                  , Treasurer

Form for Cancellation of Indebtedness

The receipt of _____ shares of this corporation to

_____ for the cancellation

by_____ of a current loan

outstanding to this corporation, dated _____, with a remaining

unpaid principal amount and unpaid accrued interest, if any, totalling

$_____ is hereby acknowledged.

Dated: _____   _____

Bill of Sale for Items of Property

In consideration of the issuance of _____ shares of stock in and by

_____, _____

hereby sells, assigns, conveys, transfers, and delivers to the corporation all right, title and

interest in and to the following property:

Dated:_____   _____

                                                                                    , Transferor

Receipt for Services Rendered

In consideration of the performance of the following services actually rendered to, or

labor done for, _____,

_____,

the provider of such services or labor done, hereby acknowledges the receipt of

_____ shares of stock in _____ as

payment in full for these services:

Dated:_____   _____

Certificate of Incorporation

of

_____

UNDER SECTION 402 OF THE BUSINESS CORPORATION LAW

The undersigned, in order to form and organize a corporation under Section 402 of the Business Corporation Law of the State of New York, hereby certify that:

1. The name of such corporation shall be _____
_____.

2. The purposes of this corporation shall be to engage in any lawful act or activity for which corporations may be organized under the Business Corporation Law. The corporation is not formed to engage in any act or activity requiring the consent or approval of any state official, department, board, agency or other body without such consent or approval first being obtained.

3. A director of the corporation shall not be liable to the corporation or its shareholders for damages for any breach of duty in such capacity except for:

(a) liability if a judgment or other final adjudication adverse to a director establishes that his or her acts or omissions were in bad faith or involved intentional misconduct or a knowing violation of law or that the director personally gained in fact a financial profit or other advantage to which he or she was not legally entitled or that the director's acts violated BCL Section 719, or

(b) liability for any act or omission prior to the adoption of this provision.

4. The aggregate number of shares which the corporation shall have the authority to issue is _____ shares, all of which are to be common shares without par value.

5. The office of the corporation is to be located in _____ County, State of New York.

6. The Secretary of State of the State of New York is hereby designated as agent of the corporation upon whom process against it may be served. The post office address to which the Secretary of State shall mail a copy of any process against the corporation served upon him is:

_____

_____

_____

The undersigned incorporator, or each of them if there are more than one, is of the age of eighteen years or over.

IN WITNESS WHEREOF, this certificate has been subscribed this _____ day of _____, 19_____, by the undersigned who affirm(s) that the statements made herein are true under the penalties of perjury.

_____   _____
Type name of incorporator   Signature

_____
                    Address

_____   _____
Type name of incorporator   Signature

_____
                    Address

_____   _____
Type name of incorporator   Signature

_____
                    Address

Certificate of Incorporation

of

_____

Filed by

_____

_____

_____

Stock Registration Certificate
Under Section 275-a Tax Law

Number of shares authorized: Common Stock: _____ shares

I, _____ the President of _____
_____ , do hereby certify that this corporation keeps a
place for the sale, transfer, or delivery of its stock at _____
_____ , in the _____
of _____, County of _____, State of New York.

I further certify that this corporation was incorporated on the _____of
_____, 19___, pursuant to the laws of the State of New York.

Date:_____   _____
                                                    , President

County of _____)
) ss
State of New York   )

On this _____ day of _____ , 19___, before me personally came
_____ to me known, and who being by me duly sworn, did
depose and say that s/he is the President of the corporation above named and that s/he
executed the foregoing certificate on behalf of the above corporation pursuant to authority
vested in him/her by a vote of the board of directors of said corporation.

                                        _____
                                                                    , Notary Public

Statement of Incorporators in Lieu of Organization Meeting

The undersigned, being all the incorporators of _____
_____, do hereby certify as follows:

1. The Certificate of Incorporation of this corporation was duly filed in the office of the Department of State of the State of New York on the _____ day of
_____, 19___. A copy of the Certificate of Incorporation and the filing receipt received from the Department of State are both attached to this Statement and are to be inserted in the Minutes of the corporation.

2. The undersigned have adopted the attached Bylaws as the Bylaws of this corporation. The Bylaws shall be inserted in the official records of the corporation.

3. The following are elected to be directors of the corporation, to serve until the first annual meeting of the shareholders of this corporation.

_____
, Director

_____
, Director

_____
, Director

The directors assumed their offices.

Dated:_____   _____
, Incorporator

_____
, Incorporator

_____
, Incorporator

Bylaws

of

_____

ARTICLE I
OFFICES

SECTION 1. NAME

The legal name of the corporation (hereinafter referred to as the corporation) is
_____.

SECTION 2. PRINCIPAL OFFICE

The principal office of the corporation shall be located at _____
_____,
County of _____, New York.

The corporation may change the location of its principal office, or designate other offices within or without the state, as the business of the corporation may require, or as the board of directors may, from time to time, determine to be desirable.

ARTICLE II
SHAREHOLDERS' MEETING

SECTION 1. PLACE OF MEETING

All meetings of the shareholders shall be held at the principal office of the corporation, or at such other place as may be determined by the board of directors, as stated in the notice of meeting.

SECTION 2. ANNUAL MEETING

The annual meeting of the shareholders shall be held on the _____
of _____ of each year, at _____ __.M. If such day shall fall on a holiday, then the meeting shall be held on the following business day at the same hour.

a. Purpose. The annual meeting shall be held for the purpose of electing the board of directors, and the transaction of any other proper business.

b. Notice. The secretary of the corporation, either personally or by mail, shall give each shareholder entitled to vote at such meeting written notice stating the place, date and hour of the meeting. Such notice shall be given not less than ten (10) nor more than fifty (50) days before the date of the meeting. If such notice is mailed, it shall be sent pre-paid by first class mail addressed to the shareholder at his or her address as it appears on the official records of the corporation, unless the shareholder has previously notified the secretary, in writing, that notices should be mailed to him or her at another address, in which case the notice shall be mailed to that address. Notice of any annual meeting may be waived by the submission by a shareholder or shareholders entitled to vote at such meeting of a signed waiver either before or after the meeting, or by attendance at the meeting.

SECTION 3. SPECIAL MEETINGS

Special meetings of the shareholders may be called by the board of directors, or the president of the corporation, and must be called by the president upon the written request of the holders of _____ of the outstanding shares entitled to vote at such a meeting.

Written notice of such meetings must be given to each shareholder of record by the secretary not less than ten (10) nor more than fifty (50) days before the date set for such special meeting. The notice shall be given in the same manner as the notice of the annual meeting. Such notice shall state the place where the meeting will be held, the date and hour of the meeting, the purpose or purposes for which it is being called, and the name or names of the person or persons who have called the meeting. No business other than that specified in the notice shall be transacted at the meeting. If, at this meeting or at an annual meeting of the shareholders, action is proposed to be taken which, if taken, will entitle shareholders fulfilling the requirements of Section 623 of the Business Corporations Law to receive payment for their shares, the notice of meeting shall include a statement of this purpose and shall be accompanied by a copy of Section 623. Notice of any special meeting may be waived by the submission by a shareholder or shareholders entitled to vote at such meeting of a signed waiver either before or after the meeting, or by attendance at the meeting.

SECTION 4. QUORUM AND SHAREHOLDER ACTION

The presence of the holders of a majority of the outstanding shares entitled to vote, either in person or by proxy, shall constitute a quorum for the transaction of any business at all meetings of the shareholders. If a quorum is present, the affirmative vote of a majority of shares, represented at the meeting and entitled to vote, shall be the act of the shareholders unless the vote of a greater number is required by the Business Corporation Law, the Certificate of Incorporation, or these Bylaws. Notwithstanding the above provisions of this section, if a special meeting for the election of directors is called pursuant to Section 603 of the Business Corporation Law, a majority of the shareholders in attendance, regardless of whether they are sufficient to be deemed a quorum, shall be sufficient for the purposes of electing directors only.

The shareholders present at a duly called or held meeting at which a quorum is initially present may continue to transact business until adjournment notwithstanding the withdrawal of enough shareholders to leave less than a quorum, if any action is approved by at least a majority of the shares required to constitute a quorum. If less than a quorum of shareholders entitled to vote is present, those shareholders present may vote to adjourn the meeting to some future time. At such adjourned meeting, any business which may have been transacted at the meeting, as originally called, may be transacted. The secretary shall send notice of the date, place and time of the adjourned meeting to all shareholders entitled to vote who were absent from the original meeting at least three (3) days before the date of the adjourned meeting.

SECTION 5. RECORD DATE

The directors may fix a date as the record date for determining the shareholders entitled to notice of, or to vote at, any meeting of shareholders, or to approve or disapprove any corporate action without a meeting, or for purposes of determining shareholders entitled to receive payment of any dividend, or the allotment of any rights with respect to any change, conversion, or exchange of stock, or for the purpose of any other lawful action. Such date shall not be less than ten (10) nor more than fifty (50) days before the date of any such meeting, nor more than fifty (50) days prior to any other action.

If no record date is fixed:

a. the record date for determination of shareholders entitled to notice of, or to vote at, a meeting of shareholders shall be at the close of business on the day next preceding the day on which notice is given or, if no notice is given, the day on which the meeting is held;

b. the record date for determining shareholders for any purpose other than that described in (a) above shall be the close of business on the day on which the resolution of the board of directors to determine shareholders is adopted.

SECTION 6. VOTING AND VOTING AGREEMENTS

Every shareholder entitled to vote at a meeting may vote at such meeting either in person or by proxy. Each shareholder entitled to vote shall be entitled to one vote for each share held, as determined by the official records of the corporation.

Any number of shareholders may enter into a written agreement which states that in exercising any voting rights, the shares held by them shall be voted as therein provided or shall be voted in accordance with procedures agreed upon by them.

SECTION 7. PROXIES

Every shareholder may authorize another person or persons to act for him or her by proxy in all matters in which a shareholder is entitled to participate. Every proxy must be signed by the shareholder or his or her attorney-in-fact. No proxy shall be valid after the expiration of eleven (11) months unless otherwise provided in the proxy. Every proxy shall be revocable at the pleasure of the shareholder executing it except as otherwise provided in Section 609 of the Business Corporation Law.

SECTION 8. CONSENT TO ACTION WITHOUT MEETING

Any action which may be taken at any annual or special meeting of the shareholders may be taken without a meeting and vote upon written consent, setting forth the action taken, and signed by the holders of all outstanding shares entitled to vote on such action.

SECTION 9. LIST OF SHAREHOLDERS

The secretary shall prepare and certify, at least _____ days before every meeting of shareholders, a complete list of the shareholders as of the record date for the meeting, arranged in alphabetical order, and indicating the address of each shareholder. The list shall be brought to each meeting of shareholders and kept there during the entire meeting, or any adjournment thereof. It may be inspected by any shareholder present at the meeting, either in person or by proxy.

SECTION 10. INSPECTORS OF ELECTION

The board of directors, in advance of any meeting of shareholders, may appoint one or more inspectors of election to act at the meeting or any adjournment thereof. The inspectors shall determine the number of shares outstanding, the number of shares represented at the meeting, the existence of a quorum, the validity of all proxies, shall receive all votes, and do all other acts which are proper to conduct the election or vote.

ARTICLE III
DIRECTORS

SECTION 1. NUMBER, QUALIFICATION, TERM AND MANNER OF ELECTION

The authorized number of directors shall be _____. A director shall not be less than eighteen (18) years of age when elected. The corporation shall have at least three (3) directors, except, however, if the shares of the corporation are held by less than three (3) shareholders, the number of directors shall be at least equal to the number of shareholders. No director is required to be a shareholder of the corporation.

At each annual meeting of the shareholders, the directors shall be elected by a plurality vote except as otherwise prescribed by law. The term of each director shall be from the date he or she is elected and qualified and shall end on the date his or her successor is elected and qualified at the next annual meeting of the shareholders.

SECTION 2. DUTIES AND POWERS OF THE BOARD OF DIRECTORS

All business of the corporation shall be managed by the board of directors. The directors shall in all cases act as a board, regularly convened. The directors may adopt such rules and regulations for the conduct of their meeting and the management of the corporation as they may deem proper, provided that they do not act in a manner inconsistent with the laws of New York, the Certificate of Incorporation of the corporation, or these Bylaws.

SECTION 3. MEETINGS

Regular meetings of the board may be held within or without the State of New York at such times and places as the board of directors may from time to time determine. The board shall hold a regular meeting each year for the purpose of the election of officers, if appropriate, and the transaction of any other business immediately after the adjournment of the annual meeting of shareholders.

Special meetings of the board may be called by the president of the corporation or the chairperson of the board of directors at any time, or upon the written consent of _____ of the directors. Such special meetings must be held within _____ days after receipt of such request or such notice by the president or chairperson of the board.

SECTION 4. NOTICE OF MEETINGS

No notice of a regular meeting of the board shall be required. If notice of a regular meeting of the board is not given, such meetings shall take place at the principal office of the corporation. Written notice of a special meeting of the board must be delivered to each director, either personally or by mail to his or her last known address not less than _____ days before the date of the meeting. It shall specify the time and place of the meeting and the business to be transacted. Notice of a special meeting need not be given to any director who submits a signed waiver before or after the meeting or who attends the meeting without protesting the lack of notice to him or her at any time before the meeting commences.

SECTION 5. QUORUM AND BOARD ACTION

A majority of the entire board shall constitute a quorum for the transaction of business. In the event a quorum is not present, a lesser number may adjourn the meeting to some future time.

In the transaction of business, except as otherwise provided under the laws of New York, the Certificate of Incorporation, or these Bylaws, the affirmative vote of a majority of the directors present at a meeting shall be considered the act of the board, provided however, that a quorum is present. A meeting at which a quorum is initially present may continue to transact business notwithstanding the withdrawal of directors, if any action taken is approved by at least a majority of the directors required to constitute a quorum.

SECTION 6. VOTING

Each director shall be entitled to one vote, regardless of the number of shares of the corporation such director may hold.

SECTION 7. COMPENSATION

Each director shall be entitled to receive a reasonable fee for each meeting attended. The amount of such fee shall be fixed by the board of directors.

SECTION 8. VACANCIES AND REMOVAL OF DIRECTORS; RESIGNATION

Any vacancy occurring in the board, for any reason, shall be filled within _____ days, or at the next regularly scheduled meeting of the board, whichever occurs first. A majority of the remaining directors shall elect the person to fill the vacancy. The director so chosen shall hold office for the remainder of the term of his or her predecessor and until his or her successor has been elected and qualified.

Any director may be removed, with or without cause, by the vote of the holders of a majority of shares present and entitled to vote on removal at any special meeting of shareholders called for that purpose at which a quorum is present.

Any director may resign his or her office at any time. Such resignation shall be in writing and shall be effective upon its receipt by the secretary of the corporation.

SECTION 9. COMMITTEES

A majority of the entire board of directors may designate, from its members, an executive or other committee as deemed necessary by the board. Each committee shall consist of no less than three (3) members, all of whom shall be directors of the corporation. Each committee shall fix its own rules and procedures, but in every case a majority of its members shall be necessary to constitute a quorum. The affirmative vote of a majority of the members present at a meeting at which a quorum is present shall be necessary to adopt any resolution. All actions undertaken by any committee shall be reported to the board of directors at the next meeting of the board, and shall be subject to revision or alteration by the board. Each committee shall serve at the pleasure of the board of directors. The members of each committee shall receive such compensation for their services as the board of directors may, from time to time, determine and fix.

The executive committee shall have the power and authority of the board of directors in the management of the corporation to the extent provided in the resolution establishing the executive committee and to the extent such power and authority may be delegated under the laws of New York.

ARTICLE IV
OFFICERS

SECTION 1. OFFICERS AND QUALIFICATIONS

The officers of the corporation shall be a president, one or more vice-presidents, a secretary, and a treasurer, and such other officers as determined by the board of directors. Except for the offices of president and secretary, any two or more offices may be held by the same person. Where only one person holds all the shares of the corporation, he or she may be both president and secretary.

SECTION 2. ELECTION AND TERM OF OFFICE

All officers of the corporation shall be elected _____ at a regular meeting held by the board of directors immediately following the annual meeting of the shareholders. All officers shall hold office from the date they are elected until the next regular meeting of the board at which their successors are elected and have been qualified, or until they have been removed or have resigned pursuant to these Bylaws.

SECTION 3. REMOVAL AND RESIGNATION OF OFFICERS

Any officer may be removed, either with or without cause, by the vote of a majority of the board of directors, or by the vote of the holders of a majority of shares present and entitled to vote on such removal at any annual or special meeting of the shareholders at which a quorum is present.

Any officer may resign at any time upon written notice to the corporation given to the chairperson of the board, the president, or the secretary of the corporation. Any such resignation shall take effect on the day of receipt of such notice or at any other time specified herein.

The provisions of this section are subject to the terms of any duly authorized written employment contract entered into by the corporation and any officer of the corporation.

SECTION 4. DUTIES OF OFFICERS

The duties and powers of the officers of the corporation shall be as follows, or as hereafter determined by resolution of the board of directors:

a. President. The president shall preside at all meetings of the board of directors and all meetings of the shareholders; shall present at each annual meeting of the shareholders and directors a report on the condition of the corporation's business; shall call regular and special meetings of the shareholders and directors as required by these Bylaws or the laws of New York; shall appoint, discharge, and determine the compensation of all employees and agents of the corporation, other than the elected officers, subject to the approval of the board of directors; shall sign and execute all contracts in the name of the corporation, and all notes, drafts and other orders for the payment of money; shall sign all certificates representing shares of the corporation; shall cause all books, reports, statements, and certificates to be properly kept and filed as required by law; shall enforce these Bylaws and perform all the duties which are incident to his or her office and as required by law; and shall supervise and control the business and affairs of the corporation.

b. Vice-President. If the president is incapacitated, absent, or otherwise unable to perform his or her duties or exercise his or her powers as set forth in these Bylaws, then the vice-president shall perform and exercise the same. When so acting, the vice-president shall have all of the powers, and be subject to all of the responsibilities, given to or imposed upon the president. In the event there are two or more vice-presidents, the one senior in order of election shall exercise these powers.

c. Secretary. The secretary shall keep minutes of meetings of the directors and the shareholders in appropriate books; shall give and serve all notices of the corporation as required by these Bylaws or by the laws of New York; shall sign all certificates representing shares of the corporation; shall present to the board of directors at its meetings all communications addressed to him or her officially by the president, or any officer or shareholder of the corporation; and shall perform all duties incident to the office of secretary.

In addition, the secretary shall keep the stock ledger and transfer books of the corporation at the principal office of the corporation, which books shall show the names, alphabetically arranged, of all the shareholders of the corporation, their places of residence, their mailing addresses, the number and class of shares held by each, and the date such shares were acquired. All such books shall be subject to the inspection of any shareholder, or any other person authorized by law to inspect such books.

In addition, the secretary shall have custody of the seal of the corporation. At such times as he or she is directed by the board of directors, or when a document has been signed by the president or vice-president pursuant to their authority under these Bylaws, the secretary shall affix the seal of the corporation to such document and attest to the same with his or her signature.

d. Treasurer. The treasurer shall have the care and custody of, and be responsible for, all the funds and securities of the corporation, and deposit all such funds in the name of the corporation in such banks, trust companies, of safe deposit vaults as the board of directors may designate; shall sign, make and endorse in the name of the corporation all checks, drafts, warrants, and other orders for the payment of money, and pay out and dispose of same as directed by the president or the board of directors; shall keep accurate books of account of the business and transactions of the corporation and exhibit them to any director of the corporation upon request during normal business hours of the corporation; shall render a full report on the financial condition of the corporation at each regular meeting of the board of directors, and at such other times as may be required by him or her; shall give a full report on the financial condition of the corporation at the annual meeting of shareholders; and shall perform all other duties incident to the office.

The treasurer shall give to the corporation a bond as security for the faithful discharge of his or her duties if requested to do so by the board of directors, in the amount designated by the board of directors.

SECTION 5. VACANCIES

All vacancies in any office shall be filled within _____ days by the board of directors, either at their regular meeting, or at a special meeting called for that purpose.

ARTICLE V
SEAL

SECTION 1. SEAL

The seal of the corporation shall be as follows:

ARTICLE VI
SHARE CERTIFICATES

SECTION 1. DESCRIPTION OF CERTIFICATES

The shares of the corporation shall be represented by certificates signed by the president or, in his or her absence, the vice-president, and by the secretary, and be sealed with the seal of the corporation or a facsimile thereof, and shall not be valid until so signed and sealed. Each certificate shall be in a form consistent with the laws of the State of New York, the Certificate of Incorporation, and these Bylaws, and shall contain the statement prescribed by Section 508, or where applicable, Sections 506, 616, 620, 709 and 1002 of the Business Corporation Law. The certificates shall be numbered consecutively and in the order in which they are issued. The stock certificates shall be bound in a book until issued. Said book shall contain a page or a stub on which shall be entered the name of the person who owns the shares, together with the number, class or series of shares owned and the date they were acquired. Each certificate shall state upon its face that the corporation has been formed under the laws of New York, the name of the person or persons to whom it has been issued, and the number and class of shares, and the designation of the series, if any, which such certificate represents.

SECTION 2. TRANSFER OF SHARES

The shares of the corporation shall be assignable and transferable on the books of the corporation only by the registered owner or his or her legal representative, and only upon surrender of the certificate endorsed with evidence of authority to transfer. No new certificate shall be issued until the former certificate has been cancelled.

SECTION 3. RETURNED CERTIFICATES

All certificates returned to the corporation for transfer shall be marked "cancelled" by the secretary, and marked with the date of cancellation. The transaction shall be recorded in the certificate book of the corporation.

ARTICLE VII
DIVIDENDS

SECTION 1. DECLARATION AND PAYMENT OF DIVIDENDS

The board of directors shall vote to declare dividends payable out of the surplus profits of the corporation whenever, in their opinion, the conditions of the corporation's finances render it appropriate to do so. The amount of any dividend, and the time and manner of payment shall be determined by the board of directors. Such dividend may be paid in cash, property or shares of the corporation. No dividend shall be declared or paid when the corporation is insolvent or if the payment of such dividend would render the corporation insolvent, or if the declaration or payment of the dividend is in violation of any provision of the laws of the State of New York.

ARTICLE VIII
TAX YEAR

SECTION 1. DATE

The tax year of the corporation shall end on _____ of each year, and begin on the next succeeding day, or shall be for such other period of time as the board of directors may from time to time designate with the consent of the Department of Taxation and Finance of New York and the Internal Revenue Service, if such consent is required.

ARTICLE IX
BILLS, NOTES, ETC.

SECTION 1. EXECUTION

All bills payable, notes, checks or other negotiable instruments of the corporation shall be made in the name of the corporation and shall be signed by those officers directed to do so by the board of directors. No officer or agent of the corporation shall, either singly or jointly with others, have the power to make any bill payable, note, check, draft or warrant or other negotiable instrument, or endorse the same in the name of the corporation, or contract, or cause to be contracted, any debt or liability in the name of or on behalf of the corporation except as may be authorized by the board of directors, or by these Bylaws.

ARTICLE X
INDEMNIFICATION

SECTION 1. INDEMNIFICATION RIGHTS

The indemnification and advancement of expenses granted pursuant to, or provided by, the Business Corporation Law shall not be deemed exclusive of any other rights to which a director or officer seeking indemnification or advancement of expenses may be entitled. The corporation is authorized to provide for indemnification and advancement of expenses of directors and officers of the corporation by (i) a resolution of shareholders, (ii) a resolution of directors, or (iii) an agreement providing for such indemnification, pursuant to, and in accordance with, the provisions of Section 721 of the Business Corporation Law.

ARTICLE XI
AMENDMENTS

SECTION 1. MANNER OF AMENDMENT

These Bylaws may be altered, amended, repealed or added to at the annual meeting of shareholders or at a special meeting called for that purpose by the affirmative vote of the holders of a majority of all of the outstanding shares of the corporation, provided that a written notice shall have been sent to each shareholder at his or her last known mailing address no less than ten (10) days prior to the date of the annual or special meeting at which such changes are proposed to be made. Such notice shall state the alterations, amendments, changes, or additions proposed to be made. Only such changes may be made as have been specified in the notice. The shareholders may, if they choose, vote to permit a majority of the directors to take this action as well.

CERTIFICATION

This is to certify that the foregoing is a true and correct copy of the Bylaws of
_____,
and that such Bylaws were duly adopted by the incorporators of the corporation
pursuant to a Statement of the Incorporators in Lieu of Organization Meeting dated the
_____ day of _____, 19___.

Dated: _____   _____

                                                                              , Secretary

Waiver of Notice of Directors' Meeting

The undersigned, being all of the directors of _____

_____,

a New York corporation, do hereby waive, pursuant to Section 711 of the Business

Corporation Law, notice of the time, place and purposes of the first meeting of directors

of said corporation, and do hereby consent that the meeting be held at

_____,

_____, County of _____, State of

New York, at _____ ___.M. and do further consent to the transaction thereat of

any and all business that may properly come before the meeting.

Dated: _____   _____

                                 _____

                                 _____

Minutes of the Meeting of the Board of Directors

of

_____

The board of directors of _____
held its first meeting on _____, 19___, at _____ ___.M.,
at _____,
_____, _____ County, New
York.

The following directors, constituting a quorum of the full board of directors , were present at the meeting:

_____

_____

_____

_____

The following directors were absent:

_____

_____

_____

_____

The meeting was called to order and _____
was designated to act as temporary chairperson and _____
as temporary secretary.

The chairperson stated that the purpose of the meeting was to take all steps necessary to complete the organization of the corporation and to enable it to commence business.

The chairperson announced that the meeting was being held pursuant to written waiver of notice signed by each of the directors. Upon motion duly made and seconded and unanimously approved, the waivers were made part of the minutes of this meeting.

The first order of business was the election of officers of the corporation. By unanimous vote, the following were elected to serve as officers for a period of _____ year(s) and until their successors are elected and qualify:

Name:

President _____

Vice-President _____

Secretary _____

Treasurer _____

The president and secretary assumed their offices in the places of those who had temporarily acted as chairperson and secretary, respectively, for this meeting.

The Statement of the Incorporators in Lieu of Organization Meeting, dated _____, 19___, was read and it was unanimously

RESOLVED, that the actions and business transacted by the incorporators in the Statement of the Incorporators in Lieu of Organization Meeting dated _____, 19___, be, and hereby are, ratified and adopted by this board.

Corporate Seal

The board next considered the adoption of a proposed form of seal for the corporation. Upon motion duly made, seconded and unanimously approved, it was

RESOLVED, that the form of the corporate seal presented to this meeting be, and hereby is, adopted as the seal of this corporation, and the secretary of the corporation is directed to place an impression thereof in the space provided.

Stock Certificates

The board next considered the adoption of a proposed form of certificate representing shares of stock in the corporation. Upon motion duly made, seconded, and unanimously approved, it was

RESOLVED, that the form of certificate presented to this meeting be, and hereby is, adopted for use by the corporation, and the secretary is directed to attach a copy thereof to the minutes of this meeting.

Registration of Stock

The board next considered authorizing the president of the corporation to execute and deliver to the State Tax Commission a Stock Registration Certificate under Section 275-a of the New York Tax Law. Upon motion duly made, seconded, and unanimously approved, it was

RESOLVED, that the president shall execute and cause to be delivered to the State Tax Commission a Stock Registration Certificate pursuant to Section 275-a of the New York Tax Law and shall attach a copy thereof to the minutes of this meeting.

Accounting Period

The board next considered the question of the accounting period of the corporation. After discussion, a motion was made, seconded, and unanimously approved, and it was

RESOLVED, that the accounting period of this corporation shall end on

_____ of each year and shall begin on the next succeeding day.

Principal Office

The board next considered the question of the address of the principal office of the corporation. After discussion, a motion was made, seconded and unanimously approved, and it was

RESOLVED, that the principal office of this corporation shall be at

_____ ,

_____ , _____ County, New York.

Bank Account

The board next considered the question of opening a corporate bank account. After discussion, a motion was made, seconded, and unanimously approved, and it was

RESOLVED, that the funds of this corporation be deposited with

_____ bank, at its

branch located at _____, and it was further

RESOLVED, that the president and secretary shall execute the banking resolution attached to these minutes, and it was further

RESOLVED, that any officer of this corporation be, and hereby is, authorized to endorse checks, drafts, or other evidences of indebtedness made payable to this corporation, but only for the purpose of depositing same in the above bank, and it was further

RESOLVED, that all drafts, checks, and other instruments obligating this corporation to pay money be signed on behalf of the corporation by any _____ of the following:

_____

_____

_____

Payment and Deduction of Expenses

The board next considered the question of paying the expenses incurred in the formation of this corporation. A motion was made, seconded and unanimously approved, and it was

RESOLVED, that the president and the treasurer of this corporation are authorized and empowered to pay all of the expenses incurred in the incorporation and organization of this corporation, including, among others, filing, licensing, attorney's and accountant's fees, and it was further,

RESOLVED, that the corporation elect to deduct on its first federal income tax return the foregoing expenses ratably over a sixty-month period, starting in the month the corporation begins its business, pursuant to Section 248 of the Internal Revenue Code of 1986, as amended.

Issuance of Stock

The board next took up the matter of the sale and issuance of stock to provide capital for the corporation. The Certificate of Incorporation authorizes the issuance of _____ shares of stock with no par value.

Allocation to Surplus Resolution

The board discussed the question of allocating the consideration to be received for each no par value share between stated capital and surplus as permitted by Section 506 of the Business Corporation Law. Upon prior advice and recommendation by the corporation's accountant, and upon motion duly made, seconded and unanimously approved, it was

RESOLVED, that the amount of consideration received by the corporation for each no par value share which is to be allocated to surplus shall be $_____.

Issuance for Cash

The secretary presented to the board the following proposal:

That the following persons have offered to purchase the number of shares of stock listed opposite their names set forth below for the sums of money set forth opposite their names.

A motion was made, seconded, and unanimously approved, and it was

RESOLVED, that this corporation shall sell and issue to the persons listed below the shares of stock listed opposite their names for the sums of money listed opposite their names

Name of Purchaser	Number of Shares	Dollar Amount

and it was further,

RESOLVED, that the president and secretary execute and deliver to each of the purchasers certificates stating the amount of shares purchased by each, and take all other action they deem necessary and appropriate to effectuate the sale and issuance of the certificates after receipt by the corporation of all money to be paid for said shares.

Issuance for Cancellation of Indebtedness

The secretary presented to the board the following proposal:

That the following persons have offered to cancel the indebtedness owed to them by this corporation in return for the issuance of the number of the shares of stock listed opposite their names set forth below.

A motion was made, seconded, and unanimously approved, and it was

RESOLVED, that this corporation shall issue to the persons listed below the shares of stock listed opposite their names in consideration for the cancellation of indebtedness as indicated:

Name of Purchaser	Number of Shares	Dollar Amount Owed and Description of Indebtedness (principal and accrued interest)

and it was further

RESOLVED, that the president and the secretary execute and deliver to each of the above named persons certificates stating the amount of shares issued to each and take all other action they deem necessary to effectuate the issuance of the certificates after receipt by the corporation of evidence of the cancellation of the indebtedness.

Issuance for Property Actually Received

The secretary presented the following proposal for consideration by the board:

That the following persons have offered to sell to this corporation all of their right, title and interest in and to the following property in return for the issuance of the following number of shares of the corporation:

Name of Offerer	Number of Shares	Description and Dollar Value of Property Offered

A motion was made, seconded, and unanimously approved, and it was

RESOLVED, that it is the judgment of the board of directors of this corporation that the value of the property offered equals the value indicated above, and that this corporation should accept the offer, and it was further

RESOLVED, that the president and secretary execute and deliver to each person a certificate representing the number of shares of this corporation listed opposite the name of each person above, and take all other action they deem necessary and appropriate to effectuate the sale and issuance of the stock after the receipt from each of the persons of the property and of all documents necessary for the transfer of the property to this corporation.

Issuance for Services Actually Rendered

The secretary presented the following proposal to the board:

Services have been previously rendered to this corporation by the following persons, which services are set forth in his or her bill to the corporation in the amounts set forth opposite each. Each of these persons has expressed his or her willingness to accept the number of shares of stock in the corporation opposite his or her name in full satisfaction of such bills:

Name of Person	Number of Shares	Dollar Amount and Description of Bill

A motion was made, seconded, and unanimously approved, and it was

RESOLVED, that in the judgment of the board of directors, such services are reasonably worth the amount set forth in the bill presented by each, and it was further,

RESOLVED, that the president and secretary of the corporation execute and deliver to each named person a certificate representing the number of shares of stock listed opposite their names above, and take all other action they deem necessary and appropriate to effectuate the sale and issuance of the stock after the bill is marked "Paid in Full" by each named person.

Issuance for Assets of a Business

The secretary next presented the following proposal to the board:

The following persons have offered to transfer to this corporation the assets of a business, described below, in return for the number of shares listed opposite each of their names:

Name of Offerer	Number of Shares	Description and Dollar Value of Assets

A motion was made, seconded, and approved, and it was

RESOLVED, that it is the judgment of the board of directors of this corporation that the value of the assets offered is the same as indicated above, and it was further

RESOLVED, that the president and secretary of the corporation be authorized to accept said offer on behalf of this corporation, and it was further

RESOLVED, that the president and secretary execute and deliver to each offerer a certificate representing the number of shares of stock listed opposite each of their names above, and take all other action they deem necessary and appropriate to effectuate the sale and issuance of the stock after receipt from each of the offerers of all documents necessary for the transfer of the offered property to this corporation after ascertaining that the requirements of the Bulk Sales Act have been fulfilled.

Federal S Corporation Tax Treatment

The board of directors next considered the advantages of electing to be taxed under the provisions of Subchapter S of the Internal Revenue Code of 1986, as amended. After discussion, upon motion duly made and seconded, it was unanimously

RESOLVED, that this corporation hereby elects to be treated as a Small Business Corporation for federal income tax purposes under Subchapter S of the Internal Revenue Code of 1986, as amended.

RESOLVED FURTHER, that the officers of this corporation take all actions necessary and proper to effectuate the foregoing resolution, including, among other things, obtaining the requisite consents from the shareholders of this corporation and executing and filing the appropriate forms with the Internal Revenue Service within the time limits specified by law.

Qualification of Stock as Section 1244 Stock

The board next considered the advisability of qualifying the stock of this corporation as Section 1244 Stock as defined in Section 1244 of the Internal Revenue Code of 1986, as amended, and of organizing and managing the corporation so that it is a Small Business Corporation as defined in that section. Upon motion duly made and seconded, it was unanimously

RESOLVED, that the proper officers of the corporation are, subject to the requirements and restrictions of federal, New York and any other applicable securities laws, authorized to sell and issue shares of stock in return for the receipt of an aggregate amount of money and other property, as a contribution to capital and as paid-in surplus, which does not exceed $1,000,000.

RESOLVED FURTHER, that the sale and issuance of shares shall be conducted in compliance with Section 1244 so that the corporation and its shareholders may obtain the benefits of that section.

RESOLVED FURTHER, that the proper officers of the corporation are directed to maintain such records as are necessary pursuant to Section 1244 so that any shareholder who experiences a loss on the transfer of shares of stock of the corporation may qualify for ordinary loss deduction treatment on his or her individual income tax return.

Compensation of Officers

The board next discussed the compensation to be paid by the corporation to its officers. A motion was made, seconded, and unanimously approved, and it was

RESOLVED, that the following annual salaries be paid to the officers of the corporation:

President	$_____
Vice-President	$_____
Secretary	$_____
Treasurer	$_____

Certificate of Assumed Name

The board next considered the question of whether the corporation would operate its business under a name other than that which is set forth in the Certificate of Incorporation. Upon motion duly made, seconded, and unanimously approved, it was

RESOLVED, that the corporation shall do business under the assumed name of

_____,

and that the president shall execute and cause to be delivered to the Secretary of State a Certificate of Assumed Name and shall attach a copy thereof to the minutes of this meeting.

Since there was no further business to come before the meeting, on motion made, seconded, and unanimously approved, the meeting was adjourned.

_____
, Secretary

NUMBER _____

SHARES _____

INCORPORATED UNDER THE LAWS OF THE STATE OF NEW YORK

The Corporation is authorized to issue _____ Common Shares without par value, of one class

This Certifies that

the owner of _____ *is* _____ *fully*
paid and non-assessable Shares of the above Corporation transferable only on the
books of the Corporation by the holder hereof in person or by duly authorized
Attorney upon surrender of this Certificate properly endorsed.

In Witness Whereof, the said Corporation has caused this Certificate to be signed by its duly
authorized officers and to be sealed with the Seal of the Corporation.

Dated _____

_____ , *President*

_____ , *Secretary*

For value received, the undersigned hereby sells, assigns and transfers to _____

_____

PRINT OR TYPE NAME AND ADDRESS OF ASSIGNEE

_____

_____ *Shares*

represented by the within Certificate, and does hereby irrevocably constitute and appoint

_____ *Attorney to*

transfer the said shares on the books of the within-named Corporation with full power of sub-stitution in the premises.

Dated _____

        In presence of

_____   _____

NOTICE: The signature to this assignment must correspond with the name as written upon the face of this certificate in every particular without alteration or enlargement, or any change whatever.

NUMBER _____

SHARES _____

INCORPORATED UNDER THE LAWS OF THE STATE OF NEW YORK

The Corporation is authorized to issue _____ Common Shares without par value, of one class

This Certifies that _____ is

the owner of _____ fully

paid and non-assessable Shares of the above Corporation transferable only on the books of the Corporation by the holder hereof in person or by duly authorized Attorney upon surrender of this Certificate properly endorsed.

In Witness Whereof, the said Corporation has caused this Certificate to be signed by its duly authorized officers and to be sealed with the Seal of the Corporation.

Dated _____

_____ , President

_____ , Secretary

For value received, the undersigned hereby sells, assigns and transfers to _____

_____

PRINT OR TYPE NAME AND ADDRESS OF ASSIGNEE

_____   _____

_____ *Shares*
represented by the within Certificate, and does hereby irrevocably constitute and appoint

_____ *Attorney to*
transfer the said shares on the books of the within-named Corporation with full power of substitution in the premises.

Dated _____

        In presence of

                                      _____

_____

NOTICE: The signature to this assignment must correspond with the name as written upon the face of this certificate in every particular without alteration or enlargement, or any change whatever.

This Certifies that _____

the owner of _____
paid and non-assessable Shares of the above Corporation transferable only on the books of the Corporation by the holder hereof in person or by duly authorized Attorney upon surrender of this Certificate properly endorsed.

In Witness Whereof, the said Corporation has caused this Certificate to be signed by its duly authorized officers and to be sealed with the Seal of the Corporation.

Dated _____

_____, President

_____, Secretary

The Corporation is authorized to issue _____ Common Shares without par value, of one class

INCORPORATED UNDER THE LAWS OF THE STATE OF NEW YORK

NUMBER _____

SHARES _____

Certificate Number _____

For _____ Shares

Issued To:

_____

Dated _____ 19 _____

From Whom Transferred

Dated _____ 19 _____

No. Original Shares	No. Original Certificate	No. of Shares Transferred

Received Certificate No. _____

For _____ Shares

This _____ day of _____ 19 _____

For value received, the undersigned hereby sells, assigns and transfers to _____

_____

PRINT OR TYPE NAME AND ADDRESS OF ASSIGNEE

_____

_____ *Shares*

represented by the within Certificate, and does hereby irrevocably constitute and appoint

_____ *Attorney to*

transfer the said shares on the books of the within-named Corporation with full power of sub-stitution in the premises.

Dated _____

In presence of

_____

_____

NOTICE: The signature to this assignment must correspond with the name as written upon the face of this certificate in every particular without alteration or enlargement, or any change whatever.

NUMBER _____

SHARES _____

INCORPORATED UNDER THE LAWS OF THE STATE OF NEW YORK

The Corporation is authorized to issue _____ Common Shares without par value, of one class

This Certifies that _____

is _____

the owner of _____ fully

paid and non-assessable Shares of the above Corporation transferable only on the
books of the Corporation by the holder hereof in person or by duly authorized
Attorney upon surrender of this Certificate properly endorsed.

In Witness Whereof, the said Corporation has caused this Certificate to be signed by its duly
authorized officers and to be sealed with the Seal of the Corporation.

Dated _____

_____ *, President*

_____ *, Secretary*

For value received, the undersigned hereby sells, assigns and transfers to _____

_____

PRINT OR TYPE NAME AND ADDRESS OF ASSIGNEE

_____

_____ *Shares*

represented by the within Certificate, and does hereby irrevocably constitute and appoint

_____ *Attorney to*

transfer the said shares on the books of the within-named Corporation with full power of sub-stitution in the premises.

Dated _____

        In presence of

                                             _____

_____

NOTICE: The signature to this assignment must correspond with the name as written upon the face of this certificate in every particular without alteration or enlargement, or any change whatever.

NUMBER _____

SHARES _____

INCORPORATED UNDER THE LAWS OF THE STATE OF NEW YORK

The Corporation is authorized to issue _____ Common Shares without par value, of one class

This Certifies that _____

the owner of _____ *is* _____ *fully paid and non-assessable Shares of the above Corporation transferable only on the books of the Corporation by the holder hereof in person or by duly authorized Attorney upon surrender of this Certificate properly endorsed.*

In Witness Whereof, the said Corporation has caused this Certificate to be signed by its duly authorized officers and to be sealed with the Seal of the Corporation.

Dated _____

_____ , *President*

_____ , *Secretary*

For value received, the undersigned hereby sells, assigns and transfers to _____

_____

PRINT OR TYPE NAME AND ADDRESS OF ASSIGNEE

_____

_____ *Shares*
represented by the within Certificate, and does hereby irrevocably constitute and appoint

_____ *Attorney to*
transfer the said shares on the books of the within-named Corporation with full power of sub-
stitution in the premises.

Dated _____

        In presence of

                                               _____

_____

NOTICE: **The signature to this assignment must correspond with the name as
written upon the face of this certificate in every particular without alteration or
enlargement, or any change whatever.**

NUMBER _____

INCORPORATED UNDER THE LAWS OF THE STATE OF NEW YORK

SHARES _____

The Corporation is authorized to issue _____ Common Shares without par value, of one class

This Certifies that _____

the owner of _____ *fully*

paid and non-assessable Shares of the above Corporation transferable only on the books of the Corporation by the holder hereof in person or by duly authorized Attorney upon surrender of this Certificate properly endorsed.

is _____

In Witness Whereof, the said Corporation has caused this Certificate to be signed by its duly authorized officers and to be sealed with the Seal of the Corporation.

Dated _____

_____ , *President*

_____ , *Secretary*

For value received, the undersigned hereby sells, assigns and transfers to _____

_____

PRINT OR TYPE NAME AND ADDRESS OF ASSIGNEE

_____

_____ *Shares*
represented by the within Certificate, and does hereby irrevocably constitute and appoint

_____ *Attorney to*
transfer the said shares on the books of the within-named Corporation with full power of substitution in the premises.

Dated _____

      In presence of   _____

_____

NOTICE: The signature to this assignment must correspond with the name as written upon the face of this certificate in every particular without alteration or enlargement, or any change whatever.

Certificate Number ——————

For —————— **Shares**

Issued To:

——————————————————

Dated —————— 19————

From Whom Transferred

——————————————————

Dated —————— 19————

No. Original Shares	No. Original Certificate	No. of Shares Transferred
——————	——————	——————

Received Certificate No. ——————

For —————— **Shares**

This —————— **day of** —————— 19————

——————————————————

NUMBER ——————

SHARES ——————

INCORPORATED UNDER THE LAWS OF THE STATE OF NEW YORK

The Corporation is authorized to issue —————— Common Shares without par value, of one class

This Certifies that

the owner of —————— *is*

paid and non-assessable Shares of the above Corporation transferable only on the books of the Corporation by the holder hereof in person or by duly authorized Attorney upon surrender of this Certificate properly endorsed.

In Witness Whereof, the said Corporation has caused this Certificate to be signed by its duly authorized officers and to be sealed with the Seal of the Corporation.

Dated ——————

—————————————, *President*

—————————————, *Secretary*

For value received, the undersigned hereby sells, assigns and transfers to _____

_____

PRINT OR TYPE NAME AND ADDRESS OF ASSIGNEE

_____

_____ *Shares*

represented by the within Certificate, and does hereby irrevocably constitute and appoint

_____ *Attorney to*

transfer the said shares on the books of the within-named Corporation with full power of substitution in the premises.

Dated _____

      In presence of   _____

_____

NOTICE: The signature to this assignment must correspond with the name as written upon the face of this certificate in every particular without alteration or enlargement, or any change whatever.

NUMBER _____

SHARES _____

INCORPORATED UNDER THE LAWS OF THE STATE OF NEW YORK

The Corporation is authorized to issue _____ Common Shares without par value, of one class

This Certifies that _____

the owner of _____ *fully*

paid and non-assessable Shares of the above Corporation transferable only on the books of the Corporation by the holder hereof in person or by duly authorized Attorney upon surrender of this Certificate properly endorsed.

In Witness Whereof, the said Corporation has caused this Certificate to be signed by its duly authorized officers and to be sealed with the Seal of the Corporation.

Dated _____

_____ *, President*

_____ *, Secretary*

For value received, the undersigned hereby sells, assigns and transfers to _____

_____

_____

_____ *Shares*
represented by the within Certificate, and does hereby irrevocably constitute and appoint

_____ *Attorney to*
transfer the said shares on the books of the within-named Corporation with full power of substitution in the premises.

Dated _____

　　　　　In presence of

　　　　　　　　　　　　　　　　　　　　　_____

_____

NOTICE: The signature to this assignment must correspond with the name as written upon the face of this certificate in every particular without alteration or enlargement, or any change whatever.

NUMBER _____

SHARES _____

INCORPORATED UNDER THE LAWS OF THE STATE OF NEW YORK

The Corporation is authorized to issue _____ Common Shares without par value, of one class

This Certifies that _____

the owner of _____ *is* _____ *fully paid and non-assessable Shares of the above Corporation transferable only on the books of the Corporation by the holder hereof in person or by duly authorized Attorney upon surrender of this Certificate properly endorsed.*

In Witness Whereof, the said Corporation has caused this Certificate to be signed by its duly authorized officers and to be sealed with the Seal of the Corporation.

Dated _____

_____ , *President*

_____ , *Secretary*

For value received, the undersigned hereby sells, assigns and transfers to _____

_____

PRINT OR TYPE NAME AND ADDRESS OF ASSIGNEE

_____

_____ *Shares*
represented by the within Certificate, and does hereby irrevocably constitute and appoint

_____ *Attorney to*
transfer the said shares on the books of the within-named Corporation with full power of substitution in the premises.

Dated _____

      In presence of   _____

_____

NOTICE: **The signature to this assignment must correspond with the name as written upon the face of this certificate in every particular without alteration or enlargement, or any change whatever.**

From Whom Transferred

_____

Dated _____ 19 ___

No. Original Shares	No. Original Certificate	No. of Shares Transferred

Received Certificate No. _____

For _____ **Shares**

This _____ **day of** _____ 19 ___

NUMBER _____

_____ SHARES

INCORPORATED UNDER THE LAWS OF THE STATE OF NEW YORK

The Corporation is authorized to issue _____ **Common Shares without par value, of one class**

This Certifies that _____

_____ is _____

the owner of _____ fully

paid and non-assessable Shares of the above Corporation transferable only on the books of the Corporation by the holder hereof in person or by duly authorized Attorney upon surrender of this Certificate properly endorsed.

In Witness Whereof, the said Corporation has caused this Certificate to be signed by its duly authorized officers and to be sealed with the Seal of the Corporation.

Dated _____

_____ , President

_____ , Secretary

For value received, the undersigned hereby sells, assigns and transfers to _____

_____

PRINT OR TYPE NAME AND ADDRESS OF ASSIGNEE

_____

_____ *Shares*
represented by the within Certificate, and does hereby irrevocably constitute and appoint

_____ *Attorney to*
transfer the said shares on the books of the within-named Corporation with full power of sub-stitution in the premises.

Dated _____

In presence of

_____

_____

NOTICE: The signature to this assignment must correspond with the name as written upon the face of this certificate in every particular without alteration or enlargement, or any change whatever.

Stock Ledger Sheet

Name of Stockholder	Address	Date of Ownership	Certificates Issued		Transferor	Amount Paid
			Certificate Number	Number Shares		

INDEX

A

Accident and health insurance premiums, and taxes, 4/21
Accountants, 5/1, 7/2-3
Accounting Period Resolution, 5/29
Accounting periods, 4/12-13. —See also— Tax year
Accumulated earnings credit, 1/6-7n, 4/4, 4/21-22
Active directors, 2/6
Allocation to Surplus Resolution, 5/30
"A.n." —See— Assumed name statement; Certificate of Assumed Name
Application for Reservation of Corporate Name, 5/10-11
  sample, 5/11
Assets, of corporation, valuing, 2/19-20
Assumed Name Certificate. —See— Certificate of Assumed Name
Assumed name statement, 5/2, 5/8n. —See also— Certificate of Assumed Name
Attorney General
  and corporate name, 5/4
  and dealer registration requirements, 3/9, 3/12
  and dissolution, 2/22
  and offering prospectus exemptions, 3/10, 3/11

B

Backing sheet
  for Certificate of Assumed Name, 6/6
  for Certificate of Incorporation, 5/17
Bank Account Resolution, 5/29-30
Bank loans, and limited liability, 1/5
Banks, and financial advice, 7/3
Basis, of stock, 4/8, 4/25
Bill of Sale for Assets of a Business, 5/53-55
  sample, 5/54
Bill of Sale for Items of Property, 5/59
  sample, 5/59
Bill of Sale, for shareholders, 5/52-55
  samples, 5/54, 5/59
Board of directors, 2/5. —See also— Director(s)
  first meeting, 5/28-34
Bulk Sales Act, 4/26, 5/36-45, 6/1
  sample forms, 5/38, 5/40, 5/41, 5/42, 5/43
  and transfers exempted, 5/37-38
  and transfers not exempted, 5/38-44
Business Corporation Law, 1/3, 1/4, 2/14-15, 3/1-2, 3/3-4, 7/1
  and Bylaws, 5/25
  and capitalization, 2/13-14
  and corporate persons, 2/4-12
  and corporate powers, 2/3-4
  and dissolution, 2/21-22
  and dividends, 2/19
  and immunity and indemnifications rules, 2/7-10, 5/25-26
  and limitations on stocks, 2/17, 2/18
  and shareholders, 3/3-4, 3/5
Business Income Tax Return (final), 6/14
Business judgement rule, 2/6
Bylaws, 3/4, 3/5, 5/25-27
  changing, 3/5
  and corporate persons, 2/7, 2/10, 3/1
  and directors, 3/1
  and dividends, 2/19
  and shareholder voting, 2/12

C

C corporations, 4/11
Calendar tax year, 1/8n, 4/10, 4/12-13. —See also— Tax year

Capital investment, 1/10
Capital losses, 4/15
Capitalization, 2/13-16
Certificate of Assumed Name, 5/8n, 5/33, 6/1, 6/3-6
  backing sheet, 6/6
  cover letter, 6/5-6
  fees, 6/3, 6/6
  sample, 6/4
Certificate of Assumed Name Resolution, 5/33
Certificate of Authority, 6/13
Certificate of Authority Identification Numbers, 5/45
Certificate of Dissolution, 2/22
Certificate of Incorporation, 2/1, 3/3, 3/4
  and business type, 2/4
  changing, 3/4
  and corporate name, 5/1, 5/5
  and corporate persons, 2/7, 2/10, 3/1
  and cover letter, 5/17-19
  and directors, 3/1
  and dissolution, 2/21-23
  filing, 2/20, 3/1, 5/16-20
  filing fees, 5/17
  and limitations on stocks, 2/17, 2/18
  and number of shares, 2/18
  and personal liability, 2/8-9
  preparation of, 5/12-16
  return of, 5/19-20
  review of, by accountant and/or lawyer, 5/1
  sample, 5/13-14
  and shareholder voting, 2/12, 3/3
  special handling, 5/19
Certificate of limited partnership, 1/2
Certificate of Registration, 6/13
Certificate of Reservation, 5/12
Certificate of (Stock) Registration, 5/20-22
Charitable contributions, 1/8
Closely-held corporations, 2/10, 2/11, 2/14-15, 3/13
  definition, 3/2
  —See also— Corporations
Commercial loans, 1/10
Common stock, 2/17-18
Compensation for Officers Resolution, 5/33
Computer search, and corporate name, 5/9
Consolidation of papers, at first Board of Directors meeting, 5/34
Corporate accounting periods, 4/12-13. —See also— Tax year
Corporate accumulated earnings credit. —See— Accumulated earnings credit
Corporate bonds, 1/10
Corporate employee and shareholder returns, 6/9
Corporate estimated tax return form, 6/10
Corporate Franchise Tax Report, 6/11
Corporate franchise taxes. —See— Franchise taxes
Corporate fringe benefits, 1/4, 1/7, 1/9, 4/10
Corporate income tax, federal, 4/3-6, 6/9
  return, 6/9
  tax rate, 4/3, 4/5
Corporate name, 5/1-12, 6/1, 6/3-6
  assumed, 5/8n, 5/33, 6/1, 6/3-6
  filing, and usage, 5/1
  formal, 5/2, 6/1, 6/3
  legal limitations on, 5/2-5
  protecting, 5/10
  registration of, 5/10
  reserving, 5/10-12

about the author

Tony Mancuso is a California attorney and the author of Nolo's best-selling corporate law series, including *How to Form Your Own Corporation* (California, Florida, Texas and New York editions) and *California Incorporator*, a software package developed in conjunction with Legisoft, Inc., which takes you through the steps necessary to form a California profit corporation on your computer. Tony is also the author of *The California Professional Corporation Handbook* and *The California Non-Profit Corporation Handbook.* Tony is a professional guitarist, has a background in electronics and computer consulting, and has written microcomputer and assembly language programming manuals.

CORPORATE KITS

Nolo Press, in cooperation with Julius Blumberg, Inc. offers three superior corporate kits. The Black Beauty® Kit features a 3-ring looseleaf vinyl binder with your corporate name on a label attached to the spine. The Ex Libris® Kit features a high quality binder with your corporate name embossed on the spine. The Portfolio Kit features a handcrafted red and black simulated leather binder with your corporate name on a gold label attached to the spine. You are not required to have a corporate kit, but many people find it is a convenient addition.

The Black Beauty, Ex Libris, and Portfolio Kits include:

- **A Corporate Records Book**. The primary difference between the three books is described above. We are partial to the truly classy Portfolio book, but the other two are also excellent products for their respective costs.

- **A Stock Transfer Ledger (share register), Minute Paper** and **Index Dividers** for Certificate of Incorporation, Bylaws, Minutes, and Stock Certificates.

- **Stock Certificates**: 20 numbered, green and black lithographed stock certificates printed with your corporate name.

Black Beauty and Ex Libris are registered trademarks of Julius Blumberg, Inc. Portfolio is our name for the Syndicate® Kit, a registered trademark of Julius Blumberg, Inc.

- **A Corporate Seal**. This is a solid metal tool designed to imprint the name of your corporation on corporate documents.

ORDER COUPON   How to Form Your Own New York Corporation

Name of Corporation (print exactly as on Certificate of Incorporation)   45

☐☐☐

☐☐☐

Put one character per space (including punctuation and spaces); be sure capital and lower case letters are clear

Year of Incorporation: _____ , NY

The corporation is authorized to issue _____ Common Shares without par value, of one class
(see paragraph 4 of your Certificate of Incorporation)

☐ Black Beauty Kit   ☐ Ex Libris Kit   ☐ Portfolio Kit
$56.00 $64.00 $78.00.................................... $_____

For long corporate names (over 45 characters) add an additional $7.00.......................$_____

Regular delivery by UPS costs $5.00 and is within 3 weeks*
10-12 day expedited delivery costs $10.00*
Air Courier (within 4 days) costs $25.00*

☐ $5.00 **or** ☐ $10.00 **or** ☐ $25.00.. $_____

TOTAL ENCLOSED...$_____

Ship to:
Name:_____

Street Address **(no PO boxes)**_____

City _____   State_____   Zip_____
                                        Phone _____

Send to:
NOLO PRESS/FOLK LAW, INC. 950 Parker Street, Berkeley CA 94710
Prices are subject to change without notice
415/549-1976

*All delivery dates are calculated from the day we receive your order. Sorry, we do not accept telephone orders for corporate kits.

S O F T W A R E

California Incorporator
By attorney Mancuso and Legisoft, Inc. About half of the small California corporations formed today are done without the services of a lawyer. This easy-to-use software program lets you do the paperwork with minimum effort. Just answer the questions on the screen, and *California Incorporator* will print out the 35-40 pages of documents you need to make your California corporation legal.
California Edition (IBM) $129.00

For the Record
By attorney Warner & Pladsen. A book/software package that helps to keep track of personal and financial records; create documents to give to family members in case of emergency; leave an accurate record for heirs, and allows easy access to all important records with the ability to print out any section.
National Edition (Macintosh) $49.95

WillMaker
—a software/book package
By Legisoft. Use your computer to prepare and update your own valid will. A manual provides help in areas such as tax planning and probate avoidance. Runs on the Apple II family, IBM PC and compatibles, Commodore, Macintosh
National Edition $59.95
Commodore Edition $39.95

B U S I N E S S   &   F I N A N C E

How To Form Your Own Corporation
By attorney Mancuso. Provides all the forms, Bylaws, Articles, minutes of meeting, stock certificates and instructions necessary to form your small profit corporation. Includes a thorough discussion of the practical and legal aspects of incorporation, including the tax consequences.
California Edition $29.95
Texas Edition $21.95
New York Edition $24.95
Florida Edition $19.95

The Non-Profit Corporation Handbook
By attorney Mancuso. Includes all the forms, Bylaws, Articles, minutes, and instructions you need to form a non-profit corporation. Step-by-step instructions on how to choose a name, draft Articles and Bylaws, attain favorable tax status. Thorough information on federal tax exemptions, which groups outside of California will find particularly useful.
California only $24.95

The California Professional Corporation Handbook
By attorneys Mancuso and Honigsberg. In California a number of professions must fulfill special requirements when forming a corporation. Among them are lawyers, dentists, doctors and other health professionals, accountants and certain social workers. This book contains detailed information on the special requirements of every profession and all the forms and instructions necessary to form a professional corporation.
California only $29.95

Marketing Without Advertising
By Phillips and Rasberry. A creative and practical guide that shows small business people how to avoid wasting money on advertising. The authors, experienced business consultants, show how to implement an ongoing marketing plan to tell potential and current customers that yours is a quality business worth trusting, recommending and coming back to.
National Edition $14.00

Billpayers' Rights
By attorney Warner. Complete information on bankruptcy, student loans, wage attachments, dealing with bill collectors and collection agencies, credit cards, car repossessions, homesteads, child support and much more.
California only $14.95

Bankruptcy: Do-It-Yourself
By attorney Kosel. Tells you exactly what bankruptcy is all about and how it affects your credit rating, property and debts, with complete details on property you can keep under the state and federal exempt property rules. Shows you step-by-step how to do it yourself; comes with all necessary forms and instructions.
National Edition $17.95

The Partnership Book
By attorneys Clifford and Warner. When two or more people join to start a small business, one of the most basic needs is to establish a solid, legal partnership agreement. This book supplies a number of sample agreements which you can use as is. Buy-out clauses, unequal sharing of assets, and limited partnerships are all discussed in detail.
National Edition $18.95

Chapter 13: The Federal Plan To Repay Your Debts
By attorney Kosel. This book allows an individual to develop and carry out a feasible plan to pay most of his/her debts over a three-year period. Chapter 13 is an alternative to straight bankruptcy and yet it still means the end of creditor harassment, wage attachments and other collection efforts. Comes complete with all necessary forms and worksheets.
National Edition $17.95

Small Time Operator
By Kamoroff, C.P.A.. Shows you how to start and operate your small business, keep your books, pay your taxes and stay out of trouble. Comes complete with a year's supply of ledgers and worksheets designed especially for small businesses, and contains invaluable information on permits, licenses, financing, loans, insurance, bank accounts, etc. Published by Bell Springs.
National Edition $10.95

Nolo's Small Business Start-Up
By Business Consultant McKeever. For anyone about to start a business or revamp an existing one, this book shows how to write a business plan, draft a loan package and find sources of small business finance.
National Edition $17.95

Getting Started as an Independent Paralegal
(two audio cassette tapes)
By attorney Warner. In these two audiotapes, about three hours in all, Ralph Warner explains how to set up and run an independent paralegal business and how to market your services. He also discusses in detail how to avoid charges of unauthorized practice of law.
National 1st Edition $24.95

The Independent Paralegal's Handbook: How To Provide Legal Services Without Going to Jail
By attorney Warner. More and more nonlawyers are opening legal typing services to help people prepare their own papers for divorce, bankruptcy, incorporation, eviction, etc. Called independent paralegals, these legal pioneers pose much the same challenge to the legal establishment as midwives do to conventional medicine.

Written by Nolo Press co-founder Ralph Warner, who established one of the first divorce typing services in 1973, this controversial book is sure to become the bible of the new movement aimed at delivering routine legal services to the public at a reasonable price.
National Edition $12.95

C O P Y R I G H T S   &   P A T E N T S

Legal Care for Your Software
By attorney Remer. Shows the software programmer how to protect his/her work through the use of trade secret, trademark, copyright, patent and, most especially, contractual laws and agreements. This book is full of forms and instructions that give programmers the hands-on information they need.
International Edition $29.95

Intellectual Property Law Dictionary
By attorney Elias. "Intellectual Property" includes ideas, creations and inventions. The Dictionary is designed for inventors, authors, programmers, journalists, scientists and business people who must understand how the law affects the ownership and control of new ideas and technologies. Divided into sections on: Trade Secrets, Copyrights, Trademarks, Patents and Contracts. More than a dictionary, it places terms in context as well as defines them.
National Edition $17.95

How to Copyright Software
By attorney Salone. Shows the serious programmer or software developer how to protect his or her programs through the legal device of copyright.
International Edition $24.95

Patent It Yourself
By attorney Pressman. Complete instructions on how to do a patent search and file for a patent in the U.S. Also covers how to choose the appropriate form of protection (copyright, trademark, trade secret, etc.), how to evaluate salability of inventions, patent prosecution, marketing, use of the patent, foreign filing, licensing, etc. Tear-out forms are included
National Edition $20.95

Inventor's Notebook
By Fred Grissom and attorney David Pressman. The best protection for your patent is adequate records. The Inventor's Notebook provides forms, instructions, references to relevant areas of patent law, a bibliography of legal and non-legal aids, and more. It helps you document the activities that are normally part of successful independent inventing.
National 1st Edition $19.95

E S T A T E   P L A N N I N G , W I L L S   &   P R O B A T E

Plan Your Estate:
Wills, Probate Avoidance, Trusts and Taxes
By attorney Clifford. Comprehensive information on making a will, alternatives to probate, planning to limit inheritance and estate taxes, living trusts, and providing for family and friends.
California Edition $17.95

Nolo's Simple Will Book
By attorney Clifford. This book will show you how to draft a will without a lawyer in any state except Louisiana. Covers all the basics, including what to do about children, whom you can designate to carry out your wishes, and how to comply with the technical legal requirements of each state. Includes examples and many alternative clauses from which to choose.
National Edition $14.95
with cassette $19.95

How to Probate an Estate
By Nissley. Forms and instructions necessary to settle a California resident's estate after death. This book deals with joint tenancy and community property transfers as well as showing you how to actually probate an estate, step-by-step. The book is aimed at the executor, administrator or family member who will have the actual responsibility to settle the estate.
California Edition $24.95

F A M I L Y   &   F R I E N D S

Family Law Dictionary
By attorneys Leonard and Elias. A national reference guide containing straightforward explanations and examples of an area of law which touches all of our lives. The book is extremely useful for people who want to know how the laws of marriage, divorce, cohabitation and having children affect them, and for legal practitioners in the area of family law.
National Edition $13.95

How to Do Your Own Divorce
By attorney Sherman. This is the original "do-your-own-law" book. It contains tear-out copies of all the court forms required for an uncontested dissolution, as well as instructions for certain special forms.
California Edition $14.95
Texas Edition $12.95

A Legal Guide for Lesbian/Gay Couples
By attorneys Curry and Clifford. Here is a book that deals specifically with legal matters of lesbian and gay couples: raising children (custody, support, living with a lover), buying property together, wills, etc. and comes complete with sample contracts and agreements.
National Edition $17.95

The Living Together Kit
By attorneys Ihara and Warner. A legal guide for unmarried couples with information about buying or sharing property, the Marvin decision, paternity statements, medical emergencies and tax consequences. Contains a sample will and Living Together Contract.
National Edition $17.95

California Marriage and Divorce Law
By attorneys Ihara and Warner. This book contains invaluable information for married couples and those considering marriage or remarriage on community and separate property, names, debts, children, buying a house, etc. Includes prenuptial contracts, a simple will, probate avoidance information and an explanation of gift and inheritance taxes. Discusses "secret marriage" and "common law" marriage.
California only $15.95

Social Security, Medicare & Pensions:
A Sourcebook for Older Americans
By attorney Matthews & Berman. The most comprehensive resource tool on the income, rights and benefits of Americans over 55.Includes detailed information on social security, retirement rights, Medicare, Medicaid, supplemental security income, private pensions, age discrimination, as well as a thorough explanation of social security legislation.
National Edition $14.95

How to Modify & Collect Child Support in California
By attorneys Matthews, Segal and Willis. California court awards for child support have radically increased in the last two years. This book contains the forms and instructions to obtain the benefits of this change without a lawyer and collect support directly from a person's wages or benefits, if necessary.
California only $17.95

How to Adopt Your Stepchild
By Zagone. Shows you how to prepare all the legal forms; includes information on how to get the consent of the natural parent and how to conduct an "abandonment" proceeding. Discusses appearing in court and making changes in birth certificates.
California only $19.95

The Power of Attorney Book
By attorney Clifford. Covers the process which allows you to arrange for someone else to protect your rights and property should you become incapable of doing so. Discusses the advantages and drawbacks and gives complete instructions for establishing a power of attorney yourself.
National Edition $17.95

How to Change Your Name
By attorneys Loeb and Brown. Changing one's name is a very simple procedure. Using this book, you can file the necessary papers yourself, saving $200 to $300 in attorney's fees. Comes complete with all forms and instructions for the court petition method or this simpler usage method.
California only $14.95

Your Family Records:
How to Preserve Personal, Financial and Legal History
By Pladsen and attorney Clifford. Helps you organize and record all sorts of items that will affect you and your family when death or disability occur, e.g., where to find your will and deed to the house. Includes information about probate avoidance, joint ownership of property and genealogical research. Space is provided for financial and legal records.
National Edition $14.95

LANDLORD/TENANT

Tenants' Rights
By attorneys Moskovitz, Warner and Sherman. Discusses everything tenants need to know in order to protect themselves: getting deposits returned, breaking a lease, getting repairs made, using Small Claims Court, dealing with an unscrupulous landlord, forming a tenants' organization, etc. Sample Fair-to-Tenants lease, rental agreements, and unlawful detainer answer forms.
California Edition $14.95

The Landlord's Law Book: Rights and Responsibilities
By attorneys Brown and Warner. Now, for the first time, there is an accessible, easy to understand law book written specifically for landlords. Covers the areas of discrimination, insurance, tenants' privacy, leases, security deposits, rent control, liability, and rent with-holding.
California only $24.95

The Landlord's Law Book: Evictions
By attorney Brown. This is the most comprehensive manual available on how to do each step of an eviction, and the only one to deal with rent control cities and contested evictions including how to represent yourself in court if necessary. All the required forms, with directions on how to complete and file them, are included. Vol. 1 covers Rights and Responsibilities.
California only $24.95

Landlording
By Robinson (Express Press). Written for the conscientious landlord or landlady, this comprehensive guide discusses maintenance and repairs, getting good tenants, how to avoid evictions, record keeping and taxes.
National Edition $17.95

REAL ESTATE

All About Escrow
By Gadow (Express Press). This book gives you a good understanding of what your escrow officer should be doing for you. Includes advice about inspections, financing, condominiums and cooperatives.
National Edition $12.95

The Deeds Book
By attorney Randolph. Adding or removing a name from a deed, giving up interest in community property at divorce, putting a house in joint tenancy to avoid probate, all these transactions require a change in the way title to real estate is held. This book shows you how to choose the right deed, fill it out and record it.
California Edition $15.95

Homebuyers: Lambs to the Slaughter
By attorney Bashinsky (Menasha Ridge Press). Written by a lawyer/broker, this book describes how sellers, agents, lenders and lawyers are out to fleece you, the buyer, and advises how to protect your interests.
National Edition $12.95

For Sale By Owner
By Devine. The average California home sold for $130,000 in 1986. That meant the average seller paid $7,800 in broker's commissions. This book will show you how to sell your own home and save the money. All the background information and legal technicalities are included to help you do the job yourself and with confidence.
California Edition $24.95

Homestead Your House
By attorney Warner. Under the California Homestead Act, you can file a Declaration of Homestead and thus protect your home from being sold to satisfy most debts. This book explains this simple and inexpensive procedure and includes all the forms and instructions. Contains information on exemptions for mobile homes and houseboats.
California only $8.95

RESEARCHING THE LAW

California Civil Code
(West Publishing) Statutes covering a wide variety of topics, rights and duties in the landlord/tenant relationship, marriage and divorce, contracts, transfers of real estate, consumer credit, power of attorney, and trusts.
California only $17.00

California Code of Civil Procedure
(West Publishing) Statutes governing most judicial and administrative procedures: unlawful detainer (eviction) proceedings, small claims actions, homestead procedures, wage garnishments, recording of liens, statutes of limitation, court procedures, arbitration, and appeals.
California only $17.00

Legal Research: How to Find and Understand the Law
By attorney Elias. A hands-on guide to unraveling the mysteries of the law library. For paralegals, law students, consumer activists, legal secretaries, business and media people. Shows exactly how to find laws relating to specific cases or legal questions, interpret statutes and regulations, find and research cases, understand case citations and Shepardize them.
National Edition $14.95

RULES & TOOLS

Make Your Own Contract
By attorney Elias. Provides tear-out contracts, with instructions, for non-commercial use. Covers lending money, selling or leasing personal property (e.g., cars, boats), leasing and storing items (with friends, neighbors), doing home repairs, and making deposits to hold personal property pending final payment. Includes an appendix listing all the contracts found in Nolo books.
National Edition $12.95

The Criminal Records Book
By attorney Siegel. Takes you step-by-step through the procedures available to get your records sealed, destroyed or changed. Detailed discussion on your criminal record what it is, how it can harm you, how to correct inaccuracies, marijuana possession records and juvenile court records.
California only $14.95

Everybody's Guide to Small Claims Court
By attorney Warner. Guides you step-by-step through the Small Claims procedure, providing practical information on how to evaluate your case, file and serve papers, prepare and present your case, and, most important, how to collect when you win. Separate chapters focus on common situations (landlord-tenant, automobile sales and repair, etc.).
National Edition $14.95
California Edition $14.95

Fight Your Ticket
By attorney Brown. A comprehensive manual on how to fight your traffic ticket. Radar, drunk driving, preparing for court, arguing your case to a judge, cross-examining witnesses are all covered.
California only $16.95

The People's Law Review
Edited by Warner. This is the first compendium of people's law resources ever published. Contains articles on mediation and the new "non-adversary" mediation centers, information on self-help law programs and centers (for tenants, artists, battered women, the disabled, etc.); and articles dealing with many common legal problems which show people how to do-it-themselves.
National Edition $8.95

How to Become a United States Citizen
By Sally Abel. Detailed explanation of the naturalization process. Includes step-by-step instructions from filing for naturalization to the final oath of allegiance. Includes a study guide on U.S. history and government. Text is written in both English and Spanish.
National Edition $12.95

Draft, Registration and The Law
By attorney Johnson. How it works, what to do, advice and strategies.
California only $9.95

JUST FOR FUN

Murder on the Air
By Ralph Warner and Toni Ihara. An unconventional murder mystery set in Berkeley, California. When a noted environmentalist and anti-nuclear activist is killed at a local radio station, the Berkeley violent crime squad swings into action. James Rivers, an unplugged lawyer, and Sara Tamura, Berkeley's first female murder squad detective, lead the chase. The action is fast, furious and fun. $5.95

29 Reasons Not to Go to Law School
By attorneys Ihara and Warner, with contributions by fellow lawyers and illustrations by Mari Stein. A humorous and irreverent look at the dubious pleasures of going to law school. 3rd Ed. $8.95

Poetic Justice
Edited by Jonathan & Edward Roth. A compendium of the funniest, meanest things ever said about lawyers with quotes from Lao-Tzu to Lenny Bruce. $8.95

self-help law books

ORDER FORM

Quantity	Title	Unit Price	Total

Prices subject to change

Subtotal _____

Tax (CA only): San Mateo, San Diego, LA, & Bart Counties 6 1/2%
Santa Clara & Alameda 7%
All others 6%

Tax _____

Postage & Handling

No. of Books	Charge
1	$2.50
2-3	$3.50
4-5	$4.00

Over 5 add 6% of total before tax

Postage & Handling _____

Total _____

Please allow 1-2 weeks for delivery.
Delivery is by UPS; no P.O. boxes, please.

Name _____

Address _____

_____

☐ VISA   ☐ Mastercard

_____ Exp. _____

Signature _____

Phone ( ) _____

ORDERS: Credit card information or a check may be sent to:

Nolo Press
950 Parker St.
Berkeley CA 94710

Use your credit card and our **800 lines** for faster service:

ORDERS ONLY
(M-F 9-5 Pacific Time)**:**

US:	800-992-NOLO
Outside (415) area **CA:**	800-445-NOLO
Inside (415) area **CA:**	(415) 549-1976

For general information call: **(415) 549-1976**

☐ Please send me a catalogue

H A L T
A law reform organization worthy of your support

HALT (Help Abolish Legal Tyranny)—An Organization of Americans for Legal

Reform —is a nonprofit public interest group whose activities are primarily

funded by its 200,000 individual members. Like Nolo Press, HALT advocates a

number of changes in the legal system to make it possible for the average

American to reasonably and affordably manage his or her legal life. To name but

a few of their admirable activities, HALT lobbies to increase disciplinary

sanctions against dishonest and incompetent lawyers, reduce probate fees and

simplify procedures, increase the role of non-lawyer (independent paralegal)

legal service providers, and expand small claims court. To keep its members

abreast of major legal reform developments, HALT also publishes a quarterly

magazine, holds law reform conferences, and publishes excellent position

papers on legal reform issues.

Nolo Press supports HALT and its members and urges all interested citizens to

join for a $15 annual membership fee. For more information write to:

H A L T
1319 F Street, NW
Suite 300
Washington, D.C. 20004
(202)347-9600

NEW YORK CORPORATE FORMS
D I S K   S E R V I C E

Let your computer do the work! Nolo Press offers the following New York incorporation forms on disk:

Application for Reservation of Corporate Name
Bylaws
Certificate of Incorporation
Cover Letter to Department of State
Minutes of First Meeting of the Board of Directors
Notice of Bulk Sales Forms:
    List of Creditors
    Notice If Debts Are Not Going to Be Paid in Full
    Notice If Debts Will Be Paid as They Come Due
    Schedule of Property
Request for Name Availability Check
Statement of Incorporators in Lieu of Organization Meeting
Stock Issuance Receipt/Bill of Sale forms for:
    Assets of a Business
    Cancellation of Indebtedness
    Cash Payment
    Items of Property
    Services Rendered
Stock Ledger sheet
Stock Registration Certificate Under Section 275-a Tax Law

The Nolo New York Corporate Form disk is offered in one of three disk formats:

Apple Macintosh. This is a Macintosh 3 1/2 " disk with a 800k (double-sided) disk format. Two sets of files are provided: one set is in Text-Only format (with a Carriage Return at the end of each paragraph) and a duplicate set of files in Macintosh Microsoft Word 3.01 document format.

IBM PC/MS-DOS: There are two choices here: 1) a 5 1/4" disk (360k, double-sided, PC/MS-DOS v. 2.0 format) <u>or</u> 2) a 3 1/2" disk (720k, PC/MS-DOS 3.13 format). Two sets of files are provided on each disk: one set is in Text-Only format (with a Carriage Return/Line Feed at the end of each paragraph) and a duplicate set of files in MS-DOS Microsoft Word 3.0 document format.

Please make sure you understand the disk and file format capabilities of your computer before ordering.

Select one disk format (see description above):

☐ Macintosh   or ☐ 5 1/4" IBM PC/MS-DOS or ☐ 3 1/2" IBM PC/MS-DOS $ 29.95

Shipping & Handling...$ 1.50
(Delivery is by first class mail and is within 10 days*)

           TOTAL ENCLOSED (make check payable to Nolo Press).............$ 31.45

Ship to:
Name: _____

Street Address_____

City_____   State _____   Zip_____

                  Phone_____

Send to: NOLO PRESS, Att: NY Disk Service, 950 Parker Street, Berkeley CA 94710 • 415-549-1976
Prices are subject to change without notice. To order toll-free by phone: 800-992-6656.

*Delivery date is calculated from the day we receive your order.